SHIP TO SHORE, INC.

SEA TO SHORE

CARIBBEAN CHARTER YACHT RECIPES

A COOK'S GUIDE TO FISH COOKERY

Publisher and Editor.............................Capt. Jan Robinson
Associate Publisher..........................Waverly H. Robinson
Illustrator/Cartoonist..Raid Ahmad
Photographer..Harry Rowell

If you are unable to obtain **SEA TO SHORE** through your local store, please write to:

SHIP TO SHORE, INC.
10500 Mt. Holly Road
Charlotte, NC 28214-9219

or

P.O. Box 10898
St. Thomas, U.S. Virgin Islands 00801

or call

1-800-338-6072

First Printing: February, 1989
Second Printing: July, 1991
Third Printing: September, 1993
Fourth Printing: December, 1994

SEA TO SHORE   Copyright 1988

ACKNOWLEDGEMENT

The author would like to thank Dr. John Tracy and Dr. Hal Hatfield for their expertise. Also many thanks to Monica Tepsick, Henry Pierce, Cindy Elliott, Mildred Thompson and Bess Lentz for their editing, and to the Virgin Island Charteryacht League, Caribbean Seafood Industries Co., Kroger Sav-on, and Burnt Cove Seafood, Inc. for their assistance.

Printed in the United States of America

ISBN 0-9612686-3-8

INTRODUCTION

SEA TO SHORE is a unique collection of fish and shellfish recipes from 80 international Caribbean Charter Yacht Chefs. These chefs have earned an outstanding reputation for creating superb meals in a limited space that satisfy even the most discriminating guests. Their recipes are easy to prepare, requiring a minimum of time and ingredients. However, the end results are elaborate and delicious creations.

While writing this book I have travelled to many places, visiting markets, libraries, and talking with fisherman, suppliers and chefs. Fish are often a mystery, but have been pleasing human palates for thousands of years. SEA TO SHORE is a cook's guide to identifying, buying, cleaning, cutting, cooking and serving these many different fish. SEA TO SHORE has over 250 mouth-watering recipes from bountiful breakfasts, delectable appetizers and zesty soups, chowders and stews to tantalizing entrees, casseroles and souffles.

Some of the fish used in the recipes are available locally, others are imported from around the world. One problem encountered is the excessive number of common names. SEA TO SHORE overcomes this by listing the other names and alternative species. The Finfish Chart on page 9 will also help you to determine which fish are interchangeable. These features enable you to have an understandable successful recipe, regardless of which of the Seven Seas produced your fish. So, wherever you are, the recipes will work for you. Each variety is carefully illustrated to help you to "fish at the market".

In recent years, the seafood renaissance, interest in nutrition, gourmet cooking and home entertaining have caused tremendous increases in seafood consumption. It is for this reason I bring you SEA TO SHORE, the fourth easy to use, informative, fun cookbook from the SHIP TO SHORE collection.

Use this book and discover the pleasure of seafood cookery and imagine cruising in the beautiful Caribbean aboard a yacht with captain, chef and crew, catering to your every whim. These delicious dishes will delight you on SEA or SHORE.

Bon appetit and bon voyage!

DEDICATION

This book
is dedicated to the
Caribbean Charter Yacht Chefs
who made this collection
of seafood recipes
possible.

TABLE OF CONTENTS

INTRODUCTION 3

NUTRITION 6

FINFISH SELECTION GUIDE 9

SHOPPING AT THE MARKET 10

GALLEY GADGETS & COOKWARE 16

DRESSING & CUTTING TECHNIQUES 17

COOKING METHODS 22

SUGGESTED SEASONINGS 27

HOW TO USE SEA TO SHORE 28

SEA TO SHORE RECIPES A - Z 29

METRIC TABLE 269

INDEX 270

CONTRIBUTING YACHTS 280

ABOUT THE ARTIST..286

ORDER FORMS...287

OTHER SHIP TO SHORE COOKBOOKS 289

ABOUT THE AUTHOR ....BACK COVER

NUTRITION

Fish and shellfish are among the most nutritious foods available to us. Fish and shellfish contain less saturated fat and more of the minerals our bodies need, like magnesium, calcium, potassium, copper, iron and phosphorus. Saltwater species are also a rich source of iodine.

Fish and shellfish are low in sodium. Saltwater species have no more sodium in their flesh than freshwater species, even though they live in a highly saline environment. Fish and shellfish are generally low in calories, rich in minerals and an excellent source of the B vitamins, vitamin A and D.

Fish are often divided into three classes "fat, medium and lean". This is a broad generalization, as the maximum amount of fat present, in any one species of fish is still considered **low fat** in any other foods. Fish flesh is a complex mixture of protein, water, free amino acids, mineral salts, fat and vitamins. The easily digested protein and low-fat content of seafood makes it an ideal nutrient for people with digestive disorders.

Japanese fishermen and eskimos who eat a great deal of fish rarely die of coronary artery disease. These groups seem to be protected by the high amount of fish oil in their diets. Apparently the oil has a unique chemical composition, known as **Omega-3**, a group of fatty acids found in fish oil and can, when consumed regularly, reduce levels of cholesterol and other heart threatening fats that circulate in our blood streams. Also, that by making blood platelets less "sticky" **omega -3** can help prevent formation of blood clots that cause heart attacks. Possible additional benefits: Consuming moderate amounts of **omega-3** may also minimize migraine headaches, lower blood pressure, ease eczema and psoriasis, relieve arthritic inflammation and even help prevent breast cancer.

NUTRITION (cont'd)

Where to get Omega-3:

Highest-fat fish (more than 5 percent body fat): anchovies, albacore, bluefin herring, mackerel, pompano, salmon, sardines, shad, tuna, rainbow trout and whitefish.

Medium-fat fish (2 to 5 percent): catfish, Pacific halibut, swordfish, brook trout and striped bass.

Lowfat fish (less than 2 percent): cod, flounder, grouper, haddock, pike, red snapper, sea bass, tilefish and whiting.

For many years it was believed that fatty fish, such as mackerel, tuna, and salmon should be avoided. Now all that has changed. Fatty fish are to be sought out. In fact, if you eat fat rich fish once or twice a week it appears that you can actually help prevent coronary heart disease.

Fish and shellfish are high in protein and contain a fat content 20% lower than most red meat. The fat these fish contain is highly polyunsaturated. About half of a person's daily protein requirement can be supplied from 1/4 pound of lean fish. Nutritive and caloric value of some of the more popular species of seafood, is shown on the following chart.

Some noted nutritionists suggest that we would be in better health if we consumed fish more often, and recommend at least four to six times per week.

NUTRITIVE AND CALORIC VALUE

TYPE OF FISH (3.5 Oz. or 100 gms.)	CALORIES	PROTEIN (gms.)	FAT (gms.)	CARBOHY-DRATES (gms.)	IRON (gms.)
Clams - canned (including hard, soft razor and unspecified)					
Solids and liquids	52	7.9	.7	2.8	4.1
drained solids	98	15.8	2.5	1.9	--
liquor, bouillon or nectar	19	2.3	.1	2.1	--
Cod	78	17.6	.3	--	.4
Flatfish (flounder, sole, sanddab)	79	16.7	.8	--	.8
Grouper	89	20.1	1.0	--	1.6
Haddock	79	18.3	.1	--	.7
Halibut	100	20.9	1.2	--	.7
Lobster (whole)	91	16.9	1.9	.5	.6
Mackerel	159	21.9	7.3	--	2.1
Oysters -					
Eastern	66	8.4	1.8	3.4	5.5
Pacific and Western	91	10.6	2.2	6.	7.2
Pollock	95	20.4	.9	--	--
Scallops	81	15.3	.2	3.3	1.8
Shrimp	88	18.1	.8	1.5	1.6
Snapper	88	19.4	1.1	--	4.3
Whitefish	155	18.9	8.2	--	.4
Whiting	105	18.3	3.0	--	--

FINFISH SELECTION GUIDE

White Meat - *Very light, delicate flavor*

Cod
Cusk
Dover Sole
Haddock
Lake Whitefish

Pacific Halibut
Pacific Sanddab
Petrale Sole
Rex Sole
Southern Flounder

Spotted Cabrilla
Summer Flounder
Witch Flounder
Yellowtail Flounder
Yellowtail Snapper

White Meat - *Light to moderate flavor*

American Plaice/Dab
Arrowtooth Flounder
Butterfish
Catfish
Cobia
English Sole
Lingcod

Mahimahi
Pacific Whiting
Red Snapper
Rock Sole
Sauger
Snook
Spotted Sea Trout

Starry Flounder
White King Salmon
White Sea Trout
Whiting
Winter Flounder
Wolffish

Light Meat - *Very light, delicate flavor*

Alaska Pollock
Brook Trout
Giant Sea Bass
Grouper

Pacific Ocean Perch
Rainbow Trout
Smelt
Tautog

Walleye
White Crappie
White Sea Bass

Light Meat - *Light to moderate flavor*

Atlantic Ocean Perch
Atlantic Salmon
Black Drum
Buffalofish
Burbot
Carp
Chum Salmon
Crevalle Jack
Croaker
Eel
Greenland Turbot
Jewfish

King(Chinook)Salmon
Lake Chub
Lake Herring
Lake Sturgeon
Lake Trout
Monkfish
Mullet
Northern Pike
Perch
Pink Salmon
Pollock
Pompano

Rockfish
Sablefish
Sand Shark
Sculpin
Scup/Porgie
Sheepshead
Silver(Coho)Salmon
Spot
Striped Bass
Swordfish
Vermillion Snapper

Light Meat - *More pronounced flavor*

Atlantic Mackerel

King Mackerel

Spanish Mackerel

Darker Meat - *Light to moderate flavor*

Black Sea Bass
Bluefish

Chinook Salmon
Ocean Pout

Sockeye(Red)Salmon

SHOPPING AT THE MARKET

QUALITY

Fish and shellfish are our most perishable foods. From the moment a fish leaves the water, bacteria begins to break down the flesh. In an unfrozen form, but properly iced, most fish have a shelf life of about 5 days, but even under the best conditions they should be used as quickly as possible after being caught.

The quality of fish depends not only on how long it has been out of the water, but also on how it is handled. Some fishermen are very good about taking the time to dress and chill their catch. Others are not. Wholesalers also vary as far as quality of their product is concerned, and retailers may mix several catches in the same batch.

You, as the cook, must learn to shop carefully. When buying fish at the market there is, of course, some element of chance in finding a perfectly fresh product. Evaluate each fish on its own merits. Buy round (whole) fish, if possible, as it is easier to judge the quality. Most fish markets will clean round fish, for little or no charge and you can use the head, bones and trimmings for stock. The following are a few pointers to keep in mind when shopping at the fish market:

FOR A WHOLE FISH, DRAWN OR IN THE ROUND

1. **Flesh** should be firm and elastic to the touch; it must not feel so soft that your finger leaves an indentation.
2. **Eyes** should be clear and full, not sunken and milky. (Some eyes of deep-water fish, such as grouper, may turn cloudy as they are raised from the bottom.)
3. **Gills** should be bright red or pink, rather than a muddy grey colour.
4. **Odor** should be clean and pleasant.
5. **Skin** colour should be unblemished and brightly coloured, with scales firmly attached.

FILLETS AND STEAKS

Fillet or steak flesh must have a clean-cut appearance and a firm moist texture. There should be no leathery traces of yellowing or browning around the edges. Must have a clean, fresh odor. There are fewer clues to freshness once a fish has been cut up. If you feel doubtful as to its freshness, have these cuts custom made from a fresh fish, drawn or in the round.

LIVE FISH

Some freshwater species are often kept alive in tanks. Choose only the lively ones.

SHELLFISH

Shellfish fall into three main categories: crustaceans (lobster, shrimp, crab, crayfish); cephalopods (squid, octopus); and mollusks (including bivalves - clams, mussels, scallop, oyster - and univalves - abalone, whelk, periwinkles). A clean fresh aroma is a good indication of quality. The following are a few good reminders when shopping:

Live crustaceans should be lively, the more lively the better, and should seem heavy for their size. Shrimp should be firm and smell fresh, don't be afraid to smell them. Shrimp, which are generally not sold alive, should have their head firmly attached, with no blackening of the gill area, just behind the head. Once a lobster or crab dies, it should be cleaned and iced immediately, and cooked the same day.

Cooked crustaceans should have legs, claw and tail (if any) pulled in tightly. To test a cooked lobster for freshness pull its tail out straight; when released it should snap back into its curled position. If the lobster has been sliced from head-to-tail before cooking, you won't be able to make the test. Unless you know the fish market, it is not recommended to buy a precooked, precut lobster.

AVAILABLE MARKET FORMS

A fish is "dressed" not cleaned.   Fish are dressed in many different ways according to their size, shape, skeletal structure and the intended method of cooking.

ROUND or WHOLE: The **whole** fish, as it comes out of the water. This is the least expensive form of fish to buy, about 45% of it is edible.

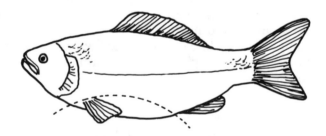

DRAWN: A **whole** fish with the gills, gut and stomach removed. The head and fins are intact and the gonads left in the body cavity. About 48% is edible.

SHOPPING AT THE MARKET(cont'd)

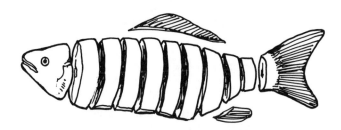

STEAKS: Cross-section cuts (1 to 1-1/2 inches thick) through the body of a dressed fish, including skin and a small piece of bone. These forms are about 84% edible.

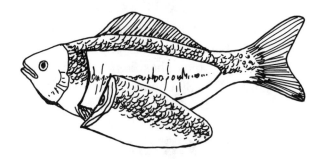

FILLETS: Meaty slices of fish, cut lengthwise from just behind the head to the tail. They are nearly boneless and with or without the skin. Fillets are almost 100% edible.

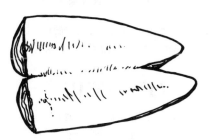

BUTTERFLY FILLETS: This is a double fillet, with the two sides connected at the backbone. It is nearly boneless. Because fish is not usually marketed in this form, you will probably have to special order it. A butterfly fillet is almost 100% edible.

SHOPPING AT THE MARKET(cont'd)

SEAFOOD SERVING SIZES
"how much to fetch per person"
(with an average appetite)

— FISH —

1 lb. whole (fish out of water)
1 lb. drawn (gutted and scaled)
1/2 lb. dressed (drawn with head, tail and fins removed)
1 steak (dressed 1-1/2 inches cross sections)
1/3 lb. fillet (boneless flesh)

— SHRIMP —

3/4 to 1 lb. "green" (shrimp out of water)
1/2 lb. raw, headless, unpeeled
1/4 lb. cooked, headless, peeled
5 jumbo (20 - 30 count) raw, unpeeled
7 medium (30 - 40 count) raw, unpeeled

— CRAB —

2 - 3 live critters per picker
1/4 lb. picked crab meat

— CLAMS —

1/2 dozen live on the half shell
1 quart shucked serves 6

— OYSTERS —

1/2 dozen live on the half shell
1 quart shucked serves 6

— SCALLOPS —

2 lbs. serves 6

PREPARATION TIPS

Storing Frozen Food
1. Keep frozen seafood frozen solid in the original wrapper.
2. For best results store at 0 degrees F.
3. Use immediately after defrosting.
4. Do NOT refreeze seafood after defrosting.

Thawing Frozen Seafood
1. Thaw fish in the refrigerator, allowing 24 hours for a one-pound package.
2. Do NOT thaw at room temperature. If thawing must be speeded up, immerse fish, wrapped in a waterproof package in cold water, or under water.
3. Use fish immediately after thawing. NEVER hold thawed fish longer than 24 hours. Dry thawed fillets or steaks before cooking.
4. Fillets and steaks may be broiled or sauteed without thawing if they are not to be breaded.
5. Frozen pre-breaded fish fillets or portions should not be thawed. Follow package directions for frying or oven finishing.

Storing Cooked Seafood
1. Place cooked fish in a covered container or wrap it in foil. Store no longer than 3 days in the refrigerator.
2. Well-wrapped, cooked seafood may be stored up to 3 months in the freezer.

SEAFOOD GALLEY GADGETS AND COOKWARE

Knives: oyster knife, fillet knife, steaking knife, clam knife cleaver and knife sharpener.

Gadgets: fish scaler or spoon, large cutting or scaling board, shears or scissors, clam opener, hammer or rubber mallet, shrimp peeler/deveiner, wide spatula/turner, basting brush, lemon squeezer, mortar and pestle, whisk, string and trussing needle, tongs, pliers, baster, some old newspapers, thermometer, timer.

Baking: baking dish, dutch oven, natural canape baking shells, fish and shellfish molds and platters, parchment paper.

Broiling or Grilling: grill, grilling racks for whole fish, skewers, fillet fish grill.

Steaming: steamer, parchment paper, wok with flat metal perforated tray.

Poaching: fish poacher, cheesecloth and cord.

Frying: heavy skillet, fryer, work with tempura rack.

DRESSING AND CUTTING TECHNIQUES

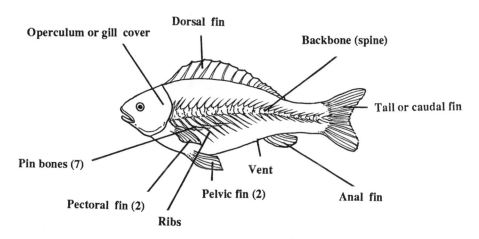

Operculum or gill cover

Dorsal fin

Backbone (spine)

Tail or caudal fin

Pin bones (7)

Vent

Pectoral fin (2)

Pelvic fin (2)

Anal fin

Ribs

TYPICAL BONE STRUCTURE OF A
* ROUND-BODIED FISH

*Round-bodied fish, refers to one of the two basic body shapes.
*Round, is a term used for whole, out of the water, undressed fish.

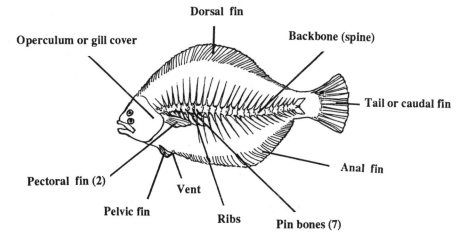

Dorsal fin

Operculum or gill cover

Backbone (spine)

Tail or caudal fin

Anal fin

Pectoral fin (2)

Vent

Pelvic fin

Ribs

Pin bones (7)

TYPICAL BONE STRUCTURE
OF A FLAT FISH

It is good to get to know the general bone structure of the two basic fish types, as shown above, before starting to work. It is important to have a sharp strong knife and make as few cuts as possible when filleting.

DRESSING AND CUTTING TECHNIQUES (cont'd)

SCALING: A fish to be cooked with the skin on, is usually scaled before dressing. First soak the fish in salt water for five minutes. Place fish on a cutting board, which has been placed on spread out newspapers, so you can collect the "flying' scales. Hold the fish tail firmly with one hand, then with either a fish scaler, spoon or knife, scrape from the tail towards the head to remove all scales. Rinse fish to remove any clinging scales. The fish may now be dressed or pan-dressed.

DRESSING: Also known as cleaning, gutting or drawing.

1. To remove entrails. Make a belly cut, with blade pointing outward, from the ventral fin to the pelvic fin.

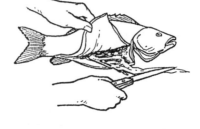

2. Make a second cut across the throat from gill to gill. If you don't wish to cook the fish with head on, remove it, but don't throw it away. They make great fish stock.

3. Use the tip of the knife to pull out and discard the internal organs, and any other material left in the cavity, and rinse well.

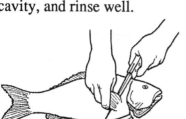

4. Remove pectoral fins by cutting behind the gills and collarbone.

DRESSING AND CUTTING TECHNIQUES (cont'd)

PAN DRESSING A FLATFISH:
1. Make one cut from just behind the vent to just behind the head. Remove head, gills and entrails in one piece. Turn fish.

2. Remove the ventral fin together with the short bones which support it and the attached strips of soft flesh. Remove the tail fin. Turn fish.

3. Two fillets are now left attached to the backbone. Remove any traces of kidney and roe. Rinse well.

FILLETING A ROUND-BODIED FISH:
1. You may fillet a fish without dressing it. Place the fish on a cutting board with dorsal fin toward you. Lift pectoral fin and cut diagonally behind gill toward the head.

2. At the end of the first cut, twist the knife until the edge is facing the tail and the point rests against the spine.

3. Hold the blade horizontally, slide the knife along the rib cage towards the tail.

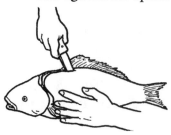

DRESSING AND CUTTING TECHNIQUES (cont'd)

FILLETING A ROUND-BODIED FISH

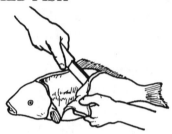

4. Peel back the fillet until you see the backbone. Cut the pin bones, but not the ribs. Slide the knife along the rib cage toward the belly.

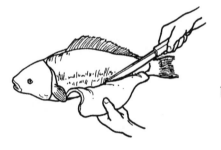

5. Continue with a smooth cut toward tail. Keep the blade flat against the bones, so you remove all the meat.

6. The fillet should come off in one piece after you sever the skin along the ventral fin. Turn the fish over and repeat the process.

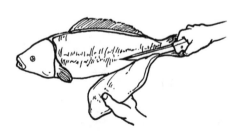

DRESS AND CUTTING TECHNIQUES (cont'd)

FILLETING A FLATFISH:

Flatfish may be filleted
similar to the process
above. Large size flatfish
are actually easier, than
most round-bodied fish.
Cut down to the backbone
behind the head. With the
knife almost horizontal,
slide it along the rib cage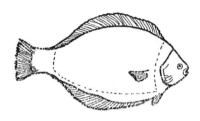
from just behind the head to the tail. Remove fillet from the
bone. Turn fish over and repeat process.

SKINNING FILLETS:

Most fillets are skinned.
Place the fillet skin side
down on the board. While
holding the tail in one hand,
make a shallow cut under
the skin. Pull the skin
against the knife and draw
knife away from tail, try to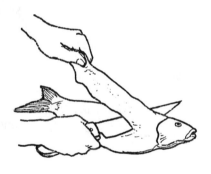
do this in one smooth cut. Save scraps for the stock pot.

CUTTING STEAKS:

With a heavy knife or cleaver,
cut 1 to 1-1/2 inch cross
sections of a dressed fish, by
slicing down the backbone.
If the backbone is thick, or
particularly large, hit the knife with a rubber mallet.

COOKING METHODS

A number of basic cooking methods are suitable for all fish, whether they are whole, filleted, or cut into steaks. But whatever cooking method is chosen, fish should be cooked for a short time only. Prolonged cooking toughens the flesh and destroys the flavor. The best and simplest rule to go by, is to measure the thickness of the fish at its thickest point (from underside to upper side) and give it 10 minutes cooking time per measured inch, whatever the cooking method. A whole salmon 4-inches thick in the center would take 40 minutes poaching; a 1/2-inch thick fillet, 5 minutes poaching or sauteing, and a 2-inch thick swordfish steak 10 minutes sauteing on each side. Double the cooking time if using fish that has been frozen.

BAKING:
This method is suitable for small whole fish and for individual cuts, such as fillets and steaks.

Brush the prepared fish with melted butter and season with lemon juice, salt and freshly ground pepper. Make 3 or 4 diagonal score marks on each side of whole round fish so that they will keep their shape. Lay the fish in a well-buttered, shallow baking dish. Bake in the center of a preheated oven at 400 degrees F. following the timing given under Cooking Methods.

During baking, baste the fish frequently - this is particularly important with white fish. Or lay slices of bacon over the fish to provide basting during cooking.

Before baking, fish may be stuffed with a filling of fine bread crumbs, seasoned with salt, pepper, herbs or parsley and bound with a little melted butter. Spoon the filling loosely into the cavity, as it tends to swell during cooking. Close the opening on round fish securely with toothpicks. For individual stuffed fillets, spread the mixture over the fillet, roll it up and secure with toothpicks.

Baking can also be done in aluminum foil, which is excellent for sealing in flavor and aroma. It also cuts down on oven cleaning. Place the prepared fish on buttered foil and sprinkle with lemon juice salt, and pepper. Wrap the foil loosely over the fish, place in a baking dish and cook in the center of a preheated oven at 450 degrees F.

GRILLING:

This is a particularly useful method for treating the fatty fishes, such as bluefish, mullet, shad and mackerel. Most grilled seafood benefits from a preliminary oil-based marinade. Additional flavor can be introduced by throwing fresh or dried herbs and herb stems on the coals as the fish cooks; rosemary, thyme and wild fennel stalks are especially appropriate for this treatment.

Oil fillets or steaks which have not had a preliminary marinade, draining off excess oil to prevent flare-ups on the grill.

Allow the pieces of fish to warm briefly to room temperature before cooking. This allows the heat to penetrate to the center more quickly without overcooking the outside.

Always preheat the grill. Fish will nearly always stick to a cold grill.

Work with a hot fire. Mexican mesquite charcoal or hardwood produces a hotter fire than briquets and imparts a nicer aroma. They say if you can hold your hand a few inches above the grill for any length of time, the fire is not hot enough. Set electric or other indoor grills to maximum heat.

Maintain the grill surface carefully during and after use. Clean the grill with a wire brush between rounds of grilling, and oil after cleaning as you would a cast iron skillet.

Position fish carefully to minimize contact with the grill Whether cooking whole fish or fillets, place them perpendicular to the grill bars rather than parallel. Start fillets skin side up for the best presentation.

Try to turn fish only once, and present the fish with the first cooked side (boneside) up. Remember that a piece may cook more or less than halfway on the first side and adjust the time for the second side accordingly. Avoid excessive handling of the fish. The more times a piece is moved, the more chances it has to stick. If the piece will not lift easily with tongs or the long edge of an offset spatula, let it sit another half minute or so before trying again.

SAUTEING:

This is one of the most popular cooking methods. It is suitable for steaks and fillets of cod, haddock, hake and flounder as well as for small whole fish such as sardines, mackerel, smelts, catfish and trout. Coat the prepared fish in seasoned flour, or dip them first in lightly beaten egg, then in dry bread crumbs, shaking off any surplus. Heat an equal amount of butter and cooking oil in a skillet over moderate heat. Put in the fish and saute until brown on one side, turn it over with a wide spatula. Allow approximately 10 minutes cooking time, depending on the thickness of the fish.. Remove the fish from the pan and drain thoroughly on paper towels.

DEEP FRYING: (fillets, catfish, whitebait)
A deep pan, ideally one fitted with a wire basket, is essential. The frying medium is vegetable oil or vegetable fat. The deep fryer should be no more than half-filled with oil and heated over moderate heat to 375 degrees F. A cooking thermometer will give the accurate temperature, if a thermometer is not available, test by dropping a 1-inch cube of day old bread in the oil. If the bread browns in 60 seconds the oil has reached the correct temperature.
Because of the high temperature required for deep frying, the fish must be coated with batter or egg and bread crumbs.

After frying fish, strain the fat or oil, using a fine mesh strainer. The food particles left in unstrained fat will cause the fat to decompose during storage. The strained oil should be stored in sealed bottles and used only for frying fish. The oil can be used again and again, provided it is always strained.

BROILING:

This quick cooking method is also suitable for small whole fish, fillets, and steaks. Whole fish should be scored with 3 or 4 diagonal cuts of a sharp knife on each side of the body. This allows the heat to penetrate more evenly and prevents the fish from splitting while cooking.

Brush the fish with melted butter or oil and sprinkle them with freshly squeezed lemon juice. Baste several times during broiling to prevent the flesh from drying out.

Broil all fish under a preheated hot broiler. Put fish on a well oiled rack or on oiled aluminum foil. The fish is cooked when the flesh separates easily into flakes when tested with a knife or fork.

During broiling, whole fish and thick steaks should be turned over once to ensure that both sides are evenly cooked. Thin fish steaks and fillets, however, need to be cooked on one side only.

POACHING

This is ideal for all types of fish, whether whole, filleted or cut into steaks. Poaching - slow simmering in liquid - can be done in a large saucepan or fish cooker on top of the stove, or in a shallow covered dish in the oven at 350 degrees F. For easy removal after poaching, tie a large fish loosely in cheesecloth or place it on a buttered wire rack.

Cover the fish completely with lightly salted water (1-1/2 teaspoons salt to 5 cups water). Add to the pan a few parsley or mushroom stalks, a good squeeze of lemon juice, a slice each of onion and carrot, together with a bay leaf and 6 peppercorns. For fish fillets, use a poaching liquid of equal amounts of milk and water, lightly seasoned with salt, freshly gound pepper and 1 bay leaf.

Bring the liquid to a boil over moderate heat, then cover the pan and lower the heat. Simmer the fish until it flakes when tested with a fork. Lift out the cooked fish with a large spatula and use the poaching liquid as the base for a sauce.

Whole fish, such as salmon, trout, and striped bass, are usually poached in a classic preparation of fish stock made with white wine and seasonings, known as court bouillon.

STEAMING:

Fillets and thin cuts of fish cooked in this manner are easily digestible and are ideal for invalids, older people and young children.

Roll the fillets or lay them flat in a perforated steamer and sprinkle lightly with salt and freshly ground pepper. Set the steamer over a pan of boiling water and cook the fish for 10-15 minutes or until tender when tested with a fork.

If a steamer is not available, place the fish on a buttered deep plate. Cover with a piece of buttered waxed paper and another plate or a lid from a saucepan. Set the plate over a pan of boiling water, cover and steam for about 15 minutes.

"STEAMING' SHELLFISH:

"Steaming" also describes a slightly different technique for cooking clams or mussels in the shell. The shellfish are placed in a saucepan with a small amount of liquid (and usually garlic and herbs), covered and brought to a boil. The shellfish cook in both the boiling liquid and the trapped steam, opening their shells when they die. The liquid released from the shells, together with the remaining cooking liquid, is then served with the shellfish or incorporated into a sauce.

BRAISING:

Large fish such as halibut and salmon, can be cooked by this method. Peel and finely chop 2 carrots, 1 onion, and 1 leek or parsnip. Saute these vegetables in a little butter and spread them over the bottom of a large baking dish. Lay the prepared fish on top and sprinkle with salt and freshly ground pepper. Add a few sprigs of fresh herbs, such as parsley and thyme, or a bay leaf. Pour over enough fish stock or white wine to come just level with the fish.

Cover the dish and cook in the center of a preheated oven at 350 degrees F. until the fish flakes when tested with a fork. Lift out the fish carefully and strain the cooking liquid. This may be used as a sauce and can be thickened with egg yolks or cream, or by fast boiling until it has reduced to the desired consistency.

PLANKING:

Shad, trout, snapper, whitefish, salmon, halibut and many other species are often cooked and seved on a hardwood oak plank. (Do not use planks made of resinous woods, such as pine.) This is a decorative way to present a whole fish, but it can also be done with thick steaks and fillets. The plank should be a grooved one so that the juices can be retained rather than being lost in the oven. Heat the plank in the oven then oil it thoroughly, preferably with olive oil. Season the fish and arrange it on the plank with bits of butter. Bake in a hot oven (400 degrees F.)

When fish is almost done, arrange creamy mashed potatoes or duchess potatoes around it. Broil until the potatoes are browned. Add some hot vegetables such as buttered green beans and broiled tomato slices. Garnish with parsley and lemon or radishes. This can be as simple or as elaborate as you like.

Fish can be planked for outdoor cooking also, but for that it will be just fish attached to the plank with wooden pegs or stainless steel nails. The plank will be placed at an angle toward the fire and should be turned once so fish is cooked evenly. Brush with basting sauce or oil during cooking.

SUGGESTED SEASONINGS FOR FISH AND SHELLFISH.

Fresh and dried herbs are used in cooking to impart additional flavor to a dish. The choice of the herb is entirely personal, but certain herbs go particularly well with certain foods. Fresh herbs are superior in taste to dried herbs, but are not as strong. If a recipe calls for dried herbs and fresh herbs are being substituted, triple the amount.

Allspice	Use when poaching or steaming fish and shellfish.
Barbecue sauce	Brush over fish and shellfish when grilling.
Basil	Use in hot butters and add to lemon juice for an easy sauce for broiled and grilled fish.
Bay leaf	Use with full-flavoredfish and in bouquet garni
Chervil	For delicate fish and shellfish. Garnish for soups.
Cilantro	or coriander (also known as Chinese parsley) is a pungent herb. Excellent in Ceviche.
Cloves	Sprinkle on fish before baking.
Curry Powder	Sprinkle over fish when broiling.
Dill	Well suited with trout and salmon. Add to dressings and mayonnaise. Use as a garnish.
Fennel	Use with full-flavored fish. Add to butters, sauces.
Ginger	Broiled and baked fish; sprinkle sparingly.
Mace	Trout; and add to sauces and stews.
Marjoram	Use in olive oil marinades for grilled fish May be used as a substitute for oregano.
Oregano	Use in chowders, sauces and stuffings; add with melted butter for a shellfish sauce.
Paprika	Use as a garnish.
Parsley	The traditional garnish with fish and most soups. Use to flavor sauces. A necessary ingredient of bouquet garni.
Rosemary	Sprinkle sparingly on flavorful fish when broiling, grilling or baking.
Sage	Use when cooking halibut and salmon. Mainly used in stuffings.
Savory	There is a summer and winter savory. Summer has a more delicate flavor. Both are used to flavor salads, soups and broiled fish.
Tarragon	Use with any fish, also in salad dressings and mayonnaise
Thyme	Use in any fish dishes, soups and stews, stuffings and marinades. A traditional ingredient of a bouquet garni.
Turmeric	Use in a marinade when broiling salmon, lobster, shrimp.

HOW TO USE SEA TO SHORE

SEA TO SHORE includes over 65 species of fish and shellfish, with 39 detailed drawings and informative introductions. Each one gives you the accepted common **name** of the fish, description, size, habitat, flavor, preparation and **other names** (localized common names; i.e. other names the fish is known by).

All of the recipes have been prepared and served onboard the charter yachts. Each cook prepares four meals a day, (breakfast, lunch, hors d'oeuvres and dinner) seven days a weeks, for 4 - 8 guests, plus crew. They know what it takes to prepare elegant meals without a lot of effort. Here are 250 tried and tested recipes we would like to share with you.

Each recipe includes a notation for *Preparation time* (preparation and mixing of all ingredients) and *Cooking time* (the length of time the dish cooks in the oven, on top of the stove, in the microwave oven, or on the barbecue). They show *Marinating time* and/or *Chilling time* when appropriate. By adding the times together, you can calculate the time required to complete a dish from initial preparation to serving time.

Most recipes suggest a garnish, vegetable accompaniment and in some cases a full menu and choice of a wine. The cooks have also given useful notes and helpful hints at the end of their recipes.

Beginning on page 280 you will find a short review about each individual yacht and chef from which these scrumptious recipes come.

There are lots of cartoons to go along with the recipes to entertain you while "slaving in the galley"!

HOW TO LOCATE THE RECIPES

There are five places in this book to find recipes for a given species.

1. The species are **alphabetically listed throughout the book.**

2. In the index, under the accepted common **name.**

3. In the index under the **other names** (by which the fish is locally known).

4. In the index under the **alternative** name (the fish which may be substituted in a recipe.) This recipe will be in *italics*.

5. In the index under breakfasts, lunches, pastas and appetizers.

ABALONE

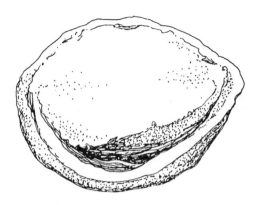

Description: Large univalve mollusk. The beautiful inner shell has opalescent blues and greens and irridescent shades of pink. Whereas the outside shell is roughly oval, and often encrusted with barnacles.

Size: From 6 to 8 inches long, lined with mother-of-pearl

Habitat: The highest concentrations of the edible species are found along the coasts of Japan, Australia, New Zealand and California clinging firmly to rocks with a large muscular foot.

Flavor: Once the delicate white meat is tenderized it has an unforgettable fresh flavor. Some say that it is superior to the conch or whelk.

Preparation: The dark outer layer of flesh requires tenderizing by beating with a mallet to break up the fibers. The flesh has high iodine content which causes a flavor loss and toughness if overcooked. Remember, the most important rule for cooking is to **avoid overcooking.** If steaks are to be sauteed, they require no more than 30 seconds on each side. Abalone also makes great seviche and is considered a delicacy when served raw.

Other names: Paua (New Zealand)

ABALONE IN CHILLI SAUCE

Preparation time: 20 minutes   *Chef: Jan Robinson*
Cooking time: 15 minutes   *Yacht: Vanity*
Serves: 4

1 lb. fresh abalone, tenderized	1 cup fish stock
1/2 lb. pork fillet, lean	1 Tblsp. cornstarch
2 cloves garlic	1 Tblsp. water
1 tsp. chopped fresh ginger	1 tsp. chilli sauce
2 Tblsp. olive or peanut oil	pepper

Cut the abalone and pork into thin strips. Crush the garlic, and finely chop the ginger. Heat the oil in a frying pan with the garlic and ginger. Add pork slices, and stir-fry until lightly cooked. Remove from pan.

Stir-fry the abalone slices for only about 10 seconds, stirring quickly. Remove from pan. Mix cornstarch with water until smooth. Add chilli sauce. Season with pepper. Return cooked pork and abalone to frying pan to quickly heat through. *Serve over rice or pasta.*

Alternatives: conch, whelk

ABALONE "PAUA" FRITTERS

Preparation time: 15 minutes   *Chef: Jan Robinson*
Cooking time: 15 minutes   *Yacht: Vanity*
Serves: 4

5 large abalone, tenderized   **1/4 cup oil**
3 egg whites   **2 oz. butter**
4 Tblsp. flour   **Garnish: lemon wedges**
fresh ground pepper   **and sprigs of parsley**

Finely chop the abalone, or mince. Beat the egg whites until they hold soft peaks. Sift flour, and fold into egg whites. Lightly mix in finely chopped abalone. Season with pepper.

Heat the butter and oil in a heavy frying pan. Place tablespoonfuls of the mixture into the pan. Cook until golden on both sides. Drain on paper towels. Serve hot. Garnish.

Alternatives: Conch, whelk

BLUEFISH

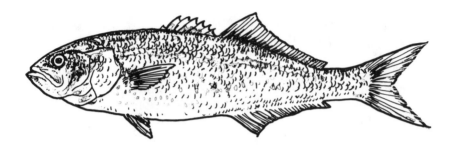

Description: Bluefish are greenish-blue along the back and silver on the sides and belly. The shape of the body is similar to that of the jacks. It has a projecting lower jaw and prominent canine teeth and will attack and eat anything in its path. They are fished commercially for food.

Size: A mature Bluefish (5 years old) is about 30" long and weighs from 7 to 9 pounds.

Habitat: In the United States, off the Atlantic Coast from Florida to Cape Cod. Bluefish are also found in other parts of the world. Off the east coast of South America, off the west African shelf in the Mediterranean and Black Seas, in the Indian Ocean and off Australia.

Flavor: Bluefish have extremely powerful digestive enzynes which cause the meat to spoil quickly (within a few hours of being caught). It must be cleaned and iced as soon as possible when taken from the water to hold the delicate flavor. At its best the Bluefish has a very smooth and mild taste, with a soft-textured long flake. The bones are large and easily removed.

Preparation: The meat has a high oil content indicating that other oils should be added very sparingly. The best cooking methods use neutralizing acids such as tomatoes and onions, or citrus fruits such as the lemon and lime. Also be sure to remove the dark strip of muscle before cooking. The smaller fish should be fried, sauteed or baked while the larger are best broiled or smoked.

Other names: Snapper, Blue, Chopper,

BREAKFAST BLUEFISH

Preparation time: 20 minutes   *Chef: Pero Robinson*
Cooking time: 13 minutes   *Yacht: Vanity*
Serves: 4

4 bluefish fillets	**12 cooked asparagus spears**
1/2 cup butter, softened	**1 or 2 eggs per person**
1 cup grated Parmesan cheese	**chopped fresh parsley**

Preheat oven to 400 degrees F. Spread half the butter over bottom of individual baking-serving platters (or over one large platter) and sprinkle evenly with half the Parmesan. Lay fillet over cheese, dot with butter and bake 10 minutes in 400 degree oven. Take from oven, break one or two eggs alongside each fillet, frame with asparagus, sprinkle over remaining Parmesan, spoon drippings over egg and bake 2 more minutes, until egg is set. Sprinkle with parsley. *A wonderful way to start the day. Serve with hot buttered English muffins, and a chilled Mimosa!*

GREEK STYLE BLUEFISH

Preparation time: 15 minutes   *Chef: Jan Robinson*
Cooking time: 20 minutes   *Yacht: Vanity*
Serves: 4

4 Tblsp. olive oil	**16 pitted black olives, sliced**
1 medium onion, sliced	**1 tsp. dried oregano**
1 green bell pepper,	**1 tsp. dried basil**
seeded and sliced	**black pepper**
1 red bell pepper, seeded	**1-1/2 lbs. bluefish fillets, or**
and sliced	**other firm-fleshed fish**
1 medium zucchini, sliced	**1/3 cup crumbled feta cheese**
2 garlic cloves, minced	**1/4 cup seasoned dry**
1 medium tomato, sliced	**breadcrumbs**

Preheat oven to 375 degrees. F. Lightly oil 10x14 inch glass baking dish. Heat 3 tablespoons oil in heavy skillet over medium heat. Add next 5 ingredients and cook until onion is translucent, stirring occasionally, about 8 minutes. Stir in tomato, olives, oregano and basil. Season with pepper. Cook until tomato is softened, 2 minutes.

Place fish in prepared baking dish. Spoon vegetables over. Sprinkle with cheese and breadcrumbs. Bake until fish is opaque, about 10 minutes per inch of thickness.

BONEFISH

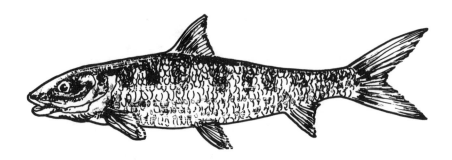

Description: The Bonefish is the only living member of very primitive boney fishes which date back 125 million years. The color is bright silvery on the sides and bottom. The back and upper sides are blue-green, punctuated by numerous faint horizontal lines that extend from the head to the tail. It has a pig like snout which is used to root in the sand and marl. The mouth is located under the snout. They are tremendously fast swimmers and regarded as one of the best saltwater game fish.

Size: Average size runs from 4 to 6 pounds with 8 pounds considered a large Bonefish

Habitat: Throughout the world in tropical and semi-tropical climates.

Flavor: The Bonefish meat is white, firm and nutlike in flavor. To experience the delicate taste the fish should be baked at a low heat. Some claim that smoking produces the best flavor.

Preparation: Bonefish, as the name implys, contains a lot of bone. However, the Y shaped structure allows for a substantial amount of near boneless meat in the larger fish. Preparation should include deboning and dressing by cutting along the back to remove the backbone and rib cage. Remember that marinating in lime or lemon juice will neutralize the oils and bring out the delicate flavor of this fish.

Other names: Macabi (West Indies), 'O'io (Hawaii)

CARIBBEAN BONEFISH

Preparation time: 15 minutes
Marinating time: overnight
Cooking time: 5 hours
Serves: 6

Chef: Jan Robinson
Yacht: Vanity

1 (6 lb.) bonefish scaled and butterflied
12 key limes, or lemons
freshly ground black pepper
2 large onions, diced
1 green pepper, diced
1/4 cup peanut oil
1-1/2 cups tomato sauce

1/4 cup Worcestershire sauce
1 tsp. dried tyme
1 tsp. crushed red pepper
1/4 cup minced parsley

Garnish: Hibiscus flowers

Lay bonefish, skin side down, on a piece of foil large enough to be folded over the fish later. Place foiled fish in baking pan. (Heat limes in microwave before slicing - you will get twice as much juice). Slice limes and squeeze juice over flesh side of fish, rubbing some of the pulp over the fillets until they are thoroughly soaked. Sprinkle with pepper, to taste. Store the fish in the refrigerator overnight to marinate.

When ready to cook, saute onions and green pepper in peanut oil in a large skillet until onions are transparent. Add tomato sauce, Worcestershire sauce, thyme and crushed red pepper, to taste; let simmer until flavours blend. Spoon sauce over entire fish, sprinkle with parsley, and fold the foil over to cover. Place fish in oven and cook at 200 degrees F. for 5 hours. *Serve hot or cold. Serve on wooden plates using bamboo fans for placemats.* Garnish with Hibiscus Flowers.

Note: The Bahamian cooks I spoke with stretch the bonefish, so all the bones lie in one direction. This makes bone removal easier after cooking. Their recipe is:- Preheat oven to 375 degrees F. Place split bonefish, skin down in an oiled baking pan. Place sliced onions and green peppers over it. Sprinkle with pepper, thyme, and a little chopped fresh bird pepper. Cover and bake 30 minutes

I like to introduce my friend, Caribbean Bonefish!

CARP

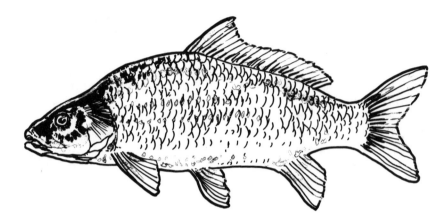

Description: Carp was the first fish to be aquacultured some 2500 years ago in China and is one of the most versatile freshwater fish. It is gold to olive brown, fading to pale yellow and has red highlights.

Size: Its average length is 12 - 20 inches and weighs from 2 to 8 pounds.

Habitat: This fish lives in the slow moving rivers, ponds and lakes of the world. It favors the warm temperate climates and is available year round.

Flavor: The flaky, mild-flavored white meat of the Carp reaches its best taste during the months between November through March. If used during other months the fish should be skinned and soaked in mild saltwater for 3 to 4 hours before cooking.

Preparation: The meat has a moderate fat content indicating that any other oils or oil - based sauces should be added sparingly. It is available fresh, frozen, or smoked: whole, or as steaks or fillets. This fish can be baked, poached, deep- fried, steamed, stewed or braised.

CARIBBEAN CARP

Preparation time: Could take days   *Chef: Gerry Hostetler*
Cooking time: 72 hours   *Yacht: Artistic*
Serves: Whomever

1 carp, freshly caught   **lots of butter**
1 medium board
salt and pepper   **Garnish: fresh flowers**

Drop fishing line in water and wait patiently for carp to grab hook.
When cork on line goes down, run backward with cane poll and
pull carp out of water. Land catch on bank. Take home.

Preheat oven to 600 degrees F. Place carp on medium board.
Butter, salt and pepper to taste. Place in hot oven and bake for 72
hours. Remove from oven. Garnish with fresh flowers. Discard
carp and eat board. *Serve with Mad Dog 20/20.*

CATFISH

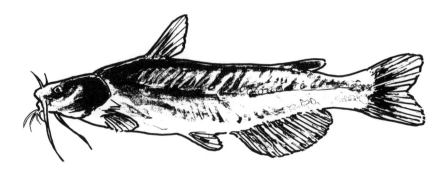

Description: The Catfish is quickly becoming known as the fish of the future. Tens of millions of pounds are grown annually yet the supply is short because of the great demand. There are many species but generally Catfish are a dark gray which fades into white on the belly. Some have irreglar black spots. Except for the armored Catfish, all are scaleless. All the North American species have whiskers around their mouths which helps them taste, touch and smell.

Size: Even though there are 28 species of Catfish in North America they mostly average about 1 to 3 pounds.

Habitat: In most of the rivers throughout North America and Mexico. Many catfish are now farm-raised commercially under clean and ideal conditions.

Flavor: The meat is snow white, flaky and has a moist texture. The flavor is sweet with a mild fresh water taste.

Preparation: Until recently, cultural prejudice has kept many Americans from trying Catfish, but now they are being consumed outside the narrow regional and ethnic market of the past. People are discovering its fine cooking qualities. It is well suited for frying, sauteing, steaming or braising. Regardless of size all Catfish should be skinned. They must be handled carefully as they have sharp spinous rays on the leading edge of their dorsal and pectoral fins which contain poison in some species.

Other names: Channel Cat, Sharpies, Fiddlers

CATFISH CARIBBEAN

Preparation time: 10 minutes
Cooking time: 30 minutes
Serves: 6

Chef: Jan Robinson
Yacht: Vanity

Vegetable cooking spray
1 cup chopped onion
3 cloves garlic, minced
1-1/4 cups water
1 (8 oz.) jar picante sauce
3/4 cup uncooked parboiled
    rice
6 (4 oz.) catfish fillets,
    preferably farm-raised

2 tsp. minced fresh cilantro
1/2 cup chopped tomatoes
1/4 cup plus 3 Tblsp.
    grated sharp cheddar
    cheese
3 Tblsp. sour cream
1 Tblsp. minced green
    onions

Coat a large heavy skillet with cooking spray. Place over medium heat until hot. Add onion and garlic, and saute 5 minutes or until tender. Add water and picante sauce; bring to a boil Add rice, cover, reduce heat and simmer 10 minutes.

Rinse fillets under cold, running water, pat dry. Arrange fillets over rice, sprinkle with cilantro. Cover and simmer 15 minutes or until fish flakes easily. Remove from heat. Top each serving with tomato, cheese, sour cream and green onions.

Alternatives: Tautog (Blackfish), Snook

No, I'm not a catfish this is my Halloween costume

Hint: Thaw fish and shellfish in milk. The milk draws out the frozen taste and provides a fresh caught flavor.

BROILED CATFISH STEAKS

Preparation time: 10 minutes
Cooking time: 12 minutes
Serves: 4

Chef: Jan Robinson
Yacht: Vanity

8 (2oz.) catfish steaks*
1/4 cup tomato sauce
1/4 cup vinegar
1-1/2 tsp. sugar
3/4 tsp. minced fresh dill
1/4 tsp. paprika
Fresh ground black pepper

**1/2 tsp. Worcestershire
   sauce**
1 tsp. Vegetable oil
Vegetable cooking spray

**Garnish: lemon slices and
   fresh dill sprigs**

* Preferably farm-raised

Rinse catfish steaks under cold, running water. Pat dry, set aside.
Combine tomato sauce and next 7 ingredients in a small bowl. Stir
well. Brush half of mixture over one side of steaks. Coat rack of
a broiler pan with cooking spray. Place steaks on rack; broil 4 to
5 inches from heat for about 6 minutes. Carefully turn fish over.
Brush with remaining tomato mixture. Broil an additional 6
minutes or until fish flakes easily when tested with a fork. Garnish.

Alternatives: Black Sea Bass

This time I'm going for Catfish!

CAVIAR

From the Turkish word *khavyah*, the derived word **caviar** refers to a lightly salted sturgeon fish roe (eggs). The Beluga being the largest egg, is considered the most highly regarded caviar in the world. Today it is very rare.

For a long time the United States brokers called all black fish roe caviar. However, now only the Sturgeon roe may be called caviar.

Caviar is usually served on a thin toast or bread and is highly regarded as a true delicacy. **The food of kings and queens.** Today caviar is used in many recipes, but, once cooked it looses its true flavor.

Most caviar in the United States is marketed in sealed jars so it is very hard to judge the quality as this is determined by the condition of the berry (uncrushed) and how well the coating of fat is attached to each berry. Color and size has no bearing on the quality of the caviar. The firmness and the lack of fishy   smell are other very important conditions that help determine the quality of the caviar.

The most common substitute for sturgeon roe "caviar" is Lumpfish roe, which is more familiar to people than the genuine item. The Lumpfish is found on both sides of the North Atlantic.

CAVIAR POTATO SALAD

Preparation time: 20 minutes   *Chef: Marilyn Stenberg*
Cooking time: 25 minutes   *Yacht: Sheerwill*
Serves: 8

6 potatoes, peeled   1 cup mayonnaise
1/4 cup cider vinegar   1/2 cup sour cream
1/2 cup finely chopped onion   2 Tblsp. fresh dill, snipped
2 oz. red caviar   small
black pepper

Cook the potatoes (do NOT overcook). Cool potatoes and slice 1/2-inch thick. Add vinegar and onions and gently toss. Combine the caviar, pepper, mayonnaise, sour cream and dill. Pour over the potatoes and gently toss again.

RUSSIAN EGG SALAD

Preparation time: 15 minutes   *Chef: Marilyn Sterberg*
Cooking time: 5 minutes   *Yacht: Sheerwill*
Serves: 6

6 eggs   Dressing:
1 (5-1/2 oz.) jar red caviar   4 Tblsp. mayonnaise
1 (5-1/2 oz.) jar black caviar   2 Tblsp. sour cream
Garnish: finely chopped lettuce   2 tsp. lime juice
     6 tomato wedges   5 drops Tabasco
     6 lime wedges   salt and pepper

Hard boil the eggs, cool. Cut them in half, lengthwise and arrange on a bed of lettuce. **Dressing:** Combine ingredients for the dressing and mask the eggs generously. Put a lavish teaspoonful of caviar onto each egg, alternating the black and red colours. Complete the garnish with the tomato and lime wedges.

Note: This simple appetizer always creates a sensation with our guests. You can substitute the less expensive brands of lumpfish caviar, if your budget doesn't run to the "real McCoy"!

CAVIAR SOUFFLE

Preparation time: 30 minutes   *Chef: Jan Robinson*
Chilling time: overnight   *Yacht: Vanity*
Serves: 4-6

1 scant Tblsp. of gelatin	1/2 tsp. lemon zest*
4 oz. whipping cream	1/4 tsp. salt
4 oz. cream cheese	3 shallots, pressed
1 egg white	1 (3-1/2 oz.) jar caviar
2 egg yolks	3 Tblsp. chives, minced
2 Tblsp. cream	1/2 cup onions, finely chopped
2 Tblsp. lemon juice	12 lemon wedges

Place gelatin in measuring cup. Add cold water to dissolve. Place over hot water to melt. Beat whipping cream until stiff and press cream cheese through a sieve. Beat egg white until stiff. Put egg yolks and two tablespoons of cream in a saucepan. Beat over low fire until creamy. Remove from flame. Add melted gelatin and slowly combine sieved cream cheese, lemon juice and zest, salt and shallots. Fold in whipped cream and beaten egg whites.

Put in a souffle dish and refrigerate overnight. Unmold the souffle on a large plate. Spread caviar over the top and sprinkle chopped chives around the base. Offer a small bowl of chopped onions, if desired, and lemon wedges on the side. *Serve with melba toast.*

* finely grated lemon peel.

Get ready, this recipe requires lots of beating!

POTATO CAKES WITH CAVIAR

Preparation time: 15 minutes   *Chef: Jan Robinson*
Cooking time: 12 minutes   *Yacht: Vanity*
Serves: 4

2 lbs. potatoes, peeled,   pepper to taste
   boiled and mashed   olive oil
1/3 cup Ricotta cheese   4 Tblsp. sour cream
1 egg   4 Tblsp. golden caviar
1 Tblsp. dill, minced   or black, or red
1 Tblsp. chopped chives
   or chopped green onion   Garnish: Fresh sprig dill

Combine potatoes, Ricotta, egg, and seasonings, mixing thoroughly. Divide the mixture into 4 cakes, about 3/4 inches thick and 3-1/2 inches in diameter. In a large skillet, pour enough olive oil to form a thin film and heat over a medium flame. Cook cakes until golden on each side. Place cakes on four small plates. Add salt and pepper to taste. Top each with 1 tablespoon of sour cream and 1 tablespoon caviar, or more according to taste. Garnish with dill. *Serve immediately as an appetizer with a Brut sparkling wine.*

CAVIAR PIE

Preparation Time: 10 minutes   *Chef: Carole Watkins Manto*
Serves: 8-10   *Yacht: Drumbeat*

1 (16 oz.) pkge. cream cheese	**1 (5 1/2 oz.) jar red caviar**
8 oz. sour cream	**1 (5 1/2 oz.) jar black caviar**
1 large red onion, chopped	**1 box melba toast**
3 hard cooked eggs, chopped	

Using a fork, combine cream cheese and sour cream, mixing well. Spread mixture into a 9-inch pie dish. Surround rim with chopped onion, then another circle of chopped egg. Use the red and black caviar to fill the center of the pie. *Serve with melba toast.*

Note: I usually make different designs with the caviar, such as the "yin and yang" symbol.

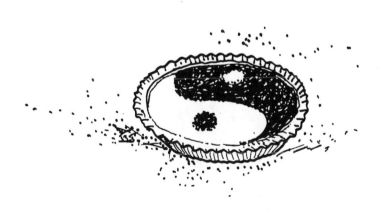

GOLDEN CAVIAR CREPES

Preparation time: 15 minutes   *Chef: Jennifer Dudley*
Cooking time: 20 minutes   *Yacht: September Morn*
Serves: 6

1 cup sour cream
1/2 cup purple onion, finely
    chopped
3 hard cooked eggs,
    finely chopped
1/4 tsp. black pepper

2 oz. black caviar
2 oz. golden caviar
12 prepared crepes
Garnish: 12 sprigs of fresh
    dill and 12 lemon wedges

In bowl, combine sour cream, onion, egg and pepper. Gently fold in caviars into sour cream mixture. Spread mixture evenly over heated crepe. Carefully roll or fold into triangle. Put 2 on serving plate and garnish with dill and lemon wedges. Sprinkle with caviars.

Note: I usually have crepes on hand as they are so versatile. For the above recipe, I add to the crepe batter:

2 tsp. fresh chives, chopped
1 Tblsp. fresh parsley, chopped
2 tsp. fresh dill, finely chopped

CLAMS

There are many species of clams that are used for food throughout the world. Along the East and West coasts there are four species of clams that are well known because of their high quality and flavor.

The Soft-Shelled Clam, also known as "the clam", is the most important commercial species from the Arctic Ocean to Cape Hatteras and central California.   You can recognize the soft-shelled clam by the relatively thin elongated gaping shell, a long neck which extends beyond the shell and is relatively easy to shuck. A soft-shelled clam may vary in color and also in thickness depending on the environment of the clam. Neither of these factors should change the flavor of the clam. This species of clams is a favorite for seafood lovers.

The Surf Clam, often referred to as the hen clam, or bar clam, is the largest in the north Atlantic. This clam often grows to about seven inches across. The shell is heavy and thick. The clam can be found in the surf just under the sands of the beaches from Labrador to the Carolinas. The meat of the surf clam is tougher than the soft-shelled clam, and is often used at clambakes and chowders because of its size. You can use the Surf clam for strips, chowders, minced clams and canned clams.

The Hard Clam, or hard-shelled clam, is also known as the littleneck, cherrystone or chowder and in Maine it is known as the quahog. You can determined the type of the clam depending on its size: necks - 2 - 2.5", cherries - 2.5-3.5", and chowders - 3 - 3.5+". The heavy rounded shell helps protect the body, which gives it a tender flavorful taste. The hard clam can grow up to 5" or more in length. The colorful purple and white inner shell of the clam is often used to make Indian Wampum Beads. This species of clam is equally delicious as the soft shell variety.

The Ocean Quahogs are often called "mahogany quahogs" or "black quahogs". These particular clams usually grow from 3 -1/ 2 " to 4" long and weighs about 1/2 pound each. It is very hard to open the shell of the ocean quahog. If you are not careful when opening, you might lose some of the fluid inside the clam. To open the ocean quahogs, it is best to steam the clam for a few minutes. You should always chop the meat of this clam because it is usually very tough. Because of the rich flavor, this clam is often used in making chowders.

Along with these are the West Coast Pismo, the Razor and the large Geoduck (pronounced gooey-duck) with its delicious neck that are commercially important.

HOW TO BUY CLAMS:

Clams that are bought in the shell must be kept alive and fresh until cooked. In buying live clams in the shell, the shells should be closed or should close tightly when tapped. Gaping shells indicate that shellfish are dead and therefore inedibile. Quahog shells when handled, should be closed tightly. Soft-shelled clams or surf clams should show muscle movement in the neck when touched (these clams gape naturally) . Clams can be kept alive for 7 to 10 days if stored in a moist, cool place.

You can usually buy shucked clams either by the pint or quart. When purchased they should be plump and creamy with clear liquid and free from ammonia odor. When refrigerated, they should remain fresh for up to 10 days.

HOW TO SHUCK CLAMS:

Use only fresh live clams for shucking. Hold the clam in the palm of one hand with the shell's hinge against the palm. Insert a slender strong knife between the halves of the shell and cut around the shell, slicing both muscle free from the two halves of the shell. If you are serving on the half shell, remove only one half of the shell (you can save the liquids to use in chowders).

Another way to shuck clams is to place the hard shells in a small amount of boiling water. Cover and steam for 5-10 minutes until they are partially open. Remove the meat from the shell. You can also freeze the clams and then wash under tap water for several minutes. These shells will then open wide enough to allow you to shuck.

The soft-shelled clams and surf clams do not have tight fitting shells, so they are much easier to open.

TIPS:

Clams are available canned as whole meats, minced, in prepared chowders, and in the shell.

Always freeze immediately after shucking due to a short shelflife or store in small containers in their own liquid and packed in ice. They can be kept under refrigeration for 7-10 days.

Frozen clams can be thawed under cold running water or in a refrigerator. Never thaw at room temperature or under warm water and never refreeze. To retain quality, clams should be thawed quickly and used immediately.

Place Clams in blender and combine with favorite batter for fritters.

Clam juice cocktail makes an excellent Bloody Mary.

SPICY CLAMS IN OYSTER SAUCE

Preparation time: 20 minutes   *Chef: Jan Robinson*
Cooking time: 15 minutes   *Yacht: Vanity*
Serves: 4

4 dozen medium-size clams   **2 Tblsp. dry sherry**
4 cups water   **2 Tblsp. soy sauce**
2 Tblsp. grated ginger   **1/4 cup oyster sauce**
4 small hot chiles, chopped   **1 Tblsp. sugar**
4 Tblsp. grated lemon peel   **1/3 cup olive or peanut oil**
1/4 cup cooked black beans   **2 Tblsp. cornstarch mixed**
4 - 6 cloves garlic, chopped   **with 6 Tblsp. water**
                                                 Garnish: fresh cilantro

Scrub the clams. Bring 4 cups of water to a boil in a large pot, or
wok. Add the clams, cover and steam just until they open. Remove
immediately to a bowl of ice water to stop the cooking. Save the
clam broth. Drain clams and set aside. Combine ginger, hot chiles
and 2 Tblsp. lemon peel. Chop the black beans and combine with
the garlic and sherry. Combine the reserved clam stock, soy sauce,
oyster sauce, remaining lemon peel and sugar.

Heat the oil in a large skillet, or wok. Add the ginger mixture, stir
10 seconds and add the black bean mixture. Cook 30 seconds and
add the clam stock-soy sauce mixture. When sauce boils, add the
corn starch mixture. Cook until thickened, then add the clams. Stir
until clams are heated and coated with the sauce.

*Serve the clams in their shells with the sauce. I also serve a big
bowl of steamed brown rice, and a fresh green salad, with a good
chilled bottle of wine .*

BABY CLAMS CHINA CLOUD

Preparation time: 15 minutes
Cooking time: 35 minutes
Serves: 4-6

Chef: Nancy Raye
Yacht: China Cloud

1/4 cup olive oil
2 Tblsp. chopped parsley
1 medium size onion, chopped
4 anchovy fillets, chopped
2 clove garlic, minced
1/2 cup celery, chopped
3 medium size potatoes, cut
  in small cubes
1 Tblsp. tomato paste
1 bay leaf
freshly ground pepper

2 cups chopped tomatoes,
  fresh or canned
1 cup white wine
2 cups boiling water
1/4 tsp. thyme, oregano
1/2 tsp. red pepper flakes
1 (10 oz.) can baby clams
  including liquid
toasted or fried Italian
  bread
Garnish: chopped parsley

Heat oil in heavy pot. Saute the parsley, onion, anchovies, and garlic. Stir and heat until lightly golden but not brown. Add celery, carrots, green pepper and herbs. Cook 3 more minutes. Add tomatoes, water, tomato paste, and wine. Mix well. Add potatoes. Keep on low simmer for 20 minutes. Add the can of clams, heat 5 more minutes to blend flavors. *Serve in bowls containing Italian bread and sprinkle parsley on top.*

Alternative: Oysters

Eliminate sticking: When pan frying or sauteing always heat your pan before adding the butter or oil. Not even eggs stick with this method.

CLAM - STUFFED MUSHROOMS

Preparation time: 15 minutes   *Chef: Susan David*
Cooking time: 13 minutes   *Yacht: Wishing Star*
Makes: 36 mushrooms

36 large mushrooms   **1/2 cup dry bread crumbs**
  (about 2 lbs.)   **1/3 cup parsley, chopped**
1 (8 oz.) can minced clams   **3/4 tsp. salt**
1/2 cup butter or margarine **1/4 tsp. pepper**
1 clove garlic, minced   **Garnish: Endive lettuce**
                                      and lemon wedges

Remove mushroom stems, chop and set aside. Place caps, rounded side down, on rack of broiler. Drain liquid from clams and reserve. In a 10" skillet, over medium heat, melt butter and brush on caps. In remaining butter cook chopped stems, garlic and clam liquid for 5 minutes. Stir in clams and remaining ingredients. Spoon into caps and broil 8 minutes until tender. Place on bed of endive and use lemon wedges as garnish.

Note: This way of preparing stuffed mushrooms is a great change from the usual cheese stuffed mushrooms.

CLAMS LINGUINE

Preparation time: 10 minutes   *Chef: Silvia & Stanley Dabney*
Cooking time: 20 minutes   *Yacht: Native Sun*
Serves: 4

1 lb. Linguine	1/3 cup butter
6 cups water	2 cups clams (2 large cans)
1- 1/2 cups clam juice	(reserve liquid)
1/3 cup olive oil	1/4 cup chopped parsley
1 Tblsp. chopped	fresh ground pepper
and smashed garlic	1/8 tsp. hot red peppers flakes

Boil linguine in 6 cups of water and 1-1/2 cups clam juice. Meanwhile, heat oil, add garlic and cook briefly. Add butter and stir, don't brown. Add clams, parsley and hot peppers. Taste! Adjust seasonings. Toss or serve over linguine. Rub plate with a little butter before plating pasta. (Spaghetti could be substituted for linguine).

Note: Aside from the linguine cooking, this takes all of 5 minutes to prepare. It's so simple that you might be tempted not to try it, but that would be a mistake and you would miss out on a really delicious meal.

Caesar salad and french bread (to soak up the sauce) make this an elegant dinner. Don't forget the champagne and a chocolate mousse for dessert. Oh la la..... I've talked myself into making this for din-din tonight.

Alternative: Conch

ELEGANT CREAM CLAM CHOWDER

Preparation time: 30 minutes   *Chef: Mardy Array*
Cooking time: 45 minutes   *Yacht: Emerald Lady*
Serves: 6

6 strips bacon	**2 cups clam broth**
1/3 cup chopped green onion	**1 tsp. salt**
1/4 cup chopped green pepper	**1/2 tsp. pepper**
1 stalk celery	**1 tsp. Worcestershire sauce**
1 sliced carrot	**good shake Tabasco sauce**
1 garlic clove, minced	**2 cups chopped clams**
5 potatoes, peeled and cubed	**2 cups light cream**
1/4 cup sherry	

In a large kettle, cook bacon until crisp. Remove, drain and chop. Add green onions, green peppers, celery, carrots, garlic and potatoes, mixing well. Add sherry and simmer briefly. Add clam broth, salt, pepper, Worcestershire sauce and Tabasco. Bring to a boil, reduce heat and simmer 15-20 minutes. Potatoes should be tender. Add bacon and clams to broth, then add cream and stir until well blended and piping hot. Hint: *Complete this hearty meal with a crusty loaf of bread!*

BASIC CLAM CHOWDER

Preparation time: 30 minutes
Cooking time: 45 minutes
Serves: 4-6

Chef: Jan Robinson
Yacht: Vanity

4-1/2 lbs. littleneck or
   cherrystone clams,
   well drained
1 cup water
2 Tblsp. (1/4 stick) butter
1 medium onion, minced
1 1/4 lbs. boiling potatoes,
   peeled and cut into
   1/2 inch cubes
1 1/4 to 1 1/2 cups whipping
   cream
1/2 to 3/4 cup milk

1 tsp. fresh thyme or 1/4
   tsp. dried, crumbled
1 tsp. snipped fresh chives
   (optional)
1/2 tsp. minced fresh
   tarragon or 1/8 tsp.
   dried, crumbled
   (optional)
Pinch of cayenne pepper
Salt and freshly ground
   pepper
Garnish: fresh parsley

Place clams in large saucepan; add water. Cover and cook over medium-high heat just until shells open, about 10 minutes. Remove opened clams. Cook remaining clams 2 more minutes; discard any that do not open. Drain clams, reserving cooking liquid. Remove clams from shells; chop coarsely. Strain cooking liquid through strainer lined with double layer of dampened cheesecloth; reserve clam cooking liquid.

Melt butter in heavy large saucepan over medium-low heat. Add onion and cook until softened, stirring frequently, about 10 minutes. Mix in reserved clam cooking liquid and potatoes, stirring potatoes into liquid. Cover and simmer over low heat until potatoes are just tender, stirring frequently, 10 to 12 minutes.

Transfer 1-1/2 cups potatoes to processor using slotted spoon. Add 3/4 cup potato cooking liquid and puree until smooth, about 30 seconds. Return potato mixture to saucepan. *(Can be prepared 1 day ahead. Cover potato mixture and clams separately and refrigerate.)*

Combine 1-1/4 cups cream and 1/2 cup milk. Return potato mixture to simmer, stirring occasionally. Add cream mixture and stir just until heated through; do not boil or mixture will curdle. Reduce heat to low, mix in thyme, chives, tarragon, cayenne, salt and pepper. Add clams and stir just until heated through, about 2 minutes. Thin chowder with remaining 1/4 cup milk if desired and stir until heated through. If richer chowder is desired, add remaining 1/4 cup cream and stir until heated through. Ladle into bowls. Garnish with parsley.

QUICK N' EASY CLAM CHOWDER

Preparation time: 10 minutes
Cooking time: 20 minutes
Serves: 6-8

Chef: Maureen Romagnolo
Yacht: Gracious Lady

1 stick butter (4 oz.)
2 carrots, sliced thin
1 (10-3/4 oz.) can cream of
   celery soup
1 (13 oz.) can evaporated
   milk

1 (15 oz.) can sliced potatoes
2 (7-1/2 oz.) cans minced
   clams
dash of garlic powder
salt and pepper, to taste

Melt butter in pan. Saute carrots until tender. Add all ingredients
and simmer for 15 minutes.

CLAM - CORN GRIDDLE CAKES

Preparation time:15 minutes
Cooking time: 20 minutes
Serves: 6

Chef: Pero Robinson
Yacht:Vanity

2 (7-1/2 oz.) cans of clams,
   minced
1-1/2 cups sifted flour
1 cup yellow corn meal
5 tsp. baking powder
1 tsp. salt

1-1/2 cups clam liquor
   and milk
2 eggs, beaten
1/3 cup melted fat or oil
butter or margarine
Cran-Applesauce

Drain clams. Reserve liquor and add enough milk to make 1-1/2
cups. Sift dry ingredients together. Add milk mixture, clams and
eggs. Stir only until blended. Drop 1/4 cup batter onto a hot, well-
greased griddle or fry pan. Fry 1 to 2 minutes or until brown. Turn
carefully and fry 1 to 2 minutes longer or until brown. *Serve with
butter and Cran-Applesauce.* Makes approximately 18 griddle
cakes.

SPINACH SOUP WITH CLAMS AND PLENTY OF GARLIC

Preparation time: 20 minutes   *Chef: Jan Robinson*
Cooking time: 50 minutes   *Yacht: Vanity*
Serves: 6

12 garlic cloves, unpeeled
2 Tblsp. olive oil
7 cups rich chicken stock
36 tiny fresh clams,
   scrubbed

6 cups loosely packed fresh
   spinach leaves, cut into 1
   inch wide strips
1 Tblsp. fresh lemon juice
freshly ground pepper

Preheat oven to 400 degrees F. Place garlic in small baking dish. Drizzle with 1 Tblsp. oil. Bake until toothpick pierces garlic easily, about 15 minutes. Peel and thinly slice.

Heat remaining 1 tablespoon oil in heavy large saucepan over low heat. Add garlic and cook until golden brown, stirring frequently, about 5 minutes. Add 6 cups stock and bring to boil. Reduce heat, cover partially and simmer 15 minutes.

Bring remaining 1 cup stock to boil in heavy medium skillet over high heat. Add clams. Cover and steam until shells open, 1-1/2 to 3 minutes. Remove opened clams. Cook remaining clams about 5 more minutes; discard any that do not open.

Divide clams among heated soup bowls using slotted spoon. Strain clam cooking liquid into garlic stock. Add spinach. Cover tightly and cook stock over high heat until spinach wilts, about 2 minutes. Add lemon juice. Season with pepper. Ladle stock over clams. Serve hot.

COD

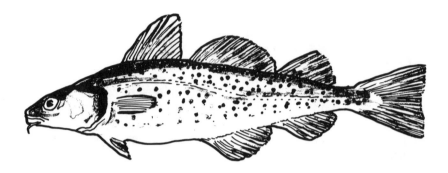

Description: There are many species of Cod. Cod have heavy, tapering bodies, three dorsal fins and two anal fins and a prominent chin barbel.   Most of the Cod are either olive-green,grey or deep red. Green, brown, or reddish spots occur along the back and sides, sometimes extending onto the fins. Cod are one of the important food fishes native to the North Atlantic.

Size: The mature Cod averages about 10 pounds.

Flavor: Fresh Cod is a lean meat with firm white flakes that divide when cooked.This produces a light flavor.

Habitat: Worldwide. The **Pacific Cod** is found from Oregon to the Bering Sea. **Atlantic Cod** are mostly caught off Iceland, Newfoundland and Greenland. The Atlantic Cod is one of many species but is the leader in commercial value.

Preparation: Cod are marketed fresh , frozen, air dried, smoked, salted and canned. They may be prepared by baking, frying,boiling or any other method you may choose. Cod are a very versatile food fish.

Other names: Pollock, Silver Hake, Atlantic Tomcod, Haddock, Atlantic Halibut, True Cod.

GOLDEN SEA FOOD PASTRIES

Preparation time: 20 minutes　　　*Chef: Anne Brown*
Cooking time: 15 minutes　　　*Yacht: Golden Skye*
Serves:

**8 squares of phyllo pastry
　6 x 6 plus extra scraps
2 Tblsp. melted butter
1 lb. cod fillets, chopped into
　1" cubes**

**3/4 lb. small shrimps, cooked
　and peeled
2 oz. cream cheese with garlic
　herbs (bousin type)
Garnish: lemon wedges and
　cucumber twists**

Preheat oven to 375 degrees F. Brush each square of phyllo pastry with melted butter, stack between sheets of waxed paper. Take one sheet at a time using an extra scrap to strengthen the center. Place 4 pieces of fish and 3 or 4 shrimps in the center of the pastry and top with a teaspoon of cheese. Draw the pastry up around the filling twisting the edges together to form a candy-type parcel. Repeat seven more times and bake in the oven for 15 minutes. Garnish and serve immediately.

Note: Do not panic if phyllo tears a little in preparation. The cooked product will look fine.

TOMATOES STUFFED WITH COD

Preparation time: 20 minutes　　　*Chef: Jan Robinson*
Cooking time: 30 minutes　　　*Yacht:Vanity*
Serves: 4-6

**8 medium tomatoes
1 lb. Cod fillets
1 tsp. pepper
1 Tblsp. butter**

**1 rasher bacon chopped
　and lightly fried
1 tsp. tomato sauce
1 tsp. white vinegar**

Poach Cod in 1 cup salted water to which white vinegar has been added. Cook about 6 minutes. Wipe tomatoes, then cut a slice off end opposite stem. Scoop out flesh discarding any woody pieces. Mix flaked fish, tomato pulp, bacon, salt and pepper. Carefully fill tomato shells with this stuffing, then place in greased baking dish. Dot with butter. Bake at 350 degrees F. for 20 minutes. *Serve hot for breakfast or lunch.*

VIRGIN ISLANDS RED COD

Preparation time: 25 minutes   *Chef: Jan Robinson*
Cooking time: 30 minutes   *Yacht: Vanity*
Serves: 4

2 lb. Cod (fillets or steaks)   2 level Tblsp. flour
1 tsp. flour   1 Tblsp. butter
2 green onions, chopped   6 blanched oysters
1/4 tsp. black pepper,   1 egg yolk
    or 2 peppercorns   1/4 cup cream
1 small carrot, sliced   1-1/2 cups mashed
1 small bay leaf   Potatoes
1/2 tsp. thyme   1 Tblsp. butter
1/4 cup white wine   1 egg yolk, beaten
1/2 cup milk   Garnish: sprigs of
1-1/2 cups water   parsley

Remove any bones from fish, cut into serving size pieces. Prepare court bouillon using salt, spring onions, carrot, pepper, bay leaf, thyme, white wine, milk and water. Simmer fish in this liquid 10-15 minutes in covered saucepan. Strain off 1 cup court bouillon, put in small saucepan.

Thicken with butter and flour which have been rubbed together. Cook sauce until creamy stirring constantly, approximately 4 minutes. Remove from heat, add egg yolk, oysters and cream. Place lid on a saucepan to keep sauce hot.

Pipe or spoon a border of potatoes on ovenware serving dish, brown at 450 degrees F., remove from oven. Arrange fish in centre of this serving dish, pour over sauce. Garnish and serve hot.

Alternatives: Sole, Rockfish

CONCH

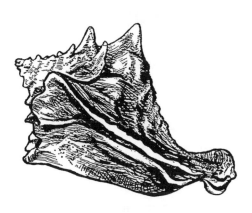

Description: The conch is a beautiful spiral shaped marine shellfish that resembles snails. The hard shell houses the soft-bodied animal which has eyes and a horn that he uses to move around the sea floor. The meat of the Conch is a valuable source of protein. Today the shells are used primarily in the manufacture of jewelry.

Size: The Queen Conch is truly the queen. Beginning as a microscopic hatchling she matures in 3-1/2 years and grows to full size in a total of about 4-1/2 to 5 years. At this stage she is about the size of a cantaloupe or small melon.

Habitat: She is scattered throughout the tropical waters of the western North Atlantic from the Florida keys and the Bahamas to the equator.

Flavor: The Queen Conch has a clean fresh taste that is very delicate and is considered more elegant than the lobster.

Preparation: Conch is sold in local areas live in the shell, cleaned, whole or ground and in one or two pound packages. Outside of the tropics most is sold frozen. When buying be sure that it has been "skinned" (removal of the heavy skin from the meat). Fresh Conch should be used within 24 hours and frozen in about one week. Allow two Conchs per person or one pound for four to six persons. Conch needs to be tenderized either by marinating or by beating with a mallet. The meat should be sliced and then beaten until its about two times normal size.

Conch is pronounced **konk**

CRISP CONCH

Preparation time: 15 minutes   *Chef:Jan Robinson*
Cooking time: 10 minutes   *Yacht:Vanity*
Serves: 4

2 large conch, cleaned   1 egg
4 medium potatoes   2 Tblsp. flour
1 green pepper   pepper to taste
2 onions   oil
dash tabasco

Put conch, potatoes, green pepper, onions in food processor, grind until course. Add tabasco, egg, flour and pepper. Make flat patties with hands. Cook in a hot iron skillet until crisp on both sides.

Note: These are great cooked in bacon grease, but not so great on the hips!!

BAHAMIAN CRACK CONCH

Preparation time: 10 minutes   *Chef: Sylvia & Stanley Dabney*
Cooking time: 10 minutes   *Yacht: Native Sun*
Serves: 4

1 tsp. allspice   2 large eggs, beaten
1/4 tsp. garlic powder   6 Tblsp. fresh lime juice
3/4 cup fine bread crumbs   1/8 tsp. Tabasco
1-1/2 lb. conch, cleaned and
  tenderized

In shallow bowl, mix allspice, garlic powder, bread crumbs. Dip conch pieces into beaten egg. Roll in bread crumb mixture and fry in hot deep oil (1" in fry pan) until golden brown. Turn and fry on second side. Mix lime juice and hot sauce together and pour over conch just before serving. *Serve with cole slaw, peas and rice.*

Alternatives: Abalone

BATTERED CONCH AND RED SAUCE

Preparation time: 15 minutes
Marinating time: 30 minutes
Cooking time: 10 minutes
Serves: 4

Chef: Jan Robinson
Yacht: Vanity

4 conch cleaned
1/4 cup lime juice
dash tabasco
1/3 cup flour
3 Tblsp. cornstarch
pinch baking powder
1/4 tsp. sugar
1/4 tsp. curry powder
2 Tblsp. grated coconut
1 egg, lightly beaten

about 1/4 cup ice water
oil for deep frying

Red Sauce:
  1/2 cup catsup
  1/4 tsp. pepper
  1 Tblsp. Worcestershire
  1 Tblsp. lime juice
  tabasco, to taste

Have conch tenderized, or cover conch with a clean piece of fabric and pound away with gusto! until conch is lacy. Marinate conch in lime juice and tabasco for 30 minutes, or more. Drain and cut into bite-size pieces, about 1-1/2 inches. Mix together flour, cornstarch, baking powder, sugar, curry powder and coconut. Stir in egg and enough ice water to make a loose batter. Immediately add conch and stir to coat. Drop into hot oil (365 degrees F.) cook until golden brown. Drain on paper towels and serve hot with Red Sauce.

Red Sauce: Mix all ingredients together

Alternatives: Abalone, Whelk

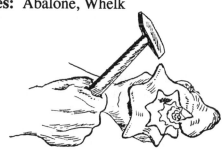

CONCH FUSION

Preparation time: 15 minutes
Cooking time: 40 minutes in a
pressure cooker
Serves: 6

Chef: Brooks Kuhn
Yacht: Rising Sun 47

2 lbs. conch, cut into bite
  size pieces
1/4 cup white vinegar

salt and pepper, to taste
1-1/2 cups water

Pressure cook all ingredients at 15 lbs. for 40 minutes or until tender. *Serve with cocktail sauce and crackers as hors d' oeuvre, or in a creole sauce over rice, or white sauce over pasta, or used in fritters - VERY CONCH FUSING !*

CARIB CONCH SALAD

Preparation time: 35 minutes
Chilling time: 1 hour
Serves: 6

Chef: Suzan Salisbury
Yacht: Gypsy

3 or 4 conchs, (about 1 lb.)
1 medium onion, finely
  chopped
1 medium cucumber,
  chopped
1 large tomato, chopped
1/2 cup celery, chopped

1/2 to 1 cup lime or
  sour orange juice
salt and pepper, to taste
Tabasco, to taste

Garnish: lemon twist or
  celery stick with leaves

Catch 3 or 4 conchs. Extract from shells, clean and cut into small pieces. Mix conch well with remaining ingredients. Chill at least one hour in sealed container. *Serve alone or on lettuce leaves.*

CONCH AND EGG SALAD

Preparation time: 30 minutes   *Chef: Sylvia & Stanley Dabney*
Chilling time: 30 minutes   *Yacht: Native Sun*
Serves: 4

1 lb. conch, cleaned   1/2 tsp. salt
6 Tblsp. diced onion   2 Tblsp. lime juice
4 Tblsp. diced celery   1/2 cup mayonnaise
2 hard boiled eggs, chopped   dash hot pepper sauce
4 Tblsp. sweet red pepper

Tenderize conch to lacy texture, or grind in a meat grinder, after boiling for 15 minutes. Toss tenderized conch with onion, celery, chopped eggs, sweet red pepper, salt, and lime juice. Add mayonnaise and hot pepper sauce. Chill before serving. *Can be served as a sandwich, appetizer or salad.*

CONCH SALAD

Preparation time: 15 minutes   *Chef: Didgie Belschner*
Chilling time: 1 hour   *Yacht: Tequila*
Serves: 4

2 large conch, cleaned   Juice of 2 lemons or limes
2 stalks celery   1/2 cup olive oil
1 green pepper   Thyme
2 scallions   Freshly ground pepper
1 large garlic clove   Dill
1 tomato

Pound conch until tender, and slice as thin as possible, cross grain. Finely chop celery, green pepper, scallions, garlic and tomato. Mix all together. Add lemon juice, olive oil, and herbs. Toss and refrigerate 1 hour at least.

Serve on top of a lettuce leaf on individual salad plates with wheat crackers. As an hors d' oeuvre, serve on a bed of lettuce on a chilled platter, along with a variety of crackers.

SWEET AND SOUR CONCH OVER RICE

Preparation time: 15 minutes   *Chef: Sylvia & Stanley Dabney*
Cooking time: 10 minutes   *Yacht: Native Sun*
Serves: 4

2 large conch, cleaned and   1 (15-1/4 oz.) can pineapple
  tenderized   chunks, with juice
2 Tblsp. butter   2 Tblsp. sugar
1 green pepper, chopped   1 Tblsp. cornstarch
1 carrot, chopped (optional)   2 Tblsp. vinegar
1 onion, chopped

Cut conch into bite-size pieces. Saute conch in butter until slightly browned. Add vegetables and drained pineapple chunks. Cook 5 minutes. Combine sugar, cornstarch, pineapple juice and vinegar and stir into conch mixture. Cook and stir until sauce is thick and clear. *Serve over rice, along with stir fried pea pods and deep fried won ton skins.*

CONCH CURRY

Preparation time: 20 minutes   *Chef:Sylvia & Stanley Dabney*
Cooking time:15 minutes   *Yacht: Native Sun*
Serves: 4

2 large conch, cleaned,   1 clove garlic, smashed
  and tenderized   1/2 tsp. lime juice
2 Tblsp. butter   2 tsp. curry
1 Tblsp. grated coconut   salt and pepper
  (optional)   dash Tabasco sauce
2 onions, chopped   1 (8 oz.) can tomato suace
1 green pepper, chopped   3/4 cup red wine

Cut conch into bite size pieces. Saute conch in butter to brown. Add all remaining ingredients except wine. Stir and allow to simmer 10 minutes. Add wine, stir. Adjust seasonings. *Serve over rice.*

MANHATTAN CONCH CHOWDER

Preparation time: 30 minutes   *Chef: Martha Purinton*
Cooking time: 1 hour   *Yacht: Iskareen*
Serves: 6-8

1/4 lb. bacon
2 potatoes
1 large onion
1 red pepper
1 green pepper
4 stalks celery
3-4 carrots
1 lb. conch, (4-5 pieces)

2 potatoes
2 (15 oz.) cans whole
   tomatoes, mashed
1 tsp. salt
1 tsp. thyme
Hot sauce, to taste
2 qts. water
1/2 cup bread crumbs

Dice bacon and potatoes. Grind onion, peppers, celery, carrots, and conch in food processor. Fry bacon in large pot until clear. Add vegetables, tomato, salt, thyme, hot sauce, conch and 2 quarts water. Cook 45 minutes until conch is tender. Stir occasionally. Add bread crumbs, stirring until blended in and thickened. Cook 3-5 minutes longer. *Serve with hot rolls or bread sticks and pass the sherry bottle.*

Note: Make ahead and freeze for any easy lunch or first course.

ITALIAN CONCH SALAD

Preparation time: 15 minutes   *Chef: Jan Robinson*
Marinating time: overnight   *Yacht: Vanity*
Serves: 4

1-1/2 conch, cleaned
2 large celery stalks,
1 cup bean sprouts
12 cherry tomatoes, halved
1/4 cup fresh parsley,
   chopped

Dressing:
   1/2 cup olive oil
   2 Tblsp. vinegar
   1 tsp. oregano
   1/2 tsp. basil
   3 cloves garlic, crushed
   freshly ground pepper

Dressing: Make this first. Combine all ingredients. Grind or mince the conch. Finely chop the celery. Place the celery and conch in the dressing and marinate overnight. Before serving, toss with the bean sprouts, parsley and tomatoes. *I serve this on Romaine lettuce leaves, with garlic French bread, and a good chilled bottle of wine.*

CONCH CHOWDER

Preparation time: 30 minutes   *Chef: Lyn Tucker*
Cooking time: 1 hour   *Yacht: Impervious Cover*
Serves: 8-10

3 large leeks
5 medium potatoes
3 Tblsp. butter
3 cups chicken broth
4 cleaned conch

3/4 cup white wine
salt and pepper, to taste
2 cups Half & Half cream
3 Tblsp. chopped fresh
   parsley

Slice leeks into 1/2" pieces. Peel and dice potatoes. Saute leeks and potatoes in butter, stirring to prevent browning. Add broth. Tenderize conch meat thoroughly with mallet. Rip into small bite size pieces. Toss into broth. Add wine, salt and pepper. Simmer 1 hour. Stir in cream and parsley. Do not boil. Garnish with fresh chopped parsley. *Goes great with corn muffins and a spinach salad.. Hearty and healthy!.*

CONCH MARINARA

Preparation time: 10 minutes   *Chef: Sylvia & Stanley Dabney*
Cooking time: 40 minutes   *Yacht: Native Sun*
Serves: 4

2 large conch, cleaned and
   tenderized
1/2 cup oil
2 sliced onions
2 cloves garlic, smashed
2 diced tomatoes or 1 (16 oz.)
   can drained

salt, pepper
dash oregano and thyme
1/2 cup sherry
1 (1-3/5 oz.) tube anchovy
   paste

Garnish: Fresh parsley

Heat oil in a skillet; brown onion and garlic lightly. Cut conch into bite-size pieces and add to skillet. Cover and simmer 20 minutes. Add tomatoes and seasonings, simmer additional 20 minutes. Taste and adjust seasonings. Add sherry, stir. *Serve over noodles or rice.* Garnish with fresh parsley. *Serve with a crisp green salad and garlic bread.*

GOOMBAY CONCH CHOWDER

Preparation time: 30 minutes   *Chef: Mardy Array*
Cooking time: 2 hours   *Yacht: Emerald Lady*
Marinating time: 1 hour
Serves: 6

1 lb. conch, tenderized, chopped or (processer ground)
4 Tblsp. lime juice
6 strips bacon
2 large onions, chopped
2 garlic cloves, chopped
3 stalks celery (with tops), chopped
3 (14-1/2 oz.) cans chicken broth
1 bottle clam juice

2 bay leaves
1 tsp. Worcestershire sauce
2 shakes Tabasco
1/3 cup sherry
2 cups new potatoes
1 (1 lb.) can chopped tomatoes
1/4 tsp. paprika
2 tsp. chopped parsley
1/4 tsp. oregano
1/4 tsp. basil
1/4 tsp. thyme
1/8 tsp. turmeric

Marinate chopped conch in lime juice for 1 hour. Strain off juice, reserving 2 tablespoons. In a large kettle cook bacon until almost crisp. Remove, drain and chop into 1 inch pieces. In the bacon drippings, saute onion, garlic and celery until tender. Add broth, clam juice, bay leaves, Worcestershire sauce, Tabasco, sherry. Peel and cube potatoes and add. Stir to blend and simmer briefly. Add tomatoes, conch and seasonings. Simmer 1-1/2 hours. Remember to adjust the seasonings to your taste. *Serve with a shake of hot pepper sauce on top of each serving.*

Alternative: Abalone

WEST INDIAN STEWED CONCH

Preparation time: 20 minutes   *Chef: Ann Brown*
Cooking time: 1 hour 15 minutes   *Yacht: Antipodes*
        with pressure cooker
      : 2 hours 15 minutes
        without pressure cooker
Serves: 6-8

3 lbs. cleaned conch	1/2 tsp. black pepper
2 bay leaves	2 tsp. thyme
1/2 cup butter	2 tsp. marjoram
1 small onion, chopped	1 tsp. Adobo seasoning
1 medium tomato, chopped	Cayenne pepper or Tabasco
1 Tblsp. garlic, minced	sauce, to taste

Place cleaned whole conch in pressure cooker. Cover with water, add bay leaves and cook 1 hour. (If you don't have a pressure cooker use a covered pan and cook 2 hours. Check occasionally to see that water does not boil out, add more when necessary.) Fifteen minutes before the conch is cooked, simmer all other ingredients in the butter. Remove conch from heat, reserving 1 cup of the liquid. Cut conch into 1" slices and add with reserved liquid to the butter and vegetable mixture. Simmer 10 minutes. Serve over rice.

Note: If you have first time conch eaters and are not sure about serving this as a meal or the day's catch was rather small, try this for an hors d'oeuvre. Reduce the recipe to 1/3, cut the conch into bite-size pieces and serve with French bread.

STAR CONCH FRITTERS

Preparation time: 20 minutes   *Chef: Cass Stewart*
Cooking time: 10 minutes   *Yacht: Morning Star*
Chilling time: 3 hours
Serves: 4-6

1-1/2 cup flour
1 tsp. salt
1/4 tsp. pepper
1 Tblsp. cooking oil
2 beaten egg yolks
1/2 tsp. Tabasco sauce

1 tsp. parsley
3/4 cup flat beer
1 lb. conch (tenderized
   and chopped) or 1 (16
   oz.) can conch (drained,
   dried, and chopped)

Mix all ingredients and refrigerate for at least three hours. Drop by spoonfuls into hot oil and cook until golden. Serve with cocktail sauce.

CORNMEAL CONCH FRITTERS

Preparation time: 20 minutes   *Chef: Ann Brown*
Cooking time:30 minutes   *Yacht: Antipodes*
Serves: 6-8

1 lb. cleaned conch
1 small green pepper
1/2 medium onion
1/2 medium tomato
1 stalk celery with leaves
6 sprigs parsley
1 egg, well beaten

3/4 cup cornmeal
3 tsp. baking powder
salt and pepper
Oil for frying

Seafood Sauce: (See
   recipe below)

Whirl conch in food processor until it forms an almost paste-like texture. Scrape into mixing bowl and set aside. Mince pepper, onion, tomato, celery and parsley in processor. Add to conch. Stir in eggs, cornmeal, baking powder and seasonings. Drop by small spoonfuls into very hot oil that almost covers the fritter. Fry on both sides until golden brown.

Seafood Sauce: Mix together 3/4 cup catsup, 4 Tblsp. horseradish (or to taste) and a dash of Tabasco. *Easy but good!*

Note: When frying do not put too many fritters in the pan at once as this drops the temperature of the oil too much. Fry small batches keeping them warm in the oven until serving.

CAYMAN CONCH FRITTERS

Preparation time: 10 minutes
Cooking time: 10 minutes
Serves: 6

Chef: Linda Green
Yacht: Elysee

6 conch, cleaned
1 medium onion, finely diced
1 bell pepper, finely diced
2 small ribs celery, diced
1 egg, beaten
2 cups flour

2 or 3 tsp. baking powder
1-1/2 cups water
hot pepper sauce
salt and pepper, to taste
cooking oil

Grind conch very finely, then mix conch, onion, pepper and celery in bowl and set aside. Combine flour, baking powder, egg, salt and peppers, and water in large bowl. Add conch mixture and mix thoroughly. Drop by teaspoonful into hot oil. Fry till golden.

No one does conch better than the Cayman Islanders. This is a traditional recipe from Grand Cayman - simple and good!

CRABS

Crab is the collective name for a large number of marine animals that are related to the lobster and spiny lobster. Within this grouping the true crabs are characterized by having a flat broad body with the abdomen very short and reflexed in contrast to the long cylindrical body and extended abdomen of lobsters and similar creatures. Crabs have hard shells or exoskeletons. Periodically, in order to grow, they shed this external shell. One interesting fact about crabs is their ability to drop an injured leg and replace it by growing a new one. <u>It is an excellent source of easily digested protein and vitamins (especially thiamine, niacin, and riboflavin), but is low in fat and calorie content.</u>

There are several types of crabs found in the United States:

Blue Crab, also known as Softshell, is one of the most valuable crustaceans in the United States. The blue crab is a savory shellfish that spends most of its time walking along the bottom of the bays and sounds where it lives. Blue crabs, like other crabs, possess five pairs of legs with the first pair always equipped with pincers. Blue crabs, when fully grown, average five to seven inches across the back of the shell. The shell is brownish green or dark green and is drawn out on each side into a long spine. The underside of the body and the legs are white, while the tops of the claws show varying amounts of blue. The tops of the claws in the female blue crab are bright red.

King Crab, also known as Alaska King Crab, one of Alaska's most valuable resources, is a tremendous fellow. Although the average size is 11 pounds, some have weighed up to twenty-four pounds. King crabs are usually found in cold waters toward the poles and in the deep sea. Although king crabmeat has a flavor, color, and texture all its own, it may be used interchangeably with other crabmeat in most recipes. The prime meat of the king crab is in the claws, legs, and shoulders, and this is the only part that is used.

The Dungeness Crab is found along the Pacific coast from Alaska to southern California. It is light reddish-brown on the back with a pattern of lighter streaks and spots. Dungeness crab meat can be used interchangeably with other crab meat in recipes. Use Dungeness crab meat in canapes, appetizers, dips, sauces, cocktails, salads, and a variety of other entrees.

From the Northeast come several commercial varieties such as the Rock Crab, Jonah Crab, Red Crab, Sea Crab and Picked Toe Crab, each with it's own delicious taste.

HOW TO BUY:

Usually live crabs may be purchased on certain days at your local seafood store. This is due to the short shelflife of about 24 hours when stored in a refrigerator or other cool place. They can be placed in coolers for transporting but make sure the crabs don't come in contact with the ice. Cook as soon as possible.
Cooked crab meat can be purchased fresh, frozen, pasteurized or canned. All crab meat should be firm, free of shell and have a fresh odor. Discoloration or a pungent odor indicates poor quality.

Fresh crab meat is marketed as lump meat - whole lumps from the large body muscles and as flake meat - the small pieces of white meat from the body. A combination of the two is sold as flake & lump. Claw meat is sold separately as claw meat.

Quick frozen crab meat is available and should be thawed slowly in the refrigerator in approximately 12 hours.

Pasteurized crab meat is another marketing approach which does not alter the taste or texture. It is fresh and table ready. Pasteurized crab meat must be kept refrigerated until ready for use.

Canned crab meat is also available and can be used properly in sauces, appetizers, chowders, salads and dips.

PREPARATION FOR USE:

All Crabs must be cooked in their shells and must be alive when cooked. While crabs may be washed and steamed alive, the majority of the time they are simply boiled in a pot of salt water and seasonings for about twenty minutes.
If you want to keep crab meat for later use it may be frozen after it is cooked and removed from the shell.

To eat or remove the meat from a crab, break off the claws and legs, crack open and remove the meat. Save any meat attached to the end of the "arm". Pull off apron from the underside. Holding the crab in both hands, insert thumb under shell by the apron hinge. Remove the top shell from the body. With spoon, scrape soft substance from the shell into a small bowl to save. Discard shell. From the body, using your fingers, remove and discard the "dead-man's fingers" (the gray,feathered structures on either side and the soft substance in the middle of the body). With kitchen shears or both hands, break the body in half down the center. Cut off the thin shell around the edges. With your fingers and a nut or lobster pick, remove the meat between the sections.

TIPS:
Do not store live crabs in fresh water, as they will quickly use up the oxygen and die.

Never freeze whole crabs, either cooked or uncooked or refreeze thawed crab meat.

Spray cooked crab with cold water to help separate the meat from the shell for easier picking. Don't forget to let cool.

Never let a cooked crab come in contact with a container or surface that has held uncooked crabs or they might become contaminatedwith harmfull bacteria that can spoil the cooked crabs.

CRAB STUFFED CHRISTOPHENES

Preparation time: 30 minutes   *Chef: Anne Hurst*
Cooking time: 30 minutes   *Yacht: Voyager*
Serves: 8

4 Christophenes   1 Tblsp. butter
12 oz. crab meat   salt
4 Tblsp. breadcrumbs   freshly ground black pepper
8 Tblsp. swiss cheese, grated

Pre-heat oven to 375 degrees F. Boil the christophenes for about 8 minutes until tender. Cut in half length ways and remove stones and part of pulp. Chop pulp into small pieces and mix in a bowl with crab meat, 2 tablespoons of breadcrumbs, cheese, butter, salt and pepper. Stuff back into christophene skins and sprinkle with remaining breadcrumbs. Bake uncovered for 30 minutes at 375 degrees F. *Serve with crusty bread, or as a first course.*

Hint: Always peel or destone raw christophenes under water to avoid getting very sticky hands.

MARINER'S CRAB QUICHE DELIGHT

Preparation time: 15 minutes   *Chef: Suzanne Leonfellner*
Cooking time: 40 minutes   *Yacht: Luna De Peponi*
Chilling time: 10 minutes
Serves: 4-6

1 (9") pie crust   1 cup milk
1 (7-1/2 oz.) can crab meat   1/2 tsp. salt
   or 2-1/2 cups chopped   1/2 tsp. dry mustard
   crab meat   1/2 tsp. grated lemon rind
2 cups grated Swiss cheese   Garnish: 3 tsp. shelled
3 eggs, beaten   pumpkin seeds toasted
3 green onions, chopped   (very optional)

Preheat oven to 350 degrees F. Add grated cheese and chopped crab meat to bottom of pie crust. Beat 3 eggs. Add milk, salt, lemon rind, green onion and dry mustard. Mix. Place in pie. Bake in 350 degrees F. oven for 35-45 minutes. Let stand 10 minutes. *Easy!! Delicious!!*

ACORN CRABS

Preparation time: 15 minutes   *Chef: Gilhian Bethell*
Cooking time: 55 minutes   *Yacht: SS Paj*
Serves: 4

2 acorn squash   **2 tsp. orange juice**
Stuffing: **salt and pepper**
  2 cans of crab meat
  2 tsp. horseradish sauce   **Garnish: dillweed, paprika**
  1/2 cup sour cream   **and an orange slice**
  2 tsp. lemon juice

Preheat oven to 350 degrees F. Cut 2 acorn squash in half and scoop out the seeds. Rub butter on the flesh and pour a teaspoon of orange juice into each half. Bake for 40 minutes.
Stuffing: Mix together all ingredients and stuff the center of the acorn halves with this mixture and bake another 10-15 minutes. Garnish with dill, paprika, and a slice of orange.

CRAB CREPES

Preparation time: 15 minutes   *Chef: Jacqueline Cheetham*
Cooking time: 12 minutes   *Yacht: Rajada*
Serves: 8

2 Tblsp. oil   **tot of brandy**
1 large onion, chopped   **1/2 - 3/4 pint white sauce (p.**
1 green pepper, chopped   **176)**
1 garlic clove, crushed   **8 crepes**
5 oz. ham chopped   **Garnish: watercress and**
12 oz. crabmeat   **lemon slices or**
                                     tomato roses

Preheat oven to 350 degrees F. Heat oil. Add chopped onion, green pepper and crushed garlic. Cook 5 minutes. Add chopped ham and crab. Heat and add brandy. Incorporate this mixture with the white sauce. Mix well and divide between crepes. Roll up and place in oven 350 degrees F. for about 12 minutes. Garnish with watercress and lemon twirls or tomato rose.

CRAB AND ASPARAGUS MOUSSE

Preparation time: 15 minutes
Cooking time: 5 minutes
Serves: 6-8

Chef: Sue Bushnell
Yacht: Emily Morgan

1 (12 oz.) can asparagus
1 (6 oz.) can crabmeat
1 Tblsp. butter
1 Tblsp. flour
1 packet gelatin
2 Tblsp. dry white wine

1 cup mayonnaise
1/2 cup heavy cream,
  lightly whipped
Garnish: lemon slices,
  asparagus tips,
  parsley tips

Drain and reserve liquid from crabmeat and asparagus. Melt butter, stir in flour and cook for 1 minute. Stir in reserved liquids, bring to boil and simmer, stirring constantly for 2 minutes. Roughly chop crabmeat and asparagus and fold into sauce. Dissolve gelatin in wine over a low heat and stir into sauce mixture. Fold in mayonnaise and cream. Pour into a 7 inch mold and chill until set. Turn over onto a serving dish and garnish with lemon slices, asparagus tips and parsley sprigs. *Serve with hot toast.*

CHEESE CRAB DIP

Preparation time: 10 minutes
Cooking time: 2 minutes
Serves: 6 - 10

Chef: Maureen Romagnola
Yacht: Gracious Lady

4 oz. butter or margarine
2 (3 oz.) pkgs. velvetta cheese
black pepper, to taste

1 can crabmeat
pinch of paprika
Nacho chips

Melt cheese and butter, mix until smooth and creamy. Stir in pepper and paprika. Add crabmeat. Serve with nacho chips.

Note: Easy recipe - loved by all. If you have a micowave it can be made and served in the same dish.

CRAB DIP

Preparation time: 10 minutes   *Chef: Kathy Prentice*
Cooking time: 20 minutes   *Yacht: Point of Sail*
Serves: 6

8 oz. cream cheese   **8 drops Worcestershire**
3/4 cup mayonnaise   **sauce**
1 Tblsp. lemon juice   **8 oz. crabmeat**
                                    1 oz. slivered almonds

Preheat oven to 350 degrees F. Mix above ingredients with 1/2 the almonds. Spoon into a small casserole dish. Place remaining almonds on top. Bake at 350 degrees 20 minutes. Serve with plain crackers.

Note: In a pinch this can be heated in a microwave or on top of a stove.

CRABMEAT GRACIE

Preparation time: 15 minutes   *Chef: Maureen Romagnolo*
Cooking time: 30 minutes   *Yacht: Gracious Lady*
Serves: 6

2 (6 oz.) cans Alaskan King   **2 cups shredded cheese**
  Crab, drained and flaked   **2 medium onions, sliced**
2 cups stuffing mix   **2 cups sour cream**
1 (8 oz.) can water chestnuts,
  sliced

Preheat oven to 350 degrees F. Mix all ingredients together. Spoon into greased 2 quart casserole dish. Bake for 30 minutes.

Note: Can be frozen.

CRAB - SHRIMP BAKE

Preparation time: 10 minutes
Cooking time: 45 minutes
Serves: 6

Chef: Vickie Sparks
Yacht: Non Sequitur

1 (10 oz.) can cream of
   shrimp soup
2/3 cup milk
1 lb. crabmeat, drained
   and flaked
1/2 cup mayonnaise

1/2 cup grated sharp cheese
2 cups uncooked noodles
1 (6-1/2 oz.) can of shrimp or
   small bag of frozen shrimp,
   thawed and rinsed
   (optional) buttered bread
   crumbs

Preheat oven to 350 degrees F. Combine all ingredients in 2 quart casserole. Cover and bake 30 minutes. Uncover and top with buttered bread crumbs. Bake 10-15 minutes uncovered.

Note: I use colored pasta and/or peas for color.

Gee, what a coincidence we have the same Family name Bake!

BEER CRAB PUFFS

Preparation time: 30 minutes   *Chef: Sylvia & Stanley Dabney*
Cooking time: 20 minutes   *Yacht: Native Sun*
Makes: 60-80 appetizers

Beer Crab Puff:
1 cup beer   1/2 tsp. salt
1/4 lb. butter   4 eggs
1 cup flour

Preheat oven to 450 degrees F.   For the puff, bring beer and butter to a boil. When butter melts, add flour and salt all at once. Cook over low heat until mixture leaves sides of pan. Remove from heat, beat in 1 egg at a time until dough is shiny. Drop by teaspoonfuls 1" apart on buttered baking sheet. Bake 10 minutes at 450 degrees F. Then reduce to 350 degrees, and bake additional 10 minutes until browned and free from moisture. Cool, split and fill with crabmeat filling.

Crab Meat Filling:
1/2 lb. crab meat   1/2 cup mayonnaise
1 Tblsp. sliced green onions   1 tsp. lemon juice
4 oz. shredded Swiss cheese   1/4 tsp. curry

Make crabmeat filling ahead by combining all the ingredients.

CHAPARRAL CRAB CAKES

Preparation time: 20 minutes   *Chef: Jennifer Dudley*
Cooking time: 12 minutes   *Yacht: Chaparral*
Serves: 8 cakes

1 lb. lump crabmeat
1/2 cup fresh bread crumbs
2 Tblsp. chopped parsley
2 Tblsp. heavy cream
1 Tblsp. lemon juice
1 Tblsp. Tabasco sauce

1 Tblsp. Dijon mustard
Black pepper, to taste
1 large egg, plus 1 egg yolk
4 Tblsp. unsalted butter
1/3 cup dry bread crumbs
Prepared tartar sauce

Preheat oven to 250 degrees F. Place all ingredients except butter, dry bread crumbs and tartar sauce in bowl and stir until combined. Shape into small patties, squeezing out excess liquids. Coat both sides of each patty with dry breadcrumbs. Heat half of the butter in skillet. Add half the cakes and cook until golden brown (4-6 minutes) turning once. Keep in a warm oven (250 degree F). Cook remaining patties. *Serve hot with tartar sauce.*

Note: This makes a delicious hors d'oeurve served on small fish plates with a lemon wedge or it's a nice change for a starter course. Serve the crab cakes on a large serving tray atop shredded lettuce and surrounded by lemon wedges. This is also a good way to serve conch fritters.

FREEZER CRAB PUFFS

Preparation time:15 -20 mins.   Chef: Sylvia & Stanley Dabney
Cooking time: 25 minutes   Yacht: Native Sun
Makes : 5 dozen

1 (6-1/2 oz.) can crabmeat,
  drained and picked
1/2 cup shredded cheddar
  cheese
3 minced green onions,
  (whole stalks)

1 tsp. Worcestershire
  sauce
1 tsp. dry mustard
1 cup water
1/2 cup butter
1 cup flour
4 eggs

Preheat oven to 400 degrees F.   Mix crab, cheese, onion, Worcestershire, mustard, salt and pepper and set aside. In a large saucepan, heat water and butter until boiling. Remove from heat. Immediately add flour and beat until mixture leaves pan side and forms balls. Add eggs one at a time until each is completely mixed. Beat in crab mixture. Drop a teaspoon of dough 1" apart on ungreased baking sheet. Bake at 400 degrees F. for 20-25 minutes until golden. Serve immediately, or cool and freeze. *To serve: reheat puffs at 325 degrees F. for 10-15 minutes.*

MARYLAND-STYLE CRAB SALAD

Preparation time: 30 minutes   Chef: Joy Smith
Chilling time: 30 minutes   Yacht: Falcon
Serves: 6

2 lbs. crabmeat, drained
  and flaked
3 stalks celery, chopped
Mayonnaise

Old Bay seafood seasoning
9 Pita bread pockets
Alfalfa sprouts

Pick any stray shells out of the crabmeat and add celery. Add mayonnaise to moisten. Add Old Bay, tasting as you go. It's spicy! Cut pita pockets in half and fill with sprouts and crab salad. Makes great picnic food.

Hint: If the expense of crabmeat is a drawback, use "sealegs". Make sure it's good quality and well drained.

DADDY'S FAVORITE SEATTLE CRAB SOUFFLE'

Preparation time: 30 minutes   *Chef: Sylvia & Stanley Dabney*
Cooking time: 30-40 minutes   *Yacht: Native Sun*
Serves: 4-6

3 Tblsp. flour	2 Tblsp. sherry
1/2 tsp. dry mustard	1/2 tsp. dillweed
1 cup milk	1 tsp. Tabasco sauce
1 cup shredded sharp	6 egg yolks
cheddar or Swiss cheese	1 cup crabmeat, cleaned
(or combination of both)	and flaked
	6 egg whites

Bake at 400 degrees F. In a 4 quart pan add flour and dry mustard. Slowly add milk and mix till smooth, then bring to boil. Add and stir cheese, sherry, dillweed, and Tabasco until cheese melts. Remove from heat and add egg yolks (all at one time) and crab. In separate bowl beat egg whites to peaks, then fold egg whites into souffle mixture, 1/2 at a time. Pour into a well buttered 2-1/2 quart souffle dish. Bake until top is golden and center firm when tapped, about 30 minutes.

Note: I come from a long line of souffle makers and this one and the oyster are two of my family's favorites. This is good for any mealtime and only needs to be served with complementary side dishes. If you have never made a souffle, kick off your shoes, pour some wine and give this a try. It is very easy. You'll feel really proud serving a beautiful dish and you too will wonder whoever spread the rumor that souffles were only made by grand chefs!

This type of souffle (not a dessert souffle) gets a wonderful outside texture if you sprinkle the buttered souffle dish with parmesan. It's optional, but my favorite way.

CRABBIES A LA SCAMP

Preparation time: 10 minutes   *Chef: Suzi DuRant*
Cooking time: 5 minutes   *Yacht: Courvoisier*
Serves: 4-6

1 stick butter (4 oz.), softened   1/2 tsp. seasoned salt
8 oz. cheddar or Monterey   1/2-1 lb. crabmeat, flaked
  Jack cheese, grated   Curry, parsley, dry mustard
1-1/2 tsp. mayonnaise   and Tabasco sauce,
1/2 tsp. garlic salt   to taste
                                    6 English muffins, split

Blend all ingredients except muffins. Spread on muffin halves. Broil until bubbly and starting to brown. Cut in wedges. *Serve hot.*

Note: A favorite from friends who cruise the Chesapeake and Bahamas. Fresh Chesapeake blue crabs make this a treat.

HOT CRAB AVOCADO SALAD

Preparation time: 10-15 minutes   *Chef: Suzi DuRant*
Cooking time: 5 minutes   *Yacht: Courvoisier*
Serves: 4

2 cups crabmeat, flaked   Dash of Tabasco sauce
1/2 cup mayonnaise   2 avocados
Juice of 2 lemons   Garnish: 2 tomatoes,
1/4 tsp. salt   curly leaf lettuce, fresh
1 tsp. Dijon mustard   parsley or tarragon
1/4 tsp. tarragon   sprigs,

Mix crab with mayonnaise, lemon juice, salt, mustard, tarragon and tabasco in saucepan. Heat slowly, stirring once or twice. Cut avocados in half, remove seeds, but do not peel. Place avocados on lettuce and fill with hot crab mixture. Garnish with tomatoes and top with fresh parsley sprigs or tarragon.

Note: Can be served as the main course for a luncheon with hot rolls or as the first course of a dinner.

CRABMEAT 1000

Preparation time: 10 minutes   *Chef: Cass Stewart*
Chilling time: 1 hour   *Yacht: Morning Star*
Serves: 8

2 cups mayonnaise
1-1/2 cups chili sauce
3 hard boiled eggs,
   finely chopped
1-1/2 Tblsp. chervil,
   finely chopped
1 Tblsp. red pepper,
   finely chopped

1 dill pickle, finely
   chopped
2 Tblsp. Worcestershire
   sauce
Romaine lettuce
3 lbs. crabmeat
Garnish: lemon wheels

Combine and mix the first 7 ingredients. Cover and chill.
To serve: arrange Romaine lettuce on a salad plate and top with
crab and spoon dressing on top. *Serve with French bread and
Gouda cheese.*

Note: If chervil is unavailable, use parsley. This is a quick and
elegant luncheon.

CREAMY CRAB AND SPINACH FETTUCINE

Preparation time: 5 minutes   *Chef: Marjorie Lallier*
Cooking time: 10 minutes   *Yacht: Pelikan*
Serves: 4

3 Tblsp. butter
1 clove garlic, minced
2 bunches green onions,
  sliced
1/4 cup fresh parsley,
  chopped
1 lb. crab, flaked
1 cup white wine

2 tomatoes, diced
Salt and pepper
1/2 to 1 cup cream
1 lb. spinach fettucine
  noodles
1/3 cup freshly grated
  Parmesan cheese

Prepare and cut up all the vegetables first. Saute in melted butter,
the garlic, green onions, and parsley, for 3 minutes. Add crab and
saute 1 minute longer. Add white wine, tomatoes, salt and pepper
and simmer until reduced to half. Lower heat and add enough
cream to make a heavy sauce consistency. Simmer 1 minute
longer. Serve over fettucine noodles. Sprinkle fresh Parmesan
cheese over sauce and serve French bread on the side.

Note: Begin heating the pot of water for the fettucine as you begin
to melt the butter to saute vegetables for best timing.

SWISS CRAB BITES

Preparation time: 15 minutes   *Chef: Nan Gee*
Cooking time: 10-12 minutes   *Yacht: Tuff*
Makes: 30

1 (7-1/2 oz.) can crabmeat,
  drained
1 Tblsp. green onion,
  chopped
1 cup Swiss cheese, shredded
1/2 cup mayonnaise
1 tsp. lemon juice

1/4 tsp. curry powder
1 (10 oz.) package flake
  style refrigerator rolls
Garnish: sliced water
  chestnuts, red pepper
  slices, parsley

Preheat oven to 400 degrees F. Combine first six ingredients.
Separate rolls and divide each into three pieces. Place on
ungreased baking sheet. Spoon mixture on rolls. Top with water
chestnuts. Bake until golden at 400 degrees F. for 10-12 minutes.
Garnish with sliced water chestnuts, red pepper slices, and parsley.

HOT CRABMEAT CANAPES

Preparation time: 20 minutes   *Chef: Candice Carson*
Cooking time: 5 minutes   *Yacht: Freight Train*
Makes: 24

1/2 lb. fresh, frozen, or   1 Tblsp. butter
   canned crabmeat, drained   1 Tblsp. flour
1 Tblsp. dry sherry   1 egg yolk
1 tsp. salt   1 cup light cream
1/8 tsp. white pepper   6 slices bread*
1 Tblsp. fresh dill, chopped

*Fiberish bread works better than white bread.

In a large mixing bowl, combine crab, sherry, salt, pepper and dill. Set aside. Melt butter, without browning it, in a small heavy saucepan. Remove from the heat and stir in the flour. In a small bowl, beat the egg yolk with the cream and briskly stir this mixture into butter-flour roux with a wire whisk. Return the pan to the heat and cook slowly, whisking constantly for a minute or 2 until the mixture thickens. Do not let boil. Pour the sauce over the crab mixture and stir together with a spoon until ingredients are well combined.

Cut four rounds from each slice of bread using a small cookie cutter or glass. Toast the bread rounds on one side only under a moderately hot broiler. Remove and spread the untoasted side of each round generously with the crab mixture, mounding it slightly. These may be prepared in advance up to this point and refrigerated. Just before serving, place under hot broiler for a minute or so until canapes brown slightly. *Serve very hot!*

Note: This really is a simple recipe. It takes longer to write it than to do it.

AUBERGINES WITH CRAB

Preparation time: 35 minutes   *Chef: Louise Brendlinger*
Cooking time: 20 minutes   *Yacht: Ring-Anderson*
Serves: 4

2 aubergines (eggplants),   1 (16 oz.) can tomatoes
   sliced in half lengthwise   1/2 tsp. oregano
Salt, to taste   Pinch of cayenne pepper or
2 onions, sliced   Tabasco sauce
2 Tblsp. butter   1 (7 oz.) can crabmeat,
Oil   (drained and flaked)
2 tsp. paprika   2 Tblsp. Parmesan cheese
1 Tblsp. tomato puree   Garnish: watercress

Preheat oven to 400 degrees F. Split aubergines and degorge (scoop out seeds). Cut surface and sprinkle with salt to draw out bitter juices. Saute the cut surface in butter until browned. Place on a baking tray and bake until tender, about 10-15 minutes. Meanwhile, in a pan, saute onions in oil until softened. Add paprika, tomato puree, tomatoes, oregano, and cayenne. Season and cook to a rich pulp. Remove the cooked pulp from aubergine skins and add to tomato mixture. Flake in the crabmeat. Pile this mixture into aubergine skins. Cover with cheese and bake for 7 minutes at 425 degrees F.

*Serve with Chicken in Mustard Sauce, Sweet and Sour Cabbage, and Baked Alaska (**See SHIP TO SHORE II**).*

Note: This is a very good dish, but is also very rich.

GINGER CRAB AND CORN SOUP

Preparation time: 5 minutes   *Chef: Jan Robinson*
Cooking time: 15 minutes   *Yacht: Vanity*
Serves: 4-6

1 (16 oz.) pkg. frozen whole
  kernel corn, thawed and
  divided
1 Tblsp. cornstarch
1/4 cup water
3 (10-3/4 oz.) cans no-salt-
  added chicken broth

1 tsp. peeled, minced
  gingerroot
1/2 lb. fresh crab meat
1/2 cup green onions,
  chopped
1/4 tsp. white pepper
1 tsp. rice vinegar, optional

Position knife blade in food processor bowl; add half of corn. Top with cover, and process until finely chopped. Add remaining corn; stir well and set aside. Combine cornstarch and water in a small bowl; stir well and set aside.

Combine chicken broth and gingerroot in a large saucepan; bring to a boil. Add corn, cornstarch mixture, crab meat and remaining ingredients; return to a boil. Reduce heat and simmer, uncovered, 3 minutes. Yield: 7 cups

BAHAMIAN STUFFED CRAB

Preparation time: 20 minutes   *Chef: Jan Robinson*
Cooking time: 25 minutes or   *Yacht: Vanity*
            12 minutes (microwave)
Serves: 6

1 lb. crab meat (flaked)
2 slices bacon
1/2 cup chopped onion
1/2 cup chopped celery
1/4 cup chopped bell
   pepper
1 clove minced garlic
1-1/2 cups cracker crumbs
1 beaten egg

1/4 cup milk
1/2 cup melted margarine
2 Tblsp. chopped parsley
1 tsp. dry mustard
1/2 tsp. salt
1 tsp. Worcestershire sauce
drop or two of "old sour"
   (or hot sauce)

Preheat oven to 350 degrees F. Fry bacon until crisp. Crumble and set aside. Saute vegetables in bacon fat. Add all ingredients in large mixing bowl and combine well. Stuff mixture into shells or casserole dish. Bake for 25 to 30 minutes at 350 degrees F. (12 minutes on HIGH in the microwave oven).

CRAB, AVOCADO AND TOMATO SOUP

Preparation time: 20 minutes   *Chef: Marilyn Stenberg*
Chilling time: 2 hours   *Yacht: Sheerwill*
Serves: 8

2 large ripe avocados
1-1/2 pints chicken stock
3-4 Tblsp. lemon juice
2 lbs. tomatoes
1 oz. finely chopped onion
4 oz. crab meat, fresh or
   frozen

2 Tblsp. Worcestershire
   sauce
10 oz. cream
salt and pepper
Garnish: freshly chopped
   parsley

Place tomatoes in a bowl, blend to a fine pulp. Peel avocados, and remove stone. Mash, then mix with the chicken stock and the lemon juice. Add finely chopped onion. Mix together with tomatoes. Add half the crab meat, Worcestershire sauce and 3/4 of the cream. Season and chill well. To serve use the rest of the crab meat with the remaining cream and swirl into the soup. Sprinkle generously with parsley.

CRAYFISH

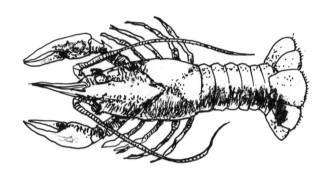

Description: The crayfish is a small lobster - like crustacean that has over 300 family members. They are a reddish brown in color when alive but turn a bright orange-red when cooked.

Size: Crayfish that are an edible size usually have a body length of 3-1/2 inches at the minimum and over 5 inches maximum. They weight between 2-8 ounces.

Habitat: In freshwater on all continents except Africa.

Flavor: Crayfish are similar to a lobster in texture and flavor. It is an important ingredient in creole and Cajun cooking.

Preparation: Wash crayfish thoroughly in salted water, then let them soak for 5 or 10 minutes. Rinse any grit that might be left on the crayfish. Pour boiling water over them and let stand for 10 minutes. Most of the meat is in the tail, but the head should be tried, it is quite tasty.

Other names: Crawfish, Crawdad

BOILED CRAYFISH

Preparation time: 5 minutes　　　　　*Chef: Jan Robinson*
Cooking time: 10 minutes　　　　　　　*Yacht: Vanity*
Serves: 4 - 6

3 gallons water
1 (3 oz.) pkg. crab and
　shrimp boil mix
4 cloves garlic

1 cup salt
2 Tblsp. cayenne pepper
3 lbs. live crayfish

In a large stew pot, bring water, crab boil, garlic, salt and pepper to a boil. Add crayfish, washed but still in shells. Cover and bring again to a boil. Cook for about for 8 minutes. Remove crayfish. Eat hot or cold.

CRAYFISH WITH GARLIC

Preparation time: 15 minutes　　　　　*Chef: Jan Robinson*
Cooking time: 35 minutes　　　　　　　*Yacht: Vanity*
Serves: 4

3 lbs. crayfish meat
1/4 lb. butter
1 large onion, chopped
2 shallots, chopped

4 cloves garlic, chopped
1/2 tsp. black pepper
pinch of cayenne
1 Tblsp. freshly chopped
　parsley

Melt the butter in a heavy skillet and add onion, shallots, cayenne and garlic. Cook over medium heat, stirring constantly, for 15 minutes. Add the crayfish meat, cover and cook over low heat 20 minutes. Season, remove from heat and add the parsley. *Serve with rice.*

CAJUN PASTA LANGOSTINE

Preparation time: 30 minutes
Cooking time: 30 minutes
Serves: 6

Chef: Mardy Array
Yacht: Emerald Lady

1-1/2 pounds raw crawfish
2 garlic cloves, minced
2 Tblsp. butter
1/4 cup onion, chopped
1/4 cup green pepper, chopped
1/2 cup celery, chopped
1 Tblsp. cornstarch
1/4 cup tomato juice
1-3/4 cup canned tomatoes, chopped
1-1/2 tsp. sugar
1 tsp. chili powder
1-1/2 Tblsp. Cajun Seasoning

Cajun Seasoning:
1 Tblsp. paprika
2 tsp. salt
1 tsp. garlic powder
1 tsp. cayenne pepper
3/4 tsp. crushed black pepper
1/2 tsp. thyme
1/2 tsp. oregano

Pasta or rice (for 6)

Cajun Seasoning: Mix all ingredients together.
Melt butter in heavy large skillet. Saute garlic, onions, green pepper and celery until tender. Blend cornstarch with tomato juice in separate bowl. Mix sugar, chili powder, Cajun seasoning into tomatoes. Add to sauted vegetables in skillet, stir to blend. Add cornstarch and tomato juice to skillet. Cook, stirring until mixture slightly thickens and clears. Add crawfish to sauce and simmer gently. Cook crawfish to pink and tender and combine the sauce flavors. About 8 to 10 minutes.

Serve over your favorite pasta: Saute cooked Pasta in a skillet with butter until well coated, add half of sauce and toss until well coated. Place on individual dishes and top each with the rest of Cajun Sauce and Crawfish. Or,

Serve with rice: Mound on large platter and pour Cajun Sauce over all.

DOLPHIN (FISH)

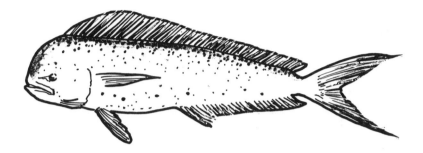

Description: This beautifully colored fish is not related to the mammal called "Dolphin" or "Porpoise."In fact, to reduce the confusion many restaurants now use the Hawaiian name "mahi-mahi" on their menus and lately some fish markets have followed suit.

That's not me

Flipper

The Dolphins coloring is of brilliant turquoise, green and orange yellow. When taken from the water these colors fade almost immediately. The males are distinguished by their bull nose and high vertical forehead.

Size: The Dolphins vary in size from 5 - 50 pounds. Although some have been caught as big as 85 -90 pounds. Dolphin are excellent eating at any size.

Habitat: Dolphin is found in all of the warm oceans of the world.

Flavor: The meat is white, large flaked and moist. The flavor is that of the finest baked white meat chicken you have ever tasted. Truly the Dolphin is a one of a kind delicacy.

Preparation: This tasty white meat fish is usually sold as filet or steaks. Sometimes the orange roe is available. The latter is considered quite a delicacy in the Caribbean Islands. The meat is firm and flavorful and can be prepared in any style. It really needs no sauce, just a squeeze of lemon or lime. This is one of my favorites because of the delicious unique natural flavor.

Other names: Mahi-mahi, Dolphin fish, Dorado

THE TRUE TAHITIAN MARINATED DOLPHIN

Preparation time: 1 hour
Chilling time: 30 minutes
Serves: 6

Chef: Madou Condon
Yacht: Tava'e

2-1/2 to 3 lbs. of 1 inch
  boneless fillet mahimahi
20 green limes
4 to 5 brown coconuts
3 tomatoes
2 green sweet peppers

1 onion
garlic, parsley, salt,
tarragon, pepper
3 boiled eggs, (optional)
Garnish: chives, baked
  bananas, boiled sweet
  potatoes

Cut fish in 1 inch pieces, soak as fast as cut in a bowl of sea water. Strain water. Cover fish with lime juice for 15 to 20 minutes (meat to be white outside, pink inside). Open coconuts in half, keep water of one, grind meat fine and squeeze it in cheese cloth to extract milk. Strain lime juice off fish. In salad bowl mix fish, vegetables, salt, pepper, garlic (to taste), tarragon. Cover with coconut milk (if not enough milk use half of coconut water). Refrigerate 15 minutes, no more. Upon serving decorate with garnish.

Note: Fish are not sticky in sea water - use fingers to mix and eat. Coconut milk will freeze or separate if chilled too long - don't add oil, lime or vinegar to milk. Any vegetables can be used except cucumbers.

Alternatives: Tuna

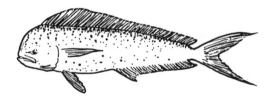

DELICIOUS DOLPHIN DISH

Preparation time: 10 minutes　　　*Chef: Jennifer Dudley*
Cooking time: 20 minutes　　　　　*Yacht: Chaparral*
Serves: 4

2 Tblsp. melted butter
1/4 cup water
1/4 cup fresh lemon juice
1/4 cup olive oil
3 Tblsp. dijon mustard

2 Tblsp. fresh herbs, basil,
　thyme (or 1 tsp. dried)
1/2 cup breadcrumbs
4 fresh dolphin fillets
Garnish: fresh basil and
　lemon wedge

Preheat oven to 400 degrees F. Place fillets in buttered baking dish. Sprinkle with lemon juice, olive oil, and herbs. Spread mustard over each fillet. Add breadcrumbs. Pour water around fillets. Bake in 400 degree F. oven for 15-20 minutes or until flakes easily. Garnish.

DOLPHIN DELIGHTFUL

Preparation time: 10 minutes　　　*Chef: Jan Robinson*
Cooking time: 20 minutes　　　　　*Yacht: Vanity*
Serves: 6

3 lbs dolphin fish fillets
2 Tblsp. butter
Juice of 1 lemon
1 Tblsp. butter
1 large onion, chopped
1/4 cup mushrooms, sliced
1/2 cup mayonnaise

1/4 cup prepared mustard,
　spicy
2 cloves garlic, crushed
4 dashes Tabasco sauce
3 oz. dry vermouth
Pepper, to taste
Garnish: paprika, lemon
　slices and fresh
　parsley

Preheat oven to 350 degrees F. Cut dolphin into 6 pieces. Bake fish with butter and lemon for 10 minutes. Saute onion and mushrooms in butter and then mix in the remaining ingredients. Pour sauce over partially cooked fish and bake 10 minutes more.

I serve this with a leafy green salad, wild and brown rice, steamed brocoli, and nice chilled bottle (or two) of Pinot Chardonnay.

BAKED DOLPHIN (MAHIMAHI)

Preparation time: 10 minutes   *Chef: Jan Robinson*
Cooking time: 15 minutes   *Yacht: Vanity*
Serves: 4

2 lbs. dolphin fillets   **pepper, to taste**
3 oz. butter, melted   **2 cloves garlic, crushed**
juice of 1 lemon   **paprika, to taste**
4 dashes Tabasco sauce   **Parmesan cheese**
1/4 cup white wine   **Garnish: lemon twists**
                                              and sprigs of parsley

Preheat oven to 400 degrees F. Cut dolphin into 4 pieces. Place in a baking dish. Mix butter, lemon juice, Tabasco, wine, pepper, garlic and paprika together. Pour over fish. Bake for 12 minutes. Sprinkle Parmesan cheese over fish. Return to oven under broiler just until the cheese browns, about 3 or 4 minutes.

DOLPHIN AND PLANTAINS

Preparation time: 15 minutes   *Chef: Brooks Kuhn*
Cooking time: 35 minutes   *Yacht: Rising Sun*
Serves: 6

6 Dolphin fillets   **salt, to taste**
6 ripe plantains, sliced   **2 cups heavy cream**
nutmeg, to taste   **Garnish: orange slices,**
ground ginger, to taste   **lemon zest, parsley,**
cinnamon, to taste   **shredded coconut**

Preheat oven to 350 degrees F. Place dolphin fillets in baking pan. Place plantains over fish. Sprinkle spices over all. Bake 25 minutes. Pour cream overall and return to oven for another 10 minutes, until cream is heated through, but not boiling (or it will curdle). Garnish.

Note: Plantains serve as the meal's starch - so all you need is a Spinach Salad and toasted garlic bagels to complete the meal. Save the broth for soup tomorrow.

Alternative: Wahoo

EEL

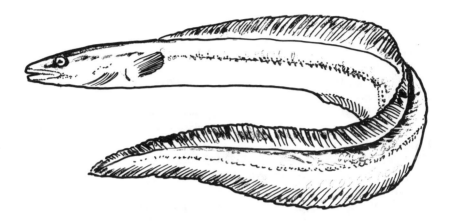

Description: Beauty is in the eyes of the beholder, but I doubt that an eel would win a "fish beauty contest". Snakelike in appearance, the eel has a pointed snout and a very large mouth. The American eel is brown to yellowish-brown with lighter undersides. They grow to about 3 feet. The conger eel, very similar to the American eel is gray and grows to about 5 to 7 feet. The Moray eel, the spotted counterpart in the more tropical climates, has sharp teeth which can cause injury to unware divers. However, contrary to the movies they seldom grow over 6 feet in length.

Size: Depending on the species the average sizes can run from about 3 feet to a large length of 5 to 6 feet.

Habitat: Coastal and inland waters throughout the world.

Preparation: Eel has been rather ignored by the American people, but it is very popular in Europe and other parts of the world. An eel has tough skin and it should be removed before cooking. Pan frying is a popular method, although it may be grilled, stewed, smoked or pickled. The meat is very firm and requires longer cooking than most other fish.

EEL STEWED IN RED BURGUNDY

Preparation time: 15 minutes   *Chef: Jan Robinson*
Cooking time: 40 minutes   *Yacht: Vanity*
Serves: 6

2 lbs. eel, cleaned and skinned	1-1/2 cups red Burgundy wine
seasoned flour	1/2 tsp. whole cloves
2 Tblsp. butter	freshly ground black pepper
2 Tblsp. olive oil	2 bay leaves
3 cloves garlic, crushed	1/2 tsp. thyme
1 medium-size onion, chopped	1/4 cup Cognac
1/4 cup chopped celery	beurre manie
1/2 cup diced carrots	Garnish: fresh parsley
2 cups fish stock	

Cut eel into 2-inch pieces, and dust with the seasoned flour. Melt butter and oil in a large skillet. Add garlic, onion, celery, carrots. Cook for about 10 minutes, until onion is soft. Add eel and brown the eel pieces. Add the fish stock, wine, cloves, pepper, bay leaves and thyme. Cover and simmer for about 35 minutes.Thicken with a little beurre manie, add the Cognac, stir a moment or two. (Find bay leaves and whole cloves and remove them!) *Serve stew over rice with a green salad and warm French bread.* Garnish with parsley.

Hi, I'm a stewed eel!

FLOUNDER

Description: There are many types and varieties of flounder. The common or left hand species (eyes on the left side when lying on the bottom) is called the Summer Flounder. Southern and Winter Flounder have a dark topside and a light bottomside. The top varies from gray and browns to nearly black while the bottom remains light.

Size: The average sizes are about 2 to 5 pounds and 8 to 10 inches in length.

Habitat: The Flounder is found worldwide while the common varieties referred to above are found in the North and South Atlantic and in the South Pacific.

Flavor: The flesh is white and flaky with a mild, almost sweet, taste. Flounder is often stuffed with crab meat to enhance the very mild flavor.

Preparation: While Flounders are an excellent eating fish, the sweet fine flaked meat with its fragile texture should be cooked lightly by simple and quick methods. Pan frying usually can produce amazing results. Baking or broiling are very popular cooking methods. Flounder fillets may be substituted for any sole recipe.

Other names: Sole, Petrale, Fluke, Plaice, Sanddab, Halibut, Turbot

LIGHT WHITE FISH CASSEROLE

Preparation time: 20 minutes   *Chef: Marita Tasse*
Cooking time: 30 minutes   *Yacht: Flower of the Storm*
Serves: 4

1 lb. flounder
1 cup plain lowfat yogurt
2 Tblsp. mayonnaise
1/4 - 1/2 cup grated Jack or
    Muenstar cheese

2 tsp. fish seasoning
6 egg whites, beaten stiff
Paprika
Garnish: lemon slices and
    parsley

Preheat oven to 350 degrees F. Poach fish, flake and set aside. Combine yogurt, mayonnaise, cheese and seasoning with fish. Fold beaten egg whites into fish mixture. Pour into 9x9x2" casserole dish. Sprinkle with paprika or some other colorful seasoning, for a touch of color on top. Bake at 350 degrees F. for 30 minutes until firm and puffy.

Alternatives: Sole or Halibut

BAKED FLOUNDER

Preparation time: 15 minutes   *Chef: Jan Robinson*
Cooking time: 17 minutes   *Yacht: Vanity*
Serves: 4

1-1/2 lbs. flounder fillets
1 cup sliced fresh
    mushrooms
1 small onion, chopped
3 Tblsp. butter
 black pepper

Juice of 1 lemon
2 Tblsp. chopped fresh
    herbs - parsley, thyme
    or chives

Garnish: lemon wedges

Preheat oven 400 degrees F. Melt 3 tablespoons butter and saute onion and mushrooms about 5 minutes until tender. Layer fillets in buttered baking dish. Pour lemon juice over fish. Dot each fillet generously with butter. Season with pepper and sprinkle with the herbs. Spoon the mushroom mixture over the fillets. Cover with foil and bake until just done, about 12 minutes at 400 degrees F.

Note: This recipe is also excellent without the mushrooms and onions.
Alternative: Sole or Petrale

FLOUNDER WITH APPLES

Preparation time: 15 minutes
Cooking time: 10 minutes
Serves: 4

Chef: Jan Robinson
Yacht: Vanity

4 flounder fillets
2 apples, peeled and sliced
flour, to dredge
pepper, to taste

4 oz. butter
juice of half lemon
fresh chopped parsley
2 Tblsp. oil
Garnish: mango chutney

Dip fish and apple in flour seasoned pepper. Cook fish in oil and butter until brown. (Do not overcook.) Sprinkle with lemon juice and chopped parsley. Add the apple slices two minutes before the flounder is done. Be careful turning the apple, which is fragile. Arrange cooked fish on platter and decorate with cooked apples. *Serve with mango chutney.*

DRUNKEN FLOUNDER

Preparation time: 20 minutes
Marinating time: 20 minutes
Cooking time: 12 minutes
Serves: 4

Chef: Jan Robinson
Yacht: Vanity

4 flounder fillets
1/2 cup butter
2 cloves garlic, crushed
1/2 cup chopped onions
1/2 cup chopped green pepper
1/2 cup sweet vermouth

1/2 cup light rum
1/2 tsp. oregano
1/4 cup toasted almond slivers
1/2 cup sherry

Garnish: lemon wedges

Preheat oven to 400 degrees F. Melt butter in shallow baking dish and sprinkle with garlic. Cut fish into 3 inch pieces and marinate in rum and vermouth mixture for 20 minutes. Arrange fish in pan on melted butter and top with onions and green pepper. Pour over the remaining rum/vermouth marinade. Sprinkle with oregano, then with toasted almond slivers and bake 10 minutes at 400 degrees F. Douse with sherry and broil 2 minutes to brown.

GOOSEFISH

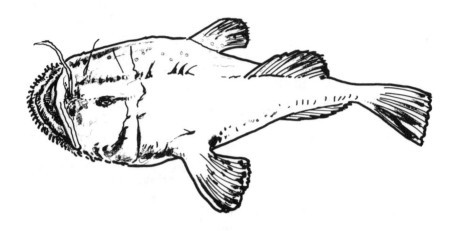

Description: When you first glance at the goosefish, it appears to be all head with tiny eyes and a huge tooth-filled mouth. Its body is quite flat and the skin, lacking scales, is thin, pliable and slippery. The upper parts are a dark chocolate-brown, with specklings of light and darker hues, while beneath it is a dirty white.

Size: Although the average goosefish found in markets are fairly small, the species grows to lengths of 4 feet and may weigh over 50 pounds.

Habitat: The goosefish is located from western Atlantic to the Grand Banks southward to North Carolina.

Flavor: The goosefish is an excellent food fish, being relatively free of bones and having sweet-flavored white flesh. Only the tail section of the goosefish contains edible meat. It is white and firm, very similar to the flesh of a puffer.

Preparation: Goosefish can be sauteed, broiled, baked, poached, or cut into fingers and deep-fried tempura style.

Other names: Monkfish, Anglerfish, Allmouth

MONKFISH BROCHETTES

Preparation time: 30 minutes
Marinating time: 1 hour
Cooking time: 10 minutes
Serves: 6

Chef: Jan Robinson
Yacht: Vanity

Marinade:
  1/4 cup olive oil
  4 Tbsp. lemon juice
  1 tsp. fresh dill, minced
  1 tsp. parsley, minced
2 lbs. monkfish fillets
2 small yellow summer
  squashes cut into
  1-1/2 inch cubes

2 sweet red peppers seeded
  and cut into 1 inch
  squares
1 green pepper cut into
  1 inch squares
1/2 tsp. paprika
1/8 tsp. cayenne pepper
6 skewers
Garnish: lemon or lime
  wedges

Cut fish into 24 cubes (about 1-1/2 inch cubes). Rinse and dry the fish. In shallow glass dish mix the oil, lemon juice and herbs and marinate fish for 1 hour, or longer. Drain and reserve marinade. Toss the cut vegetables in the marinade, mix well and then drain vegetables. Save marinade for a basting sauce.

Skewer the fish and vegetables, alternating the colors. Sprinkle kabobs with paprika and cayenne pepper. Broil 3 inches from broiler element for about 10 minutes or until fish flakes. Turn the fish often and baste with the marinade. Garnish with lemon or lime wedges. *Serve hot with brown rice.*

Hint: When marinating fish, steaks, chicken, etc., use plastic bags with ties. Makes turning easy.

BAKED GORDA GOOSEFISH

Preparation time: 10 minutes　　　　*Chef: Jan Robinson*
Cooking time: 20 minutes　　　　　　*Yacht: Vanity*
Serves: 4

1-1/2 lbs. goosefish, cut butterfly style
Stuffing:
1/4 cup bread crumbs　　　　**4 cloves garlic, chopped**
1/4 cup raisins　　　　　　　**1 Tblsp. olive oil**
2 Tblsp. fresh chopped　　　**1 Tblsp. lemon juice**
parsley
2 Tblsp. pine nuts, or　　　　**Garnish: Tomato slices and**
almonds　　　　　　　　　　　**fresh sprigs of parsley**

Preheat oven to 350 degrees F. Combine the stuffing ingredients. Spread the stuffing across the fish. Roll the fish around the stuffing, wrap tightly in foil and bake for 25 minutes, until just cooked. *To serve, slice across the roll of fish.* Garnish with tomato slices and fresh sprigs of parsley.

GROUPER

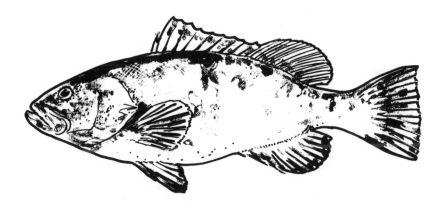

Description: Groupers are members of the Sea Bass family of which there are over 400 species. The color varies as much as the species but most have the straight line appearance of the spiny dorsal fin with a longer second spline following.

Size: While the size varies according to the species, the smaller is about 2 to 3 pounds with the overall average being 3 to 5 pounds.

Habitat: Grouper are found in temperate and tropical waters throughout the world. They are often found around the coral reefs and rock outcroppings on the ocean shelfs.

Flavor: The firm lean flesh of the Grouper is similar in taste to the Halibut, with an almost shellfish flavor.

Preparation: Having no intermuscular bones, the Grouper makes the perfect fillet. The skin is tough and strong flavored and should always be removed before cooking. Deep frying and poaching are the very popular methods of preparing this fish.

Other names: Sea Bass, Jewfish, Hind, scamp

ORANGE GINGER FISH STEAKS

Preparation time: 15 minutes　　　　*Chef: Suzan Salisbury*
Cooking time: 9 minutes　　　　　　　*Yacht: Gypsy*
Serves: 6

6 fish steaks (1 inch thick)　　　**non stick spray (Pam)**
　grouper, snapper, etc　　　　　**3 Tblsp. melted margarine**

Orange Ginger Sauce:
　3 tsp. cornstarch　　　　　　**1-1/2 Tblsp. Worcestershire**
　1-1/2 tsp. grated ginger root　　**sauce**
　3/4 tsp. instant chicken　　　　**2 green onions, thinly**
　　bouillon　　　　　　　　　**chopped**
　1-1/4 cups orange juice　　　　**black pepper**

Preheat broiler. Spray broiler rack of broiler pan with Pam nonstick spray. Place fish on rack. Brush fish with half the margarine. Salt and pepper. Broil fish 4 inches from heat for about 5 minutes. Turn fish , brush with remaining margarine, and broil for another 3 or 4 minutes.

Orange Ginger Sauce: Meanwhile, in a small saucepan combine cornstarch, ginger and chicken bouillon. Stir in orange juice and Worcestershire sauce. Cook and stir until thickened. Cook one minute more. Stir in green onions and pepper. *Place fish on serving plate. Top with sauce and serve.*

Alternatives: Snapper, Mahi-mahi

Non-smoke broiling: Add a cup of water to the bottom portion of the broiling pan before sliding into the oven. The water absorbs smoke and grease.

FESTIVE GROUPER

Preparation time: 10 minutes   *Chef: Gunilla Lundgren*
Cooking time: 10 minutes   *Yacht: Bambi*
Serves: 4

4 grouper fillets
juice from one lemon
1 cup bread crumbs
butter for frying
3 Tblsp. mayonnaise
2 Tblsp. cream

1 red onion, finely
  chopped
1 cup cooked beets,
  chopped
1 Tblsp. capers
Garnish: lemon slices
  and parsley

Sprinkle grouper with lemon juice. Beat egg. Dip grouper first in the egg, then in breadcrumbs. Fry fillets until done (about 10 minutes). Keep warm. Mix mayonnaise with cream, onion, beets and capers. Mix well. Top each grouper fillet with a "dollop" of the mayonnaise mixture. Garnish with lemon slices and parsley.

GROUPER ALMONDINE

Preparation time: 10 minutes   *Chef: Ann Landry Cast*
Cooking time: 10 minutes   *Yacht: Sonrisa*
Serves: 4

4 grouper or snapper fillets
milk
1/2 tsp. salt
2-3 dashes Tabasco
seasoned flour
salt and pepper
2 Tblsp. safflower oil
4 Tblsp. butter

Sauce:
  3/4 stick butter
  1/4 cup sliced almonds
  2 Tblsp. lemon juice
  1/4 tsp. Worcestershire
    sauce
Garnish: 2 Tblsp. chopped
  parsley

Soak grouper fillets in milk with salt and Tabasco for 30 minutes. Drain fillets and pat dry. Dust with flour, seasoned with salt and pepper. Cook in oil and butter until tender. Keep warm in oven while preparing sauce.

Sauce: Melt butter and saute almonds. Add other ingredients. Mix and pour over fish. Sprinkle with chopped parsley.

GOLDEN GROUPER

Preparation time: 15 minutes　　　　*Chef: Debbie Ulrey*
Cooking time: 10-15 minutes　　　　*Yacht: Dream Merchant*
Serves: 8

8 Grouper fillets
Spicy Mustard Sauce:
   4 oz. butter or margarine　　　**2-4 Tblsp. spicy mustard**
   1-2 onions, chopped　　　　　　**or spicy brown**
   Juice of 1-2 lemons　　　　　　**salt and pepper, to taste**

Preheat oven to 350 degrees F. Wash and pat dry grouper fillets - set aside.

Spicy Mustard Sauce: Melt butter or margarine in a saucepan. Add onions and saute until clear. Add juice of lemons, spicy mustard, salt and pepper.

Place fillets in shallow baking dish. Spoon mixture over fillets and bake at 350 degrees F. until fish is flaky, about 15 minutes. Fillets may be done over the grill, turning them frequently while brushing liberally with sauce. Fish is done when inner most area is white and flaky.

Note: This sauce can be utilized with any firm fish fillet. If your grill has a large grate - use screening material to cook your fish on.

Alternative: Snapper

Fish: Any living creature that does not call the Coast Guard when faced with the prospect of being submerged for more than one minute.

KROKEATIKOS ROFUS

Preparation time: 10 minutes   *Chef: Julie Fridlington*
Cooking time: 20 minutes   *Yacht: Knightwind*
Serves: 4

4 grouper fillets
1/2 cup olive oil
2 Tblsp. garlic, chopped
1 cup onion, chopped
2 tomatoes, peeled & chopped

1 Tblsp. oregano
salt and pepper to taste
1 cup dry white wine
8 calamata olives,
   pitted and halved

Heat oil in skillet and saute garlic and onion for a minute or two. Stir in tomatoes, oregano, salt and pepper and saute 8 additional minutes. Set aside. Place fish in large pan. Pour in wine. Spoon sauce evenly over fish and garnish with olives. Cover pan and cook 10 minutes. *This is a Greek recipe. Very easy and quick! Quite tasty too!*

ALMONDINE GROUPER

Preparation time: 15 minutes   *Chef: Beth Avore*
Cooking time: 30 minutes   *Yacht: Perfection*
Serves: 4

1/2 cup sliced almonds
1/4 cup margarine or butter
1/4 cup flour
1/4 cup corn meal
1/8 tsp. salt or Adobo

1/8 tsp. fresh ground pepper
2 lbs. thick grouper fillets
1/2 tsp. parsley flakes
1/2 cup dry white wine
1/2 lemon
Garnish: lemon wheels

Saute almonds in half of the margarine until golden. Remove and set aside. Cut fish into 4 portions. Combine flour, cornmeal, salt and pepper, and coat fish evenly. Add remaining butter to pan. Saute fish until golden on each side. Add wine, squeeze juice from lemon onto fish. Cover, simmer for 5-10 minutes. Remove fish, add almonds, reduce sauce until thickened, spoon over fish, sprinkle with parsley. Garnish with lemon wheels.

FETTUCINE AL PESCO

Preparation time: 25 minutes   *Chef: Marilyn Stenberg*
Cooking time: 20 minutes   *Yacht: Sheerwill*
Serves: 4-6

2 Tblsp. olive oil
2 medium onions, chopped
1 clove garlic, minced
1 small red pepper, chopped
1 small green pepper, chopped
1 can anchovies, chopped

black pepper
finely chopped parsley
2 cups tomato sauce
1/2 tsp. tarragon, dried
1 lb. fish fillets (grouper, sole)
1 lb. fettucine

Heat the oil and add the onion, garlic, chopped peppers, anchovies,and a good sprinkling of black pepper. Saute until soft. Stir in the chopped parsley, tomato sauce, tarragon and the pieces of fish. Simmer gently uncovered, until the fish is cooked (5-8 minutes). Meanwhile cook the fettucine. Toss gently with half the sauce. *Serve on warm plates. This makes a great lunch or light supper. Serve with a crispy green salad .*

GROUPER WEST INDIAN STYLE

Preparation time: 15 minutes   *Chef: Jan Robinson*
Marinating time: 1 hour   *Yacht: Vanity*
Cooking time: 1 hour 40 minutes
Serves: 6

3 lbs. grouper fillets
1 green pepper, diced
3 stalks celery, diced
2 tsp. dried thyme
1 cup lime juice
pepper
2 oz. butter or margarine

1/4 cup olive oil
2 cloves garlic, crushed
1 large onion, diced
4 cups canned tomatoes
6 oz. tomato paste
4 potatoes, peeled and cubed
1/4 cup Worcestershire sauce

Cut the grouper fillets into 2-1/2 inch cubes. Marinate the cubes in 3/4 cup lime juice, and a little pepper, for about an hour. In a large saucepan half-fry the marinated fish cubes, so that they are browned slightly. Remove and set aside. Add onion, garlic, pepper and celery pieces to the pan and saute in butter and oil until golden. Add thyme, tomatoes, tomato paste and potato cubes. Reduce heat and let the chowder simmer for about 1 hour. Add the half-fried fish cubes and cook another 20 minutes, or until done. Just before serving, add Worcestershire sauce and remaining lime juice. *Serve with pigeon peas and rice.*

LOBSTER

The lobster is probably the most popular of all shellfish. This crustacean is known the world over for its large body, claws, and, of course, the delicious taste. Except for minor details, the lobster is very much like its freshwater relative, the crayfish. The upper part of the body is covered by a hard shell, which has a free edge on each side projecting down to cover the gills. The color of the adult varies from greenish-blue to reddish-brown. Contrary to popular belief, its shell is red only after boiling. <u>Low in calories and fat while high in protein and nutrition.</u>

There are three varieties of lobsters that are of commercial value in the United States.

The American Lobster or Maine Lobster, located from the Northwest Atlantic down to North Carolina . This is the TRUE lobster with the large claws. Generally the upper surface of the body is speckled with greenish-black spots. The color is from greenish blue to reddish brown.

The Spiny Lobster or Southern crawfish ranges from North Carolina and Bermuda south to Brazil, Southern Gulf of Mexico and the Caribbean sea. Unlike the true lobster, it has no large claws. It is a beautifully marked species with browns, yellows, orange, green and blue mottled over the upper parts and underside of the tail.

The Small Pacific, or Rock Lobster is found on the southwest coast of the United States. The meat of this lobster is found only in its tail. Even though this lobster has claws there is almost no meat in them.

HOW TO BUY:

Whole lobsters may be purchased live or cooked.

Live lobsters should be purchased from an environmental water tank at your local seafood market or at the dock when they are brought in from the sea. The live lobster should be active. If you should purchase a lobster whose tail hangs limp and loosely, it is probably dead or near death. Watch out for a disagreeable odor if not active. This indicates deterioration. Ice, fresh water or contact with metals will quickly kill a lobster.

Once you have purchased a live lobster, be sure to take care in keeping it alive until you reach home. If you use ice in a cooler, you must separate the lobster from the fresh water. You also do not want to freeze your lobster to death.

Cooked lobsters should have a good red color and a fresh seafood odor. The tail should spring back when straightened out.
Lobster meat picked from the shell is also available in a fresh state or quick frozen. This meat should be white, not gray, and have a good odor. Any sour smell or ammonia odor is an indication of old or tainted meat.

There are several types of lobsters to choose from when purchasing:

Select Lobster: 1-1/2 lbs to 2 lbs, hard shelled and full -meated.
Chicken Lobster : small and tender, 3/4 lb. to one lb.
Culls : damaged in some way. Usually missing claw or shell damage.
Shedders : recent shedding of the shell. The new shell is soft and easily broken by hand. The body cavity is not filled with meat and the flesh tends to be soft.

HOW TO PREPARE:

Lobsters should be kept alive until the moment of cooking. Keep the lobsters in the bottom of the refrigerator until ready for cooking. Do not let them come in contact with fresh water or metals as both will kill the lobster quite rapidly. Refrigerated lobsters can be kept for several days but should be cooked as soon as possible.

Boiling is the method most used for cooking . Lobster should be boiled in enough salted water, (One tablespoon per quart) to cover. Pick up the lobster behind large, front claws. Plunge head first, into boiling water. Cover the kettle. Remove lobster when done, and submerge in cold water to stop cooking process. Rinse and drain. A one pound lobster usually takes about 7 minutes to cook. 10 minutes for a two pound lobster.

To clean and serve lobster, use a sharp, heavy knife, cut the lobster lengthwise from head to tail. Split it completely in two. Holding lobster open, remove and discard stomach and intestinal vein. The liver (green) and coral (the red spawn) are quite good to eat. You may remove them and serve them with the lobster or throw away. As soon as the lobster is clean, serve.

To serve claws, crack them with a nutcracker or smash them with a mallet and pick out the meat with a small fork.

TIPS:

If you put a few teaspoons of boiling water between the eyes of the lobster, it will kill them instantly.

Live Lobsters on a bed of ice are being frozen to death.

Small lobsters are the most tender.

To painlessly kill a lobster, pierce with a knife tip, the shell and flesh at the center of the cross-shaped mark behind the head.

LOBSTER AND PASTA SALAD WITH PESTO SAUCE

Preparation time: 10 minutes   *Chef: Anne Hurst*
Cooking time: 10 minutes   *Yacht: Voyager*
Chilling time: 2 hours
Serves: 8

4 lobsters cooked,   **Pesto Sauce:**
 (about 3 lbs. each)   **1 cup fresh basil leaves**
6 oz. pasta shells   **2 Tblsp. grated Parmesan**
1 can black olives   **cheese**
mayonnaise (homemade) **2 Tblsp. chopped pine nuts**
           or walnuts
Garnish: shredded lettuce **4 cloves garlic, chopped**
          about 1/4 cup olive oil

Pesto Sauce: Combine the basil, Parmesan, nuts and garlic in a mortar, blender or food processor. Slowly add enough olive oil to produce a thick paste.   Makes about 1/2 cup. **Hint:** I make pesto once a season (when I can find fresh basil) and keep it in the freezer all winter in small containers.

Remove lobster tails from shells and slice in half lengthways so that you have 8 crescent shaped pieces. Boil pasta until al dente. Drain and rinse. Before pasta goes sticky, add olives and pesto sauce and toss. Chill for a least 2 hours. *To serve: Arrange lobster tails like spokes of a wheel on a large platter. Fill in the gaps with pasta and put more pasta round the outside.* Finish with a ring of shredded lettuce. Put bowl of homemade mayonnaise on the table.

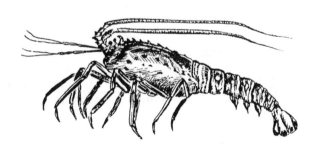

SHRIMP AND LOBSTER SALAD WITH CHAMPAGNE DRESSING IN PUFF PASTRY FISH

Preparation time: 25 minutes   *Chef: Nora Frei*
Cooking time: 25 minutes   *Yacht: Memories*
Serves: 4-6

2 lbs.(U-15 or jumbo) shrimp
1 (10 oz.) lobster tail
2 hickory smoked
buttercheese, cubed
1/2 red onion, chopped fine
2 tomatoes, chopped
Green bibb, lettuce

lemon quarters
4-5 Tblsp. capers
3 Tblsp. Chopped fresh dill
  (1 Tblsp. dried)
2 sheets puff pastry
*1 cup Champagne
  Dressing (see below)

Preheat oven to 400 degrees F. To make salad, boil shrimp and lobster tail until just cooked, let drain. Place cheese, onion, tomato, add dill and capers in mixing bowl. Shell shrimp, lobster, cut into bite size pieces, add to bowl. Make dressing and pour over salad. Cover bowl with foil, refrigerate. To make fish-shaped pastry, lay 2 sheets of puff pastry on top of each other on cutting board, cut out fish shapes with a vent cutter or with sharp knife. You can cut 8 fish from 1 sheet but I use 2 sheets on top of each other to make them thicker. Place on cookie sheet. Cook at 400 degrees F. 20 minutes or until browned on top. (Use several sheets of parchment paper on cookie sheet.) Cut hole out of fish, hollow out, fill with salad and serve.

I serve this with tropical fruit salad and pate on a bed of red and green bibb lettuce. Worth the effort. A definite show stopper. Everyone takes pictures of it. Easy if you make a big batch of dressing in advance.

Champagne Dressing: (Makes 3 cups)
1 cup Champagne vinegar
2 Tblsp. sugar
1-1/2 Tblsp. all-purpose
   flour
1 tsp. dry vermouth
1 tsp. dijon-style mustard

1 egg, beaten
3 Tblsp. heavy or
whipping cream
2 cups olive oil
salt
freshly ground pepper, to taste

Combine the vinegar, sugar, flour, vermouth, and mustard in a small saucepan. Heat to simmering over medium heat. Gradually whisk in the egg and cream over low heat. Whisk in the oil in a thin steady stream. Season with salt and pepper to taste. Remove from heat.

LANGOUSTINES IN PORTO

Preparation time: 10 minutes
Cooking time: 35 minutes
Serves: 6

Chef: Silvia Schiltz
Yacht: Kea 1

4 Tblsp. butter
30 langoustines or 3 medium
   size lobsters
pinch of celery seeds
1/3 glass of fine champagne
   or white wine
1 Tblsp. shallot, chopped

1/2 cup of porto (port)
2 egg yolks
3/4 cup of heavy cream
1 Tblsp. of mustard, Dijon
   or English
Salt and cayenne, to taste

Boil the lobsters or langoustines in a lot of water salted and spiced with some celery seeds. Cook for 10 minutes. Put the butter in a pan and add langoustines (lobsters) and saute for about 5 minutes on each side until golden brown. Pour the fine champagne in a saucepan, heat it and flambe it. Pour it over the lobsters. Make sure the alcohol burns completely. Add the chopped shallots. Add the port and cook it for 8 to 10 minutes. Beat the egg yolks with the heavy cream and mustard. Pour over lobsters. Don't boil. Season with salt and a pinch of cayenne. Stir over a very low fire. Place the lobsters into a shallow serving dish. Pour the sauce over in horizontal lines. Serve immediately. *This dish goes well with some Riesling.*

LOBSTER SOUFFLE

Preparation time: 10 minutes
Cooking time: 55 minutes
Serves: 6

Chef: Silvia Schiltz
Yacht: Kea 1

2 Tblsp. butter
1 cup sliced scallions
1-1/2 cups of cooked lobster,
    chopped in small pieces
8 Tblsp. (4 oz.) butter
5 Tblsp. four
1-1/2 cup milk

5 egg yolks
1/4 tsp. Tabasco sauce
1/2 tsp. salt
2 cups grated gruyere or
    cheddar cheese
1 Tblsp. grated Parmesan
    cheese
7 egg whites

Preheat oven to 375 degrees F. Saute scallions in two tablespoons of butter for 3 minutes. Let it cool, put it on the side. Melt 4 oz. butter in a saucepan, add the flour and mix well. Cook on medium heat for 1 minute (until slightly brown and grainy). Add the milk, bring to a boil, stirring with a whisk. Keep cooking until it comes to a boil. It will get very thick. Remove from the fire and add the egg yolks, Tabasco and salt. Add the cheese and lobster meat and mix well. Set aside. Butter a gratin dish, add flour, shake it around well, and pour the excess flour away.

Beat egg whites in a bowl with a pinch of salt until very firm. Finish beating by a hand whisk. Add a third of the whites to the other mixture. When mixed, fold remaining egg whites into the lobster mixture. Pour mixture into the gratin dish, place it in the oven and bake on 375 degrees F. for 55 minutes. *Serve immediately.*

BLANQUETTE OF LOBSTER

Preparation time: 50 minutes   *Chef: Silvia Schiltz*
Cooking time: 15 minutes   *Yacht: Kea 1*
Serves: 4

4 live lobsters, each weighing
   about 1 lb.
2 quarts of court bouillon
   (or use bouillon cubes)
4 carrots (about 6 oz.)
2 turnips (4 oz.)
3 stalks celery (4 oz.)
1 leek (white part only)
1 cucumber (6 oz.)

5 oz. mushrooms
8 oz. double cream (heavy
   or whipping)
1 oz. butter
2 egg yolks
2 branches chervil
   (or parsley)
cayenne pepper to taste
Garnish: Sprinkle over some
   chervil before serving

Bring the court bouillon to boil in a large saucepan. Plunge the lobsters into the boiling court bouillon for 10 minutes. Lift them out and keep in cool place. When they are cold, remove the meat from the claws and tails and cut the tail meat into 1/2 inch chunks.

Peel and wash the vegetables. Turn all the vegetables, except the leek and mushrooms, into pointed almond shapes. Slice the leek very finely and cut the mushrooms into quarters. Cook each vegetable separately in a little nage (court bouillon) but keep them very crunchy. Lay them on a damp tea towel.

Prepare the sauce. Pour 1 pint of the court bouillon, in which vegetables were cooked into a shallow pan. Reduce the liquid by one-third. Add the cream and bring to a boil. Put all vegetables into the nage and cook for 2 minutes before adding the lobster meat. Lower the heat and do not allow the mixture to boil.

Lightly beat the egg yolks with 1 tablespoon nage. Stir the butter and egg yolks into the sauce. Add a small pinch of cayenne pepper, then tip everything into a shallow serving dish or onto plates. Sprinkle over some chervil (or parsley) and serve immediately.

LOBSTER MEDALLIONS IN GARLIC BUTTER

Preparation time: 15 minutes   *Chef: Beth Avore*
Cooking time: 10 minutes   *Yacht: Perfection*
Serves: 6

6 (10-12 oz.) lobster tails   **1/4 - 1/2 cup melted butter**
3-4 cloves fresh garlic   **Garnish: fresh parsley,**
                                         lemon wedges

Shell tails. Trim and slice at diagonal to have slices to lay in shape of tail. Peel and chop garlic leaving it rather coarse. Melt butter. Saute garlic until beginning to brown. Add lobster slices. Cook over hot heat to keep lobster from becoming tough. Cook a few minutes. Do not overcook. *To serve, realign pieces overlapping to shape into tails.* Garnish with fresh parley and lemon wedges dusted with paprika. You can drizzle garlic butter over "tails" before garnishing.

LOBSTER AND ASPARAGUS WITH ORANGE BUTTER SAUCE

Preparation time: 20 minutes   *Chef: Helen Bromley*
Cooking time: 10 minutes   *Yacht: Golden Rule*
Serves: 4

3 lobster tails   **4 green shallots, chopped**
1 10 oz. pkg. frozen snow   **2 tsp. grated orange rind**
**   peas**   **1/2 cup orange juice**
2 lbs. fresh asparagus   **1/2 cup pine nuts**
1 oz. butter

Cut lobster tails along the underside with scissors. Remove skin. Pull lobster flesh away from shells. Cut flesh into slices. Top and tail snow peas. Peel and trim asparagus. Cut in half. Boil, steam or microwave until asparagus are just tender. Add snow peas, cook 1 minute. Drain. Rinse asparagus and snow peas under cold water; drain. Heat butter in pan. Add shallots, orange rind and juice. Add lobster. Stir until lobster is just tender. Add pine nuts, asparagus and snow peas. Stir fry until heated through.

LOBSTER AROMATIQUE

Preparation time: 20 minutes　　　*Chef: Jan Robinson*
Cooking time: 10 minutes　　　　　　*Yacht: Vanity*
Serves: 4-6

6 Tblsp. butter
2 Tblsp. shallots
4-1/2 cups lobster
1/4 cup Pernod (or brandy),
　warmed
1/4 tsp. Dijon mustard
1/4 tsp. paprika
salt and pepper, to taste
1/4 tsp. cayenne pepper

1/4 tsp. curry
dash of lemon juice
1 Tblsp. minced chives
1 Tblsp. minced parsley
1-1/2 cups cream sauce
　(white sauce p. 176)
1/2 cup whipped cream
　(no sugar)

Heat butter. Add shallots and saute. Add lobster and flame with pernod. Mix salt with spices and add lemon juice. Add chives, parsley and sauce. Cook over reduced heat for 3-5 minutes. Remove from heat. Add whipped cream. *Serve over rice.* Wonderful!! Thank you Becca!   **Variation:** Use crab, shrimp or scallops.

LOBSTER SUPREME

Preparation time: 30 minutes　　*Chef: Gisela Huffman*
Cooking time: 15-20 minutes　　　*Yacht: Nighthawk*
Serves: 8-10

4 (1-1/4 lb.) lobsters, boiled
4 Tblsp. butter
4 shallots, chopped
salt and pepper, to taste
1 cup good dry white wine

1 cup creme fraiche
2 Tblsp. flour
1 Tblsp. dijon-style mustard
Garnish: fresh dill and
　slices of lemon

Cut lobsters in half. Remove the tender meat from the claws and tail. Cut into 3/4 inch pieces. Melt 2 tablespoons of the butter in a skillet and saute the chopped shallots until soft. Add the lobster meat, season with salt and pepper, saute for 2 minutes. Add the wine or Vermouth. Bring to a boil and cook for 3 minutes. Remove the lobster meat with a slotted spoon and boil the sauce until thick. Add the creme fraiche and return to a boil. In the meantime, blend the flour and the remaining butter to make a beurre manie. Gradually add to the boiling sauce until it thickens. Return the lobster meat to the sauce and heat through. Add the mustard and blend. Transfer to ramekins or decorative seashells and serve. Garnish with fresh dill and slices of lemon.

PATTI'S LOBSTER PASTA

Preparation time: 45 minutes　　　　*Chef: Patti Messersmith*
Cooking time: 30 minutes　　　　　　　*Yacht: Scorpio 57*
Serves: 4

4 whole lobster tails　　　　　1/2 lb. angel hair pasta
3 Tblsp. sweet butter　　　　　1 cup creme fraiche
2 cloves garlic, crushed　　　　1/3 cup small capers, drained
1/4 cup cooking sherry　　　　Garnish: Parsley and
1/3 cup fresh dill, chopped　　　　lemon slices
1(12 oz.) jar marinated
　artichoke hearts, drained

Boil lobster tails whole in shells for 25 minutes or until tender. Lift lobster meat out of shells and cut into bite size pieces. Saute in butter and garlic for 1 minute. Add cooking sherry, dill and artichoke hearts. Simmer for 5 minutes. Begin cooking pasta at this time. Add creme fraiche and capers to lobster and simmer for 10 minutes. Serve pasta directly from water to warmed plates. Smother with sauce and garnish each plate with a sprig of parsley and a lemon crown. *Serve with crusty Italian bread!*

STUFFED LOBSTER

Preparation time: 30 minutes　　　　*Chef: Shannon Webster*
Cooking time: 35 minutes　　　　　　　*Yacht: Chaparral*
Serves: 6

3 whole lobsters
Stuffing:
　1 cup cheddar cheese, grated 1 onion, diced and sauteed
　1 (6 1/2 oz.) can crabmeat　　1/2 tsp oregano
　3 large potatoes, cooked and 1/2 tsp. thyme
　　mashed　　　　　　　　Garnish: lemon wedges

Stuffing: Combine ingredients for stuffing. Adjust seasonings to taste.

Preheat oven to 400 degree F. Split whole lobsters, and clean out heads. Stuff with 2-inch layer of stuffing in head and over tail. Bake at 400 degree F. for 35 minutes. Garnish with lemon wedges.

SPANISH MACKEREL

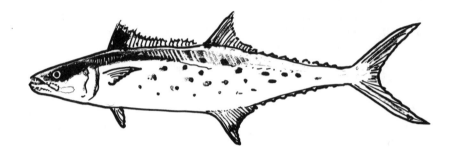

Description: The sleek Spanish Mackerel is one of the more colorful fish being green to greenish - blue on top with silver sides and bottom and with yellow spots on the sides.

Size: Market size is usually about 2 to 4 pounds

Habitat: The Atlantic Ocean from the Chesapeake Bay to Brazil including the Gulf of Mexico. In the Florida the Spanish Mackerel is very plentiful and is popular due to its light taste.

Flavor: The Mackerel species with the lean firm meat is a little strong in taste, however the Spanish Mackerel is much lighter and delicately flavored than any of the others. The best of the species.

Preparation: The Spanish Mackerel is excellent eating broiled, baked or smoked. They are easily cut into fillets and may even be fried.

KINGFISH AND FUNGI

Preparation time: 1 hour　　　　　　　　*Chef: Tuffis Byden*
Marinating time: 2 hours　　　　　　　　*Yacht: Rising Sun 47*
Cooking time: 45 minutes
Serves: 6

6 kingfish steaks　　　　　　　　**4 carrots**
Seasonall *　　　　　　　　　　　　**2 medium onions**
lemon juice　　　　　　　　　　　　**2 cups cornmeal**
1 garlic clove　　　　　　　　　　　**4 oz. unsalted butter**
1/4 cup fresh chopped parsley
2 potatoes (sweet & white)　　　**Sauce:**
1 taro　　　　　　　　　　　　　　　**1/2 cup butter**
1 plaintain　　　　　　　　　　　　**1/2 cup mayonnaise**
1/4 cabbage　　　　　　　　　　　　**juice of 1 lemon**

Season fish with Seasonall and lemon juice.   Let stand 2 hours.
Peel and cut up vegetables in large chunks. Add clove of garlic and
parsley. Cover with 2 quarts water in large pot and boil until tender.
Save broth but remove veggies. Poach fish in broth 20 minutes and
remove to veggies.

To make fungi: To about 5 cups broth, sprinkle in cornmeal
gradually while stirring constantly. Add water or cornmeal to
make it mashed-potato consistency, cook about 5 minutes. Beat in
butter. *Serve sauce over all.*

Sauce: Melt, heat and mix ingredients in saucepan.

* Seasonall (a combination of salt, pepper, oil of onion, oil of
garlic, parsley, celery seed and other spices.)

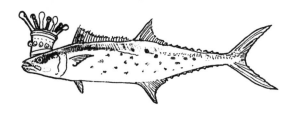

B.B.Q. MACKEREL

Preparation time: 10 minutes   *Chef: Sylvia & Stanley Dabney*
Marinating time: 2 hours   *Yacht : Native Sun*
Cooking time: 20-25 minutes
on BBQ grill

Serves: 6

3 lbs. mackerel fillets, or   **1 (8 oz.) bottle lime juice**
**   tuna, wahoo, bonito**   **Worcestershire sauce**
1 stick (4 oz.) butter

Melt butter, add lime juice and Worcestershire to make a dark sauce. Marinate fish 2 or more hours. Remove fillets, reserve marinade. Wrap fillets (skin side down) in aluminum foil, make holes every 3 inches. Lay over grill (medium-to-low heat) to cook slowly. Baste with reserved marinade during the 20-25 minutes of cooking. Do not turn.

Alternatives: Tuna, Dolphin

BROILED SPICY MACKEREL

Preparation time: 15 minutes   *Chef: Jan Robinson*
Cooking time: 10 minutes   *Yacht: Vanity*
Serves: 6

2-1/2 lbs. mackerel fillets   1 Tblsp. prepared mustard
pepper, to taste   2 tsp. prepared horseradish
4 Tblsp. melted butter   2 Tblsp. chili sauce
1 cup grated cheese

Preheat broiler. Cut fillets into serving size portions and arrange on a greased baking dish or broiler pan, skin side down. Pepper lightly, brush with butter and broil 6-8 minutes or until browned and flaky. Meanwhile, combine the cheese, mustard, horseradish and chili sauce. Spoon cheese mix on top of fillets and return to broiler for 1 or 2 minutes, until cheese melts and browns.

BAKED WEST INDIAN MACKEREL

Preparation time: 15 minutes   *Chef: Jan Robinson*
Cooking time: 15-20 minutes   *Yacht: Vanity*
Serves: 4

4 mackerel fillets   1/4 tsp. ground ginger
1 small onion, chopped   1/2 tsp. curry powder
1 large peeled tomato, chopped 1/4 cup tomato juice
2 cloves minced garlic   1 Tblsp. vinegar

Preheat oven to 375 degrees F. In a blender, mix the onion, tomato, garlic, ginger and curry powder. In a separate bowl mix the tomato juice and vinegar, then gradually add to the onion and tomato mix while the blender is running. Place fillets in a greased baking dish and pour over the sauce. Bake 15-20 minutes at 375 degrees F. until fish flakes.

SEAFOOD LINGUINE

Preparation time: 30 minutes　　　　*Chef: Kate Hinrichs*
Cooking time: 20 minutes　　　　　　*Yacht: Mystique*
Serves: 6

3 Tblsp. olive oil
3 shallots, chopped
1 garlic clove, chopped
1-2 Tblsp. flour
3/4 cup cream
1-1/2 cups clam juice or
　white wine

1-1/2 lbs. Spanish mackerel
　fillet, or other fish fillet
1 lb. linguine, cooked
salt and white pepper,
　to taste
Garnish: chopped fresh
　parsley

Saute shallots and garlic in olive oil until tender. Add flour, make roux. Cook about 1 minute. Add cream and clam juice, stir until thickened about 5 minutes. Add fish, salt and white pepper to taste. Simmer about 10 minutes until fish is firm. Serve over linguine. Garnish with chopped fresh parsley. *Serve with salad and dry white wine.*

MACKEREL VINAIGRETTE

Preparation time: 15 minutes　　　　*Chef: Jan Robinson*
Cooking time: 10 minutes　　　　　　*Yacht: Vanity*
Serves: 4

4 mackerel or wahoo steaks
1/4 cup butter, melted
pepper

Vinaigrette Dressing:
　1/2 cup olive oil
　1 Tblsp. white vinegar
　1/2 tsp. celery seed

2 tsp. lemon juice
2 cloves garlic, crushed
dash of thyme

Preheat broiler. Pepper the steaks, baste with melted butter, and broil 4 inches from oven coils 5-8 minutes per side.

Vinaigrette Dressing: Mix ingredients in small saucepan and heat. Pour dressing over the steaks and serve immediately.

MARLIN

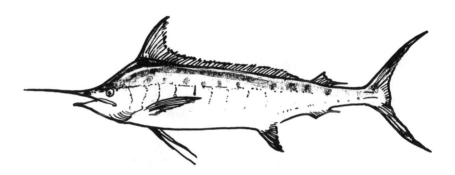

Description: The body of the Marlin is dark blue to Chocolate brown along the back and upper sides, changing to silvery white on the belly. On the sides there are approximately 15 pale blue vertical bars. The spear is more round and appears long for the body length.

Size: Marlin have been caught weighing up to one ton, but in most areas they average between 250 to 300 pounds.

Habitat: The Marlin is a fish of worldwide occurrence and is found in the warm and temperate seas.

Flavor: The red flesh of the Marlin has an excellent fresh flavor but tastes dry unless prepared properly.

Preparation: All Marlins are delicious when smoked, baked or broiled. It is a leaner meat than Swordfish, and tends to dry out unless basted and cooked just to the point of "done". Substitute marlin for any swordfish or tuna recipe.

BAKED SPORT FISH FROM THE U. S. VIRGIN ISLANDS

Preparation time: 15-20 minutes   *Chef: Debbie Ulrey*
Marinating time: 30 minutes   *Yacht: Dream Merchant*
Cooking time: 40 minutes
Serves: 6-8

3 lbs. blue marlin, white marlin, or sailfish fillets
1/4 tsp. ground cloves
1-1/2 tsp. Lawry's seasoned salt
1-1/2 tsp. Bohio* seasoning
2 cloves garlic, minced

1/2 cup water
2 stalks celery, chopped
1 small onion, chopped
2 Tblsp. lemon juice
1/2 tsp. pepper

Garnish: parsley sprigs

Preheat oven to 250 degrees F. Cut fish into 3/4" fillets. Mix all other ingredients and pour into 11x15" baking dish. Place fillets in mixture and marinate 15 minutes on each side. Bake in 250 degrees F. oven for 40-45 minutes or until fish is flaky.

*Bohio is a Puerto Rican spice, if unavailable substitute 1-1/4 tsp. garlic salt and 1/2 tsp. oregano.

FISH PARMESAN

Preparation time: 15 minutes   *Chef: Jan Robinson*
Cooking time: 30 minutes   *Yacht: Vanity*
Serves: 4

3 lbs. marlin or grouper fillets
16 oz. sour cream
1/3 cups grated Parmesan Cheese
1/4 cup onions, chopped

1 Tblsp. lemon juice
1/2 tsp. salt
dash Tabasco sauce
Paprika
Garnish: Parsley

Preheat oven to 350 degrees F. Place fillets in a single layer in a greased, overproof dish. Combine rest of ingredients except paprika and parsley. Mix well. Spread the sauce over fish and sprinkle paprika on top. Bake in oven at 350 degrees F. or approximately 30 minutes. Garnish with parsley.

MUSSELS

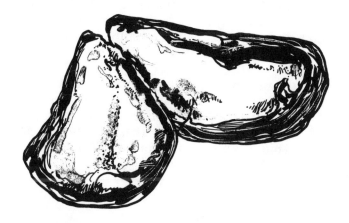

In the United States, mussels are probably one of the greatest unused seafood resources. You can usually find the wild form on just about all seacoasts. In Europe, however, mussels have been very popular for hundreds of years. The demand is so great there that for may years mussels have been propagated to augment the natural supply.

This delicate bivalve has a thin, blue-black shell, measuring two to three inches long, with a deep violet color inside. They usually spin a very strong silken black thread or beard to anchor themselves to underwater objects. The flesh is tender and has a distinctive smoky taste.

Mussels are the most common and abundant group of bivalves found on the shores of all continents.   The best mussels are harvested from colder waters, although they are found all over the world. In the summer, it is best not to collect mussels from beds which have been exposed at low tide. As with clams or oysters, a live mussel will clamp its shell shut when disturbed. Mussels are usually at their peak for eating during the fall, winter, and early spring. <u>Mussels are an excellent source of protein, vitamins and minerals.</u>

Here are three types of mussels that are commercially available today:

The Common Edible Mussel can be found hanging in masses on wharf timbers, covering sand bars, mud flats, on floating objects

The Horse Mussel is also quite common. It often grows up to six inches with the shell being a dark brown color and having a coarse texture and a wedge shape. This is an edible mussel whose flesh is usually a deep orange-red color.

The Ribbed Mussel has a brittle greenish-yellow shell that is finely scalloped around its outer edge. It is found on mud flats and sand bars that are exposed at low tide. Although there are no evidence of toxicity, the ribbed mussel has a strong and unpleasant flavor. Ribbed mussels are usually sold at bait stations to be used as flounder bait rather than for eating.

HOW TO BUY:

Mussels can be purchased in the shell alive, or canned in either brine, a barbeque sauce, or smoked. The shells of the fresh live ones should be tightly closed. If there is a gap between the shells, tap the mussel, and if alive, it will close. To check for "mudders", try to slide two halves of the shell across each other. If they budge, the shells may be filled with mud.

Mussels are very perishable, so they should be cooked and eaten the same day. One to two dozen mussels will serve one person for a main dish.

PREPARATION FOR USE:

To clean the mussel, hold under cold running water, scrub with a stiff brush to remove the mud on the outer shell and most, if not all, the beard that appears on the outer edges. Place them in a pot, cover with cold water, and let stand for two hours. Live mussels will drop to the bottom. Dead ones will float to the top. Be sure to discard any dead mussels.

To open, place a pan on the table to catch the liquid which you might want to save. Hold the scrubbed mussel over the pan. Insert knife between the shells in the bearded area and run a blade around the edge, working first toward the beard end. Remove the meat, trim away any remaining whiskers, and place the meat in a separate dish from the liquid. Strain the liquid through two layers of cheesecloth to remove sand or shells.

the edge, working first toward the beard end. Remove the meat, trim away any remaining whiskers, and place the meat in a separate dish from the liquid.   Strain the liquid through two layers of cheesecloth to remove sand or shells.

Mussels cook very quickly, so once they have opened their shells, they are done. To steam mussels, put about one inch of water into a pot. Add salt and bring to boil. Slide cleaned, unshelled mussels gently into the pot. Cover and simmer about three minutes or less (just until they open). Remove mussels carefully so as not to lose the liquid inside the shells.   Let the mussels cool, then pour the liquid from the shells through a cheesecloth to save for sauce. Remove the shell, trim whiskers, and taste for doneness. If they are not done, you can return them to the pot for one to three minutes.

TIPS:

You can keep mussels from one to two days in the refrigerator before cooking.

Cultured mussels have the best quality.

Always steam or saute shell and all for a unique flavor in sauces and stews.

Never gather mussels above the low water mark due to parasites. These mussels are subject to sunlight and are of poorer quality. Mussels can be used in just about any dish calling for clams or oysters.

PAELLA CARIBIANA

Preparation time: 20 minutes   *Chef: Nancy Thorne*
Cooking time: 45 minutes   *Yacht: Fancy Free*
Serves: 6

1 lb. mussels, cleaned
2 lobsters, cut up (shell on)
1 lb. scallops
1 lb. large shrimp, deveined
2 conch, cleaned, 1-inch pieces
2 cups rice
1 green pepper, strips
1 red pepper, strips

2 Tblsp. garlic, minced
1 onion, diced
1/2 cup olive oil
1 cup white wine
1 1/2 cup V-8 juice
2 chicken bouillon cubes
2 tsp. tumeric
1 cup peas
Garnish: chopped parsley

Saute peppers, onions and garlic in olive oil. Remove to baking dish. Saute rice in same pan till golden. Remove to baking pan. Make stock of wine, "V-8", bouillon cubes, tumeric. Heat and pour over rice-vegetable mixture. Top with raw seafood. Top with foil and bake 30 minutes. Remove foil, add peas and bake 15 minutes uncovered. Garnish with lots of chopped parsley. *Serve with a Saviginon Blanc (Kenwood, Iron Horse).*

Precede the   Paella with Gazpacho and follow with fruit and Zabaglione.

I just asked him about the mussels!

Hint: *Vinegar bought to a boil in a new frying pan will prevent foods from sticking.*

STEAMED SHELLFISH PLATTER

Preparation time: 5 minutes   *Chef: Jan Robinson*
Cooking time: 2 minutes   *Yacht: Vanity*
Serves: 4

4 cloves garlic, chopped
2 tsp. dried hot peppers
1 cup dry white wine
1 cup clam juice

2 lb. clams, washed and
   cleaned
2 lb. mussels, washed and
   cleaned
Garnish: Italian red
   peppers, parsley

In a large saucepan bring first four ingredients to a boil; add shellfish.   Cover and steam until mussels and clams open - approximately 2 minutes. Garnish with parsley and Italian red peppers. *Serve with drawn butter.*

MOLLY MALONE MUSSELS

Preparation time: 10 minutes   *Chef: Evelyn Flanagan*
Cooking time: 10 minutes   *Yacht: Vanity*
Serves: 4

2 lbs. mussels (fresh in shells),
   scrubbed and debearded
1 cup onion, finely chopped
4 cloves garlic, crushed

1/2 cup parsley
Salt and black pepper, to
   taste
1 cup white wine

Place mussels in a saucepan of boiling water.   Sprinkle all ingredients over them. Cover and bring to boil, simmer for 8 minutes. Serve in individual bowls along with lemon water finger bowls. *Serve with French bread.*

Note: A roux can be added to residue in pot to make a creamy mornay sauce.

MUSSELS DINGLE STYLE

Preparation time: 10 minutes　　　　*Chef: Evelyn Flanagan*
Cooking time: 20 minutes　　　　　　　*Yacht: Vanity*
Serves: 4

1 onion , chopped
2 cloves garlic, chopped
1/4 lb. butter
1/2 tsp. sugar
1 lb. mussels, shelled
1 cup bread crumbs

1/2 tsp. thyme
1/4 cup freshly chopped
　parsley
1/2 tsp. oregano
Salt and pepper
2 small tomatoes, sliced

Preheat oven to 350 degrees F. Saute finely chopped onions and garlic in melted butter and sugar. Arrange mussels in dish and sprinkle onions and garlic over them; then breadcrumbs and herbs. Finally, add sliced tomatoes on top to garnish and salt and pepper. Bake in moderate oven 20 minutes. *Serve with garlic bread and a salad.*

MARINATED MUSSELS

Preparation time: 10 minutes　　　　*Chef: Jan Robinson*
Cooking time: 10-15 minutes　　　　　*Yacht: Vanity*
Chilling time: 1 hour
Serves: 6

2 lbs. mussels (about 3 dozen)
1 cup water or white wine
1/4 cup parsley sprigs
1 large clove of garlic
1/4 cup olive oil

2 Tblsp. lemon juice
2 Tblsp. white vermouth
pepper, to taste

Scrub mussels, removing beards. Steam in water or white wine just until shells open. Do not over cook. Discard any mussel that does not open. Remove empty half shell and discard. Arrange mussels in shells on a serving platter. Chop parsley and garlic in blender. Add lemon juice, vermouth, pepper and blend. Pour marinade over mussels in shells. Cover and chill for 1 hour.

SCREAMING STUFFED MUSSELS

Preparation time: 1 hour   *Chef: Janet Jacobs*
Cooking time: 2 hours 15 minutes   *Yacht: Begone*
Serves: 6

50 to 60 large mussels, scrubbed and debearded
2 cups natural mussel liquid
3 cups finely chopped onion
1 cup olive oil
1/2 cup uncooked, long-grain rice
1/4 cup currants
1/4 cup pignoli (pine nuts)
1 tsp. freshly ground black pepper
1 tsp. ground allspice
1/2 tsp. ground cinnamon
Garnish: lemon wedges

Each mussel has a straight-sided "hinged" back, a large rounded end, and a short rounded end. To open the mussels for stuffing, plunge a sharp, thin paring knife midway into the back of each, with the blade facing the large rounded end. Carefully work the knife blade clockwise, taking care to catch all the mussel liquid in a mixing bowl. When the muscle of the mussel is cut through, the shell can easily be pried open with the fingers like a purse or pocketbook. Open the mussel to receive the stuffing, but take care not to break the hinged back. Measure the mussel liquid. If there is not two cups, add enough water to make two cups and a little salt to taste.

Cook the onion in oil over low heat until it is soft. Add the rice, currants, nuts, pepper, allspice and cinnamon. Use a small spoon to fill each mussel lightly with the rice mixture. Do not overfill them. Close the mussel shells and place them in layers in a deep, wide kettle. Add the mussel liquid and cover closely with an inverted plate. Add the pot lid and cook over high heat until the steam escapes from the pot, about 5 minutes. Reduce heat and cook over very low heat two hours.

Let the mussels cool thoroughly. Several hours before serving, take the mussels from the pot and reverse the layers, so that the mussels remain equally moist and marinate equally in the pot broth. To serve, remove the mussels from the pot and arrange them symmetrically on a large platter. Garnish liberally with lemon wedges.

Note: I've renamed this dish "Screaming Stuffed Mussels". Before you begin step 1, you must check that any mussels slightly open are not in fact expired. You can do this a number of ways but it all amounts to frightening them so they close the shell. Suggested method is to tap them on a counter or with a spoon etc. I found it much more fun to belt arias at them or practice voice scales, which with my voice amounts to screaming. At any rate it produced the desired results. The mussels quickly slammed shut and I had more fun than tapping with a spoon.

OCTOPUS

Description: Octopus is actually a mollusk and is a member of the same family as Squid. It has a flexible, almost circular body with 8 long arms covered by suction cups. An Octopus can discharge clouds of ink which take the shape of a dummy or "phantom" Octopus so as to fool its attackers.

Size: The weight can range from 5 to 50 pounds, with the smaller weight being more desirable.

Habitat: They are found year round in the temperate and tropical oceans world - wide.

Flavor: The meat is generally compared to chicken and requires tenderizing or long, slow cooking.

Preparation: Octopuses are marketed in fresh and frozen forms. They are eaten raw, pickled in vinegar, smoked, added to tomato - based stews and grilled. If dressing your own, invert the Octopus (It can be turned inside out like a sock) and cut away the beaks in the mouth area.
Remove or leave the ink sac according to the recipe.

Other names: Develfish, Pulpo

OCTOPUS   STEW

Preparation time: 10 minutes   *Chef: Jan Robinson*
Cooking time: 30 minutes   *Yacht: Vanity*
Serves: 4

1-1/2 lbs. octopus, tentacles   **1/2 cup white wine**
**   and body**   **2 Tblsp. chopped parsley**
2 Tblsp. olive oil   **2 canned anchovy fillets**
1 large onion, sliced   **pepper, to taste**
4 cloves garlic, chopped
1 cup fennel bulb   **Garnish: fresh parsley**

Cut octopus into 1/2-inch strips. Blanch in salted water for 5 minutes and allow to cool in liquid, then drain. Slice fennel bulb into 1/2-inch thick slices. In a large saucepan, saute garlic, onion and fennel in oil, until soft; do not brown. Add wine, octopus, parsley and anchovies. Cover and simmer for 30 minutes, or longer.

Serve in soup bowls with hot crusty French bread.

Alternative: Squid

Hint: Try charcoaling fish in grape leaves (if fortunate enought to have grapes). Have fish gutted, but leave unscaled. When leaves are unrolled skin comes off.

ORANGE ROUGHY

Description: Orange Roughy is easily recognized by its orange body and fins. It has a deep body, massive head with conspicuous bony ridges and cavities. The scales are small and irregular in shape and pattern.

Size: Resource size unknown, but definitely large.

Habitat: Orange Roughy is a deep water species, irregular in distribution and abundance. It is very common in some areas on the Chatham Rise in New Zealand.

Flavor: Orange Roughy has a pearly white flesh with a medium texture and coarse flakes. It has a delicate shellfish flavor before spawning.

Preparation: This is a good eating fish, but it requires deep skinning to remove subutaneous fat layer. It is suitable for most cooking methods.

PAN-FRIED ORANGE ROUGHY

Preparation time: 10 minutes   *Chef: Jan Robinson*
Cooking time: 6 minutes   *Yacht: Vanity*
Serves: 4

4 fillets of orange roughy,   **2 tsp. of lemon-pepper**
  (approximately 1-1/2 lbs.)   **seasoning**
2 Tblsp. of all-purpose flour   **2 Tblsp. of butter or oil**
                                         Garnish: lemon wedges and
                                           fresh sprigs of parsley

Thaw orange roughy fillets. Rinse fillets and pat dry. Combine flour and lemon-pepper seasoning. Coat orange roughy fillets with mixture and shake-off excess. Gently saute in butter or oil until cooked through. (Approximately 3 minutes on each side). Garnish. *Serve with boiled new red potatoes, sauteed peapods and steamed carrots.*

ORANGE ROUGHY FILLETS IN WHITE WINE

Preparation time: 10 minutes   *Chef: Jan Robinson*
Marinating time: 30 minutes   *Yacht: Vanity*
Cooking time: 10 minutes
Serves: 6

6 orange roughy fillets,   **1 onion, finely chopped**
  (approximately 3 lbs.)   **1 tsp. of capers (optional)**
1-1/2 cups of white wine
1/3 cup all-purpose flour   **Garnish: orange twists with**
black pepper, to taste   **fresh sprigs of dill or**
2 Tblsp. butter + 1 Tblsp.oil   **parsley**

Marinate fish in wine in refrigerator for 15-60 minutes. Drain fish and reserve wine. Pat fish dry and coat with flour seasoned with pepper. Heat butter and oil in large skillet. Gently cook onion 3-5 minutes. Add fillets to pan and fry each side for 2 minutes. Add wine and capers and cook over high heat for 2-3 minutes, until liquid is reduced by half. *Serve with steamed pea pods, and orange rice. Accompanied by a good bottle of chilled champagne, or dry white wine.*

INDONESIAN FISH

Preparation time: 15 minutes   *Chef: Mary Usmar*
Cooking time: 20 minutes   *Yacht: Voyager*
Serves: 4

Batter:
- 3 cups oil
- 1 egg lightly beaten
- 1 tsp. salt
- 1/4 cup cornstarch
- 1/4 cup flour
- 1/4 cup chicken stock
- 4 fish fillets, orange roughy snapper, or other fish fillets, about 2 lbs.

Sauce:
- 1 Tblsp. oil
- 1 tsp. chopped garlic
- 1 large green pepper, sliced
- 2 carrots, slivered
- 1/2 cup chicken stock
- 4 Tblsp. sugar
- 4 Tblsp. red wine vinegar
- 1 tsp. soy sauce
- 1 Tblsp. cornstarch dissolved in 2 Tblsp. cold water

Heat oil in wok (skillet). Mix together all batter ingredients. Cut fish into bite size pieces. Coat fish with batter, fry in batches until crisp golden brown, 3-4 minutes. Drain, keep warm. May be done in advance and reheated.

Sauce: Pour oil into wok, heat; add garlic then green pepper and carrot, stir fry 2-3 minutes. Add next four ingredients and bring to boil rapidly about 1 minute to dissolve sugar. Stir cornstarch with water and add. Cook until sauce is thick and clear. Pour over fish and serve at once.

Serve with sticky rice or noodles and a crispy vegetable. (Chop sticks for fun).   "Selamat makan"   means bon appetit.

Alternatives: Sole, Black Sea Bass

FISH FILLETS WITH SPINACH

Preparation time: 20 minutes   *Chef: Peggy Curren*
Cooking time: 25 minutes   *Yacht: Scatteree*
Serves: 4

2 Tblsp. margarine or butter
2 Tblsp flour
1 tsp. instant chicken bouillon
dash of ground nutmeg
dash of white pepper
dash of ground red pepper
1 Tblsp. paprika
1 cup milk
2/3 cup shredded Swiss or
    cheddar cheese

1 pkg. (10 oz.) frozen chopped
    spinach
1 Tblsp. lemon juice
1- 1/2 lbs. orange roughy
    fillets, or flounder or
    snapper
1/2 tsp. salt
2 Tblsp. grated Parmesan
    cheese
Garnish: lemon wedges

Heat margarine over low heat until melted; stir in flour, bouillon, nutmeg, red pepper, paprika, and white pepper. Cook over low heat, stirring constantly until mixture is smooth and bubbly - remove from heat. Stir in milk. Heat to boiling; stirring constantly. Boil and stir 1 minute. Add swiss cheese; cook; stirring constantly; just until cheese is melted. Place spinach (thawed and well drained) in ungreased baking dish - sprinkle with lemon juice. Arrange fish on spinach; sprinkle with salt and Parmesan cheese. Spread sauce over fish and spinach. Cook uncovered in 350 degree oven until fish flakes easily with fork (about 20 minutes). Garnish with lemon wedges.

Alternatives: Flounder, Snapper

ORANGE ROUGHY MICROWAVED IN LEMON BUTTER

Preparation time: 5 minutes   *Chef: Jan Robinson*
Cooking time: 12 minutes (microwave)   *Yacht: Vanity*
Serves: 4

4 (8 oz.) orange roughy fillets   2 cloves crushed garlic
  or other fish fillets   1/4 cup fresh lemon juice
1/4 cup melted butter   Garnish: lemon wedges and
freshly ground black pepper   fresh parsley sprigs

Place thawed fillets in microwave dish with thickest parts to outside edges of dish. Mix together the butter, pepper, garlic and lemon juice. Brush or pour over fillets. Cover with clear wrap. Cook on high allowing about 3 minutes for each 8 oz. Do, NOT overcook. *Serve with boiled new potatoes and steamed peapods.*

FISH WITH SOUR CREAM

Preparation time: 10 minutes   *Chef: Peggy Curren*
Cooking time: 20 minutes   *Yacht: Scatteree*
Serves: 4

4 orange roughy fish fillets   1/2 cup dairy sour cream
4 oz. mushrooms, sliced   3 Tblsp. grated Parmesan
1 small onion, chopped   cheese
1 Tblsp. margarine or butter   2 Tblsp. dry bread crumbs
1/2 tsp. salt   Garnish: paprika, snipped
1/8 tsp. pepper   parsley

Preheat oven to 350 degrees F. Rinse fillets and pat dry with paper towels; arrange in an ungreased oblong baking dish (12" x 7-1/2" x 2"). In a skillet cook mushrooms and onions in margarine until golden (3 minutes). Spoon mushroom and onion mixture over fish; sprinkle with salt and pepper. Mix sour cream and cheese; spread over mushroom and onion mixture. Sprinkle with bread crumbs. Cook uncovered in 350 degrees F. oven until fish flakes easily with fork (about 20 minutes). Sprinkle with paprika and parsley. *This goes well with boiled red potatoes.*

Alternatives: Any fish fillets

FILLETS WELLINGTON

Preparation time: 45 minutes   *Chef: Jan Robinson*
Cooking time: 25 minutes   *Yacht: Vanity*
Serves: 4

4 Orange roughy fish fillets   **Crab Stuffing:**
juice of one lemon   **1/2 lb. flaked crabmeat**
2 cloves garlic, crushed   **1 egg white**
freshly ground black pepper   **1/3 whipping cream**
1 (8 oz.) can refrigerated   **1/2 cup chopped celery**
   crescent rolls   **1/2 cup Italian bread**
1 egg yolk, lightly beaten   **crumbs**
                                                          1/4 cup melted butter
Garnish: lemon and lime slices   **1 tsp. lemon-pepper**

Preheat oven to 425 degrees F. Season fillets with lemon juice, garlic, and pepper. Set aside.

Make crab stuffing: Combine crabmeat, egg white, whipping cream, chopped celery, bread crumbs, melted butter and lemon pepper.

Separate the roll dough into 2 portions. On a lightly floured board, roll out half the dough and cut into a fish shape. Cut the second fish shape 1 inch bigger, all the way around, than the first shape. Place the first shape on a greased baking sheet and spread a thin layer of crab stuffing on it. Lay two fillets on the dough and spread half of the crab mixture on top. Layer with remaining fillets and cover top and sides with remaining stuffing. Place second fish shape on top and pinch edges together to seal. Use scrap dough to make fins, eyes and gill slits. Brush with egg yolk and water mixture. Bake for 10 minutes at 425 degrees F. then for 15 minutes at 350 degrees F. or until crust is brown and fillets are opaque and flake when tested.

To serve: Overlap orange and lime slices alternatively around the edge of a fish or large oval platter. Lay the fish shaped pastry on top, so it is surrounded by the lime and orange slices. Makes a nice presentation.

Alternatives: Any fish fillets

BAKED FISH MOZZARELLA

Preparation time: 10 minutes
Cooking time: 12-20 minutes
Serves: 6

Chef: Jean Crook
Yacht: Dileas

6 fish fillets (2lbs.) orange
   or any other fillets
salt and pepper, to taste
2 cups grated mozzarella
   cheese

1 small clove garlic, minced
2 large tomatoes, peeled
   and sliced
1 tsp. dried oregano

Preheat oven to 375 degrees F. Pat fillets dry. Arrange in single layer in buttered 13 x 9" baking dish with salt and pepper to taste. Combine cheese and garlic. Spread over fish. Arrange tomato slices on top and sprinkle with oregano, salt and pepper. Bake in oven at 375 degrees F, 12-20 minutes or until fish flakes easily with fork. With slotted spoon, transfer to serving platter.

I serve a rice pilaf and broccili casserole from Ship To Shore I. Also amaretto apples and whipped cream. A nice light dinner.

FISH AND KRAUT SANDWICHES

Preparation time: 15 minutes
Cooking time: 15 minutes
Serves: 4

Chef: Jan Robinson
Yacht: Vanity

1 cup cooked, flaked fish
1/2 cup well drained
   sauerkraut
1/4 cup chopped dill pickles
1/4 cup mayonnaise

1 Tblsp. horseradish
12 slices party rye bread
6 slices (1 oz. each) swiss
   cheese
2 Tblsp. margarine

Cook fish by baking, broiling, poaching or in the microwave oven. Cool and flake. In mixing bowl, combine fish, sauerkraut, pickles, mayonnaise and horseradish. Mix well. Portion mixture evenly on half the bread. Top with cheese. Top with remaining bread. Melt margarine in skillet. Place sandwiches in skillet and grill on each side until golden brown. *Serve with chips or relishes and a cold drink.*

Alternatives: Any cooked fish

MILD FISH CURRY

Preparation time: 15 minutes   *Chef: Mary Usmar*
Cooking time: 20 minutes   *Yacht: Voyager*
Serves: 4

4 orange roughy fish fillets   **1 Tblsp. curry powder**
1/4 cup oil   **1 bay leaf**
2 onions, chopped   **1 cup pulped tomatoes**
2 garlic cloves, chopped   **1 cup coconut milk**
1 tsp. ginger, chopped   **salt to taste**
1 small cinnamon stick

Heat oil and gently fry onions, garlic and ginger. Add cinnamon stick, curry powder and bay leaf. Cook 2 minutes. Add tomato pulp and coconut milk. Simmer uncovered until gravy has thickened. Add salt. Cut fish into 1-inch cubes and place in gravy. Simmer approximately 10 minutes. Remove cinnamon stick and bay leaf.

Serve with spoons - no knives or forks.   Have ready hot dishes of lentils or yellow rice and lots of condiments (eg. chutney, grated cucumber (drained), yogurt, pineapple chunks, sliced bananas, salted peanuts, and pappadams.)

Note: As with all curries, it is best made the day before.

Alternatives: Any fish fillets

Hint: Thaw fish and shellfish in milk. The milk draws out the frozen taste and provides a fresh caught flavor.

MARINATED ORANGE ROUGHY WITH FRUIT AND COCONUT CREAM

Preparation time: 30 minutes   *Chef: Jan Robinson*
Marinating time: 10 hours   *Yacht Vanity*
Chilling time:1 hour
Serves: 4

4 fillets of orange roughy,   **2 small onions, chopped**
**   (approximately 2 lbs.)**   **melon, mangoes or other**
juice of 4 limes*   **   colorful seasonal fruits**

Coconut Cream Mayonnaise:
1 egg, separated   **1 Tblsp. of boiling water**
1/2 tsp. of dried mustard   **2/3 cup of canned coconut**
1 Tblsp. of lime juice   **   cream**
1/4 tsp. pepper   **1/3 cup of cream**
1/2 cup of olive oil

Thaw orange roughy fillets. Rinse and pat dry. Cut fillets in 1/2 inch cubes or strips. Placed cubed fish into bowl containing lime juice and finely chopped onions. Marinate for 10 to 12 hours (or overnight) in refrigerator.

Coconut Cream Mayonnaise:
Mix 1 egg yolk with dried mustard in a small mixing bowl. Add 1 tablespoon of lime juice and pepper. Warm 1/2 cup of olive oil. Add warmed olive oil drop by drop at first, beating into mixture, and then increase flow to a slow trickle while continuing to beat mixture until the mayonnaise is thickened and smooth.

Whisk one egg-white until stiff and fold into mayonnaise with 1 tablespoon of boiling water. Take 2/3 cup of coconut cream and blend with 1/3 cup of cream. Stir enough blended coconut cream into mayonnaise mixture to give required taste and consistency. Chill at least 1 hour. I usually make it and chill it overnight in the refrigerator, while the fillets are marinating.

Presentation: Remove orange roughy from refrigerator and drain. Place on attractive platter. Make melonballs or cube fruit. Add to platter. Spoon over coconut cream mayonnaise. *This makes a great lunch, served with crusty hot bread and a chilled white wine.*

Note: This dish is really worth the effort. May be prepared andheld in the refrigerator for up to one day prior to serving.

Alternative: Scallops

* Hint: Microwave limes for about 40 seconds before squeezing, you'll get twice the amount of juice.

MEDITERRANEAN SAUCE FOR COLD FISH

Preparation time: 15 minutes   *Chef: Marilyn Stenberg*
Serves: 4   *Yacht: Sheerwill*

1 (3 1/2 oz.) can tuna, in water   salt and pepper
3 Tblsp. mayonnaise   1-2 hard-boiled eggs
1-1/2 oz. single cream,   2 tsp. capers
   (Half & Half)
1 Tblsp. lemon juice   Garnish: slices of lemon

Blend together the drained tuna, mayonnaise, cream and lemon juice. Season well with salt and pepper. Mask your fish pieces and garnish with lemon slices, eggs, and capers.

Tip: You can adjust the consistency of your sauce with the addition of more cream if it looks to stiff.

OYSTERS

Although no one knows how many centuries oysters have been enjoyed as food, it is known that oyster farming has been practiced in the West since the days of the Romans, and that oysters were cultivated in China long before the Christan Era. Today oysters are more popular than ever. <u>Oysters are one of the richest sources of iron found in nature.</u> It also supplies many other minerals and most essential vitamins.

The Oyster is a bivalve mollusk belonging to the Ostreidae family. More than a hundred living species in this large family have been described, but only a few are of economic importance. True oysters are distinguised by having dissimilar lower and upper shells. These shells or valves, are hinged together by a complex elastic ligament. The upper valve of the shell is normally flat, while the lower is concave, providing space for the body of the oyster. The two valves fit together making a watertight seal when the oyster closes, providing the shell has not been damaged or broken. Near the center of the oyster's body is an adductor muscle, attached to both valves, which controls the opening and closing of the shell. There are three important species of oysters which are enjoyed in the United States:

The Eastern or Atlantic Oyster is found along the Gulf Coast and up the Atlantic coast to Cape Cod. It makes up aproximately 85% of the commercial Oyster harvest and includes many area names such as Cheseapeake and Bluepoint. An eastern oyster will take 2-5 years to grow to marketable sizes, depending on the locality in which it lives.

The Pacific Oyster, recently called "Pacific King Oyster", is grown in coastal waters from Alaska to Northern California. This oyster is grown from seeds imported from Japan. It differs from our natural oyster in appearance by its elongated and rather fragile shell. Because of its rapid growth and high glycerin content the "Japanese" oyster is considered well-suited for canning. The flavor and appearance is inferior to our eastern oyster and cannot take its place in half-shell trade.

The Rare Western oyster, also known as Oympia oyster, is a native to the Pacific Coast. The yield of this species has declined because of predators, water pollution, and increased cost of production. It is smaller than the eastern oyster, seldom exceeding a length of 2-1/4 inches. Growth is slow in this species, 4-5 years being required to reach marketable size.

HOW TO BUY OYSTERS:
When purchasing oysters live in their shells, look for ones tightly closed. If they are open, tap them and they should quickly close. If they don't, pass them up. You can keep them for seven to ten days in the refrigerator. Large oysters have a strong flavor, while the smaller oysters have a mild flavor.

Freshly shucked oysters should be plump and have a natural creamy color and clear liquid. Plump oyster meat is a sign of good quality. They are available in pints, quarts, and gallons. Frozen oysters can be purchased and kept for up to two months in the freezer. It is not recommended that you freeze them at home; packers have "quick freeze" facilities which are not possible with a home freezer.

SHUCKING OYSTERS:
To shuck your own oysters, be sure to wash oyster shells thoroughly and rinse in cold water. Grip the thin end between thumb and fingers, rounded half against the palm. Place an oyster knife near its point, curved tip down and insert near narrow end. Press the knife firmly against the top shell half, cut through to the muscle attached to the center of the shell and then around the rim, holding the shell slightly open with thumb. Turn the blade, curved

Oysters in the shell may also be opened by steaming, but you will lose some of the flavor. Put the scrubbed and rinsed oyster in a kettle with a very small amount of water - no more than 1/2 cup for 24 medium -sized oysters. Steam them 5-10 minutes, or until the shells open. Lift them from the pan carefully so you do not spill the liquid from the shells. When precooked this way, oysters should be used in cooked dishes within two days. Avoid overcooking oysters. They are toughened by high heat or pro - longed cooking.

TIPS:

Refrigerated or packed in ice, shucked oysters will remain fresh for a week to ten days.

If you buy oysters in their shells, make sure they are tightly closed.

When you buy shucked oysters, look for nice plump oysters with no sunken areas and clear, fresh sweet smelling liquid.

Shell oysters are generally sold by the dozen or sack and must be alive when purchased.

Sometimes merchants will soak oysters in fresh water to plump them, therefore ruining their flavor and texture. The soaked oysters will burst while frying. Shucked oysters are generally sold by the pint or quart, when plumped they take up more space.

Frozen oysters should not be thawed until ready to use and should never be refrozen.

Canned oysters are flavorful and may be substituted when fresh ones are not available.

Allow nine shelled oysters per person or one quart of shucked oysters per 6 persons, or two number one cans per 6 persons.

A little lemon, or vinegar and pepper enhances the delicate flavor of oysters on the half shell.

MAMA'S FAVORITE OYSTER SOUFFLE

Preparation time: 30 minutes   *Chef: Sylvia & Stanley Dabney*
Cooking time: 15-20 minutes   *Yacht: Native Sun*
Serves: 6

18 fresh (or 1-8 oz. can)
 oysters, with liquid
6 Tblsp. butter

Souffle:

5 Tblsp. butter   **1/3 cup Parmesan cheese**
6 Tblsp. flour   **6 egg whites**
dash cayenne   **1/2 tsp. cream of tartar**
1 cup milk   **1/4 tsp. salt**
1/4 cup reserved oyster liquid
6 egg yolks

Drain oysters, reserving liquid. Divide oysters into 6 (8 oz.) individual souffle dishes. Top each with 1 tablespoon butter.

Preheat oven to 350 degrees F. Melt 5 tablespoons butter in medium saucepan. Remove from heat and add 6 tablespoons flour and dash of cayenne. Mix till smooth. Gradually add milk and reserved oyster liquid. Bring to boil and stir. Then reduce heat and simmer until mixture becomes very thick and leaves bottom and sides of pan. Remove from heat. In large bowl beat egg yolks with wire whisk. Beat in souffle mixture, mixing well. Beat in Parmesan cheese. In large bowl beat egg whites, cream of tartar and salt until peaks are formed. Fold the egg mixture into souffle mixture 1/2 at a time and fold just until combined. Spoon over oysters in souffle mixing dishes. Bake 15 minutes or until puffed and nicely browned.

Hint: Clam and oysters will be simple to open if washed with cold water, then placed in a plastic bag and put in the freezer for an hour.

OYSTER STEW NEW ENGLAND STYLE

Preparation time: 10 minutes   *Chef: Beth Avone*
Cooking time: 15 minutes   *Yacht: Perfection*
Serves: 4

2-3 cans raw oysters, save   1 quart milk
  liquid or 1 pint fresh   pepper to taste
1/4 cup butter   paprika
                             Garnish: oyster crackers

Drain oysters, saving liquid. Saute oysters in hot butter until edges
curl. Add liquid, milk and pepper. Lower heat. Warm stew but do
not boil. To serve sprinkle with paprika and garnish with oyster
crackers.

SCALLOPED OYSTERS

Preparation time: 15 minutes   *Chef: Beth Avore*
Cooking time: 30 minutes   *Yacht: Perfection*
Serves: 4

1 pint raw oysters   1/2 to 1 cup cracker crumbs
2 Tblsp. oyster liquid   1/2 cup melted butter or
2 Tblsp. milk or cream   margarine
2 Tblsp. sherry   salt and pepper
1/2 cup seasoned bread   Garnish: paprika
  crumbs

Preheat oven to 425 degrees. F. Mix crumbs and melted butter. Put
a third on bottom of oven proof shallow casserole dish. Cover with
half of the oysters and half of all liquids and spices. Repeat. Cover
top with the remaining third of crumb mixture. Sprinkle with
paprika. Bake at 400-450 degrees F. for 30 minutes.

POACHED OYSTERS IN CREAM SAUCE

Preparation time: 5 minutes
Cooking time: 10 minutes
Serves: 4

Chef: Jan Robinson
Yacht: Vanity

2 Tblsp. unsalted butter
2 shallots, finely minced
1-1/2 cups sparkling white
   wine
2 dozen fresh shucked oysters,
   reserve shells

Cream Sauce:
   1/2 cup poaching liquid
   1/3 cup heavy cream
   white pepper, to taste
   4 oz. unsalted butter

In a heavy skillet, melt the butter and saute the shallots until soft, but not brown. Add the sparkling wine and bring to a simmer. Add the oysters and cook 2-3 minutes - do not overcook. Remove oysters and set aside; reserve the poaching liquid.

Cream Sauce: In a heavy skillet, reduce the poaching liquid slightly. Add the cream and pepper, continue to reduce over high heat until there is about 1/2 cup sauce left in the skillet. Remove from heat and gently stir in butter, a little at a time.

Warm reserved oyster shells. Return oysters to the sauce just long enough to warm them. Fill reserved shells with oysters and cover with sauce. *Serve as an hors d' oeuvre or an appetizer.*

Instant White Sauce: Blend together 1 cup soft butter and 1 cup flour. Spread in an ice cube tray. chill well, cut into 16 cubes before storing in a plastic bag in the freezor. For medium-thick sauce, drop 1 cube into 1 cup of milk and heat slowly, stirring as it thickens.

OYSTER HORS D'OEUVRE

Preparation time: 15 minutes   *Chef: Jan Robinson*
Cooking time: 5-7 minutes   *Yacht: Vanity*
Serves: 6

1 pint oysters, fresh or frozen   1/3 cup flour, to dredge
2 eggs   2 cups saltine cracker
2 Tblsp. evaporated milk   crumbs
1/2 tsp. pepper   1/3 cup margarine or butter
    1/3 cup cooking oil

Thaw oysters if frozen; drain. Beat together the eggs and milk. Dip oysters into egg mixture, then lightly into flour. Dip into egg mixture again and roll in cracker crumbs. Let stand 5 to 10 minutes before frying. Heat margarine (or butter) and oil in large frypan over moderate heat, 350 degrees F. Fry oysters 5 to 7 minutes or until lightly browned, turning once during cooking. Drain on absorbent paper. *Serve with a favorite seafood sauce.*

POMPANO

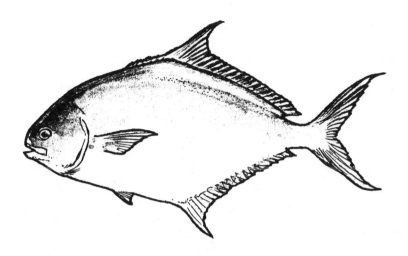

Description: The Pompano is a brightly colored fish that has a shallow body with relatively short fins. It is silvery - blue to blue - green on the top, silvery on the sides with a white belly. When removed from the water the colors become more vivid taking on a golden hue.

Size: Pompano range from 1to 2 pounds in the marketplace.

Habitat: Along the Atlantic coast from Massachusetts to Florida and the Caribbean, with a concentration between Virginia and Florida.

Flavor: The firm and rich flesh of the Pompano is considered to be the best in taste of all the warm salt water fish. This delicately flavored white meat is often used as a comparison when tasting other fish.

Preparation: Pompano is sold fresh or frozen and may be prepared by broiling or lightly frying to hold the light taste.

Other names: Sunfish

MEDITERRANEAN POMPANO

Preparation time: 15 minutes　　　　*Chef: Jan Robinson*
Cooking time: 40 minutes　　　　　　*Yacht: Vanity*
Serves: 4

4 Pompano fillets
flour
pepper
3 Tblsp. butter
1 Tblsp. olive oil
1 large onion, finely chopped
4 garlic cloves, crushed
  chopped
1 green pepper, finely
 chopped
1/4 cup capers
1 cup fish stock

3 Tblsp. Worcestershire
  sauce
1 tsp. Tabasco
 pepper, to taste
6 Tblsp. butter
6 Tblsp. flour
4 green onions, finely
  chopped
1/3 cup pimientos, minced
Garnish: lemon wedges
  and fresh parsley sprigs

Melt 3 Tblsp. butter and 1 Tblsp. olive oil in a large skillet. Add onion, garlic and green pepper. Saute for about 10 minutes. Add capers, fish stock, Worcestershire, Tabasco and pepper. Mix well. In a separate skillet or saucepan, melt the 6 Tblsp. butter, add 6 Tblsp. flour and cook until the roux is thick and turns light brown. Stir the roux into the other mixture, add green onions, stir, and cook for 20 minutes. Keep sauce hot.

Preheat broiler. Rinse the pompano, pat dry with paper towels. Dust with flour seasoned with pepper. Broil until just brown. Do NOT overcook. Keep warm.

Just before serving, stir the pimientos into the sauce. Place the pompano on warm plates, pour sauce over. Garnish.

Serve with Potatoes Anna, Petit Pois Peas and Stir Fry Carrots, followed by French Chocolate Mousse. (All these recipes in SHIP TO SHORE I)

RED DRUM

Description: The body of the Red Drum has a metallic rosy gold color fading to silver - bronze on the lower body. It has large scales with red colored pectoral fins. Most have one or two black spots on the tail section.

Size: The average size is 3 to 10 pounds, with the smaller fish being the more desirable.

Habitat: They are found along the Atlantic coast of the United States from Massachusetts to Texas.

Flavor: The meat of the Red Drum is firm but moist, white and heavy - flaked.

Preparation: Red Drum are marketed fresh and are best used in chowder form, stuffed and baked, or cut into cubes and deep - fried

Other names: Red Bass, Redfish Channel Bass, Puppy Drum

NORTH CAROLINA FISH STEW

Preparation time: 20 minutes　　　　*Chef: Jan Robinson*
Cooking time: 1 hour 15 minutes　　　　　*Yacht: Vanity*
Serves: 8

6 - 8 lbs. of Red Drum, fillets or steaks.	1/4 lb. bacon
3 lbs. white potatoes	4 cups canned tomatoes
3 lbs. yellow onions	12 oz. tomato puree or paste
bunch green onion	Tabasco, to taste
4 cloves garlic, chopped	Freshly ground pepper
	8 eggs

Cut fish into chunks, if you have steaks, leave the bones in to add flavor. Wash potatoes (and peel if you like) cut in quarters or big chunks. Slice them if you have fillets. Peel and quarter the onions. Chop the green onions. Brown the bacon in a large pot, uncovered. Add potato, onion and green onions, fish, tomatoes and tomato puree. Add Tabasco, pepper and enough water to cover everything. Simmer slowly for about 1 hour, or until the fish flakes. Crack the eggs and drop into the simmering stew. The yolks will be firm in about 10 minutes.
Note: This is a favourite of the natives of the Outer Banks and has become a favourite of my guests for lunch on board. Especially after a hard morning of snorkeling, swimming, board sailing or sunbathing!

Serve with hush puppies or hot crusty bread, to dunk into the stew. A big salad and iced beer or ice tea .

Alternatives: Flounder, Sea Trout, Weakfish,Redfish

SALMON

Description: There are seven distinct species of Salmon including King, Silver, red or sockeye, pink, chum and Atlantic. Most have blue-gray backs and silvery sides with irregular black spots. King is the most desirable followed by Silver.

Size: The weight range is from 3 to 15 pounds, with a few weighing more. The average is 3 to 5 pounds. They are usually less than 30 inches in length.

Habitat: Six of the seven Salmon species are found in the Pacific Ocean and are available mainly in the spring and fall season. The remaining species is found in the Atlantic Ocean.

Flavor: The pink to red flesh has a very distinctive and rich flavor. Oils and oil-based sauces should be used minimally because of the high fat content.

Preparation: It is particularly delicious grilled or broiled, baked with or without stuffing or poached and served hot or cold. Available fresh, or frozen or canned; whole or as steaks, fillets or chunks; smoked, kippered or salted.

Other names: Chinook, Coho

FILLET OF SALMON WITH ZINFANDEL SAUCE

Preparation time: 20 minutes
Cooking time: 4 minutes
Serves: 4

Chef: Gregor Roblsson
Yacht: Sea Cloud

4 (9 oz.) boneless salmon
   fillets
egg wash, (egg and milk)
fine seasoned bread crumbs
2 oz. clarified butter

Zinfandel Sauce:
  1/4 lb. butter
  2 large shallots, chopped
  small handful julienne
   basil
  3 oz. white zinfandel wine
  juice of 2 lemons
  2 oz. heavy cream
  salt and pepper
Garnish: tomato julienne

Submerge salmon in eggwash and lightly dredge in bread crumbs. Saute in clarified butter on medium-high heat, approximately 2 minutes on each side, to a nice even browned color. Keep warm.

Zinfandel Sauce: Saute chopped shallots in whole butter, add wine, lemon juice, 1/2 the basil and let reduce until thickened. Add cream and again reduce until thick. Remove from heat and swirl in butter in batches. Add rest of basil and adjust seasoning. Pour sauce over fillets and garnish with sliced tomato.

Salmon is a fish that should never be overcooked. Served medium -rare to medium.

Alternatives: Sea Trout

SALMON SUPREME

Preparation time: 15 minutes   *Chef: Paulette Dupuis*
Cooking time: 30 minutes   *Yacht: Rising Sun*
Serves: 6

1 cup dry white wine
1 cup chicken broth
6 salmon steaks
3 bay leaves
Beurre Manie (2 Tblsp.
   butter and 2 Tblsp. flour)
2-3 twigs fresh thyme
1 tsp. fresh marjoran

salt and cayenne pepper,
   dash
1 cup heavy cream or
   creme fraiche
1 egg yolk
lemon juice, to taste
1 lb. shrimp and truffles
Garnish: marjoran leaves
   and lemon slices

Preheat oven to 350 degrees F. Pour hot broth and white wine with bay leaves over salmon steaks in pan. Cover and bake for 20 minutes depending on thickness of steaks, or just until fish flakes. Meanwhile prepare beurre manie, blend together flour and soft butter. Peel and devein the shrimp, set aside. When steaks are done, put on a hot plate going to oven. Keep warm.

Make the sauce - strain salmon juices and wine in saucepan. Heat up, add beurre manie, stirring constantly. Beat egg yolk in cream, stir into the juices with herbs, salt and pepper then add shrimp. Cook for a few minutes. Taste for seasoning and add a little lemon juice, 1 teaspoon or more. Add truffles if desired, serve on salmon. If sauce is too thick, clear out with wine or milk depending on taste. If too clear add thicker beurre manie (more flour than butter). Garnish with fresh majoram leaves and a slice of lemon if desired

Serve with string beans, broccoli, asparagus tips, or other greens.... rice or pasta salad with tarragon vinegarette as entree. Mango sherbet for dessert.

Alternatives: Sea Trout

SIMPLE SALMON

Preparation time: 15 minutes   *Chef: Kate Young*
Cooking time: 20 minutes   *Yacht: Alize'*
Serves: 6

6 salmon steaks (1-inch thick)   **Lemon Mayonnaise:**
1/3 cup melted butter   **3/4 cup mayonnaise**
1 tsp. marjoram   **1/4 cup lemon juice**
2 cloves garlic, minced   **1 tsp. Worcestershire sauce**
salt and pepper, to taste   **salt and pepper, to taste**
                               Garnish: fluted tomato,
                                  parsley and lemon wheels

Preheat oven to 450 degrees F. Thoroughly coat steaks with butter, marjoram, garlic, salt and pepper. Bake in 450 degrees F. oven for 15 to 20 minutes or until fish flakes easily. Remove from oven, place fluted tomatoes in hollows of steaks. Drizzle prepared lemon mayonnaise sauce over steaks.

Lemon Mayonnaise: Mix mayonnaise, lemon juice, Worcestershire sauce, salt and pepper together.

Garnish with lemon wheels and fresh parsley. *Serve with your favorite green vegetable.*

Alternative: Sea Trout

I'm the one how asked before about Crabmeat 1000, Now do you have Simple Salmon?

SALMON STEAKS WITH CHAMPAGNE SAUCE

Preparation time: 10 minutes
Cooking time: 30 minutes
Serves: 6

Chef: Sally Chalker
Yacht: Green Norseman

6 salmon steaks
1 cup champagne

Champagne Sauce:
1 shallot, minced
1/2 tsp. dried thyme
1/2 tsp. ground nutmeg
1 cup champagne
1 cup chicken stock

1 cup heavy cream
2 Tblsp. cold unsalted butter
flour to thicken
1 Tblsp. champagne vinegar
Garnish: parsley

Preheat oven to 350 degrees F. Steam steaks in 1 cup champagne about 20 minutes in the oven.

Champagne Sauce: In skillet cook shallots, thyme and nutmeg in champagne and   chicken stock. Continue cooking until sauce reduces to 1/2 to 3/4 cup, about 20 to 30 minutes. Reduce heat and add heavy cream. Whisk in butter and thicken with flour to consistency. Remove from heat and stir in vinegar. Serve sauce under or over fish, which ever you prefer. Garnish with parsley. Do not overcook cream or it will separate. *A dry white wine goes well with this*.

Alternative: Tuna, Sea Trout

SALMON - ASPARAGUS DIVAN

Preparation time: 20 minutes   *Chef: Sylvia & Stanley Dabney*
Cooking time: 15 minutes   *Yacht: Native Sun*
Serves: 4

1 lb. can salmon, drained and
   flaked (reserving liquid)
1/4 lb. sliced mushrooms
5 Tblsp.(2-1/2 oz.) butter
1/4 cup flour
2 cups half-and-half

1/2 tsp. salt
1/8 tsp. white pepper
1/4 cup Parmesan cheese
2 (10 oz.) pkgs.frozen
   or 2 lbs. fresh
   asparagus, cooked
Garnish: toast triangles

Saute mushrooms in butter. Blend in flour, half-and-half, and salmon liquid. Cook stirring constantly until thickened. Add seasonings, Parmesan cheese and salmon. Heat gently. Spoon over hot cooked asparagus. Garnish with toast triangles. *Good with tomato aspic for lunch or baked stuffed tomatoes and green salad for dinner.*

SALMON WITH PEARS

Preparation time: 20 minutes   *Chef: Jennifer Dudley*
Marinating time: 30 minutes   *Yacht: Chaparral*
Cooking time: 15 minutes
Serves: 4

2 fresh Bartlett pears
4 salmon steaks
1 cup dry white wine
flour, salt, pepper

1/4 cup butter
Garnish: sugar coated
   clustered grapes and
   purple grapes with
   orange wheel

Cut pears lengthwise into halves, remove core. Marinate fish in wine for 15 minutes, turn and marinade 15 more minutes. Reserve marinade. Pat dry the steaks. Dust with flour, salt and pepper, coating both sides well. Heat butter in skillet, add salmon and brown quickly on both sides. Add reserved wine marinade. Arrange pears around salmon in skillet. Cover and simmer about 10 minutes. Put salmon on plate, arrange pear halves. Add grapes and orange slice. *Extremely pretty presentation.*

PASTA WITH SMOKED SALMON

Preparation time: 30 minutes   *Chef: Elsa Castaldo*
Cooking time: 20 minutes   *Yacht: Elsa Jane*
Serves: 4

1 lb. linguine
2 oz. butter
5 scallions (tops included),
  chopped
2 oz. smoked salmon

2 oz. champagne
12 oz. heavy cream
salt and pepper, to taste
Parmesan cheese, to taste
Garnish: parsley sprigs

Cut salmon julienne style (thin strips). Cook pasta as directed on package. Saute scallions in butter. Add 1-1/2 oz. salmon, champagne and cream. Simmer 5 minutes. Add cooked pasta. Mix well. Add salt, pepper and parmesan cheese. Use rest of salmon and parsley for garnish. *Can be served for lunch with sliced tomatoes, bread sticks and beaujolais wine.*

SALMON TETRAZZINI

Preparation time: 15 minutes   *Chef: Nancy May*
Cooking time: 25 minutes   *Yacht: Oh Be Joyful*
Serves: 4

4 oz. spaghetti
1/3 cup chopped onion
3 Tblsp. olive oil
1/4 cup flour
1/8 tsp. thyme
black pepper
2 cups half-and-half

1-1/2 Tblsp. sherry
2 (6-1/2 oz.) cans salmon,
  drained
1/2 cup black olives, sliced
1/4 cup green peppers,
  chopped
1/3 cup Parmesan
Garnish: paprika and
  parsley

Preheat oven to 350 degrees F. Cook spaghetti, drain and set aside. Saute chopped onion in olive oil. Blend in flour, thyme and pepper. Cook until bubbly. Remove from heat. Stir in half-and-half. Cook on low stirring constantly. Stir in sherry, spaghetti, salmon, olives and green pepper. Turn into baking dish. Sprinkle on cheese. Bake 20-25 minutes. Garnish.

SMOKED SALMON CANAPES

Preparation time: 15 minutes
Cooking time: 5 minutes
Serves: 6

Chef: Mary Woods
Yacht: Silent Joy

8 square slices bread, firm textured, white or rye
1/2 cup herbed cream cheese, room temperature, or 1/2 cup herbed butter, slightly chilled

1/3 lb. smoked salmon slices

Garnish: 1 lemon sliced paper thin, then halved; capers and fresh dill sprigs

Toast bread, then let cool. Spread toast with the cream cheese or herb butter, then top with salmon slices. Trim crusts and cut into thirds. Top with lemon slice halves, capers, and dill sprigs. Makes 24 canapes. *Classic, quick and simple. Looks great on a silver tray lined with doilies.*

POACHED SALMON AND ASPARAGUS SPEARS

Preparation time: 25 minutes
Cooking time: 20 minutes
Serves: 4

Chef: Jennifer Dudley
Yacht: Chaparral

1 large onion, sliced
2 fresh limes, sliced
1/2 tsp. whole peppercorns
4 cups water
4 fresh salmon steaks, 1" thick
6 sprigs fresh parsley

1/4 cup butter
1-1/2 Tblsp. fresh lime juice
1/4 tsp. paprika
16 stalks fresh asparagus, steamed
Garnish: lime and lemon wheels

Combine onion, limes, and peppercorns, in large saucepan. Add water and bring to a boil. Add salmon and parsley. When water begins to reboil, cover and reduce heat so water is just below simmering. Cook salmon 10 minutes, or until it flakes easily. Meanwhile, melt butter in small saucepan, add lime juice and paprika. Remove salmon with slotted spoon to serving dish, pour butter mixture over salmon. Garnish with lime wheels and lemon wheels alternately. *Serve with steamed fresh asparagus. A wonderful springtime meal!*

Alternative: Rockfish

INTERNATIONAL SEAFOOD CHOWDER

Preparation time: 15 minutes   *Chef: Jan Burnes*
Cooking time: 30 minutes   *Yacht: Adaro*
Serves: 4

Oil	1 tsp. curry powder
2 onions, finely sliced	salt and pepper, to taste
2 slices bacon, chopped	fish stock or water
1 (16 oz.) can Salmon or other smoked fish	1 (6-1/2 oz.) can shrimp or prawns
1 (16 oz.) can sweet creamed corn	1 (4 oz.) can smoked oysters
2 large potatoes, diced	Garnish: parsley
1 (7 oz.) can peas	

In a large sauce pan, lightly brown onion and bacon in a little oil. Add Salmon, corn, peas, potatoes, curry, salt and pepper. Cover with fish stock or water and simmer gently until vegetables are cooked. Add prawns and oysters 10 minutes before serving so that they just warm through. Garnish with parsley. *Serve with hot , crusty bread.*

Note: A store cupboard meal! Can be made a day ahead - even more delicious.

NATIVE SUN'S CANAPES

Preparation time: 10 minutes   *Chef: Sylvia & Stanley Dabney*
Serves: 4 - 6   *Yacht: Native Sun*

8 oz. smoked salmon	1/2 - 1 tsp. Worcestershire sauce
1/2 cup finely chopped chives	Party rye or pumpernickel bread
1 (8 oz.) pkg. soft cream cheese	Garnish: fresh parsley
1 (8 oz.) plain yogurt	

Cut salmon in 1/2-inch cubes. Combine with chives. In bowl, combine cream cheese, yogurt and Worcestershire, beat with mixer. Add salmon and chives to cheese mixture. Pile on serving tray. Surround with party bread and knives for spreading. Garnish with parsley.

SALMON AND AVOCADO SALAD

Preparation time: 10 minutes *Chef: Sylvia & Stanley Dabney*
Chilling time: 30 minutes *Yacht: Native Sun*
Serves: 4

1 can salmon, cleaned and drained

2 Tblsp. finely chopped celery

2 hardboiled eggs, chopped

4 Tblsp. garlic mayonnaise *

1/2 tsp. (or more) curry powder

2 avocados

juice of 1 lemon

Garnish: paprika and parsley

Flake salmon, add celery, eggs - toss. In separate bowl mix mayonnaise and curry, pour over salmon and refrigerate 30 minutes to overnight. When you're ready to eat, half avocados and brush with lemon juice, fill with salmon, place on a lettuce plate, garnish with parsley and a dusting of paprika.

A wonderful light lunch - good with crackers and an iced bottle of champagne.

* **Garlic Mayonnaise** - good and easy!
Dump 1 large bottle Hellmans into a bowl , add juice of 1 large lemon, 3 shakes of salt, add 3-4 large cloves of smashed/pureed garlic, mix well and pack back into original jar. *This is delicious with anything using mayonnaise, except Fruit Salad.*

SALMON SALAD DELIGHT

Preparation time: 20 minutes   *Chef: Jennifer Dudley*
Marinating time: 2 hours   *Yacht: Chaparral*
Cooking time: 15 minutes
Serves: 2-3

3 new potatoes, cooked
   and cut in half
2 Tblsp. minced onion
1 (16 oz.) can salmon
1 Tblsp. green onion,
1 large tomato, sliced
1/2 cucumber, sliced
2 hard-cooked eggs, peeled
   and halved
chilled lettuce

Tarragon Marinade:
   1/4 cup olive oil
   1/8 tsp. dried tarragon
   2 Tblsp. tarragon
     vinegar
   2 Tblsp. fresh lemon
     juice
   salt and pepper
   1 clove garlic, pressed
   1 Tblsp. green onion,
     chopped

Garnish: black olives

Tarragon Marinade: Mix together olive oil, tarragon, vinegar, lemon juice, salt, pepper and garlic.

Sprinkle warm potatoes with onion, then pour over tarragon marinade. Cover and refrigerate several hours. Drain, reserving marinade. Arrange salmon, tomatoes, cucumber, and eggs on lettuce lined platter, add potatoes and sprinkle with green onion and black olives. Serve with reserved marinade.

This is a great light lunch served with hot bread.

SMOKED SALMON AND MELON SALAD

Preparation time: 10 minutes
Serves: 6

Chef: Nancy Thorne
Yacht: Fancy Free

1 lb. smoked salmon,
   cut julienne
1 small honeydew melon,
   cut in chunks
1 small cantaloupe,
   cut in chunks
2 medium avocados, cut in
   chunks

Orange-Lemon Dressing:
1 egg yolk
1/2 cup fresh orange juice
1/4 cup fresh lemon juice
1 shallot, minced
1/4 cup raspberry vinegar
1 cup olive oil, extra virgin
Garnish: chopped chives

Orange-Lemon Dressing: Combine first five ingredients of dressing. Mix in blender. Slowly add oil to emulsify.

Toss salmon, melon and avocado with dressing just before serving. Sprinkle with chives. *Serve with Iron Horse Blanc De Blancs sparkling wine.*

PASTA WITH SMOKED SALMON IN DILL DRESSING

Preparation time: 10 minutes
Cooking time: 20 minutes
Serves: 4 - 6

Chef: Nancy Raye
Yacht: China Cloud

Dill Dressing:
1/3 cup safflower oil
1-1/2 Tblsp. minced shallots
1/4 cup minced fresh
  chives
2 Tblsp. freshly squeezed
  lemon juice
1/3 cup fresh dill, chopped
  salt, to taste
  freshly ground black pepper
8 oz. gemelli (twisted twin
  rods) or other fancifully
  shaped pasta

1 cup cherry tomatoes,
  halved
5 oz. (or more) smoked
  salmon, cut into small
  pieces
1 small red onion, thinly
  sliced in rings and
  separated
1 cup sour cream

Garnish: fresh dill sprigs

Dill Dressing: Combine oil, shallots, lemon juice, dill, salt and pepper: whisk well and set aside.

Cook pasta in 4 quarts boiling water until very al dente. Drain and rinse well in cold water, then drain again. Place in a large bowl and cool to room temperature, stirring occasionally to keep pasta from sticking together. Add tomatoes, chives, and reserved dressing to the pasta and mix gently. Arrange salmon, onion rings, and sour cream on top of pasta. Garnish with dill sprigs.

SALMON EN PAPILLOTE WITH GINGER LIME BUTTER

Preparation time: 15 minutes
Cooking time: 10 minutes
Serves: 6

Chef: Nancy Thorne
Yacht: Fancy Free

6 (7 oz.) salmon fillets
3 green onions, julienne
1 carrot, julienne
1/2 red pepper, julienne
parchment paper

1/2 cup butter
2 Tblsp. ginger, grated
2 limes, juiced
salt and pepper

Cut six parchment circles 12" in diameter. Fold in half to make half-moons. Against fold on inside place one piece of salmon. Top with a sprinkling of julienne vegetables, ginger, lime juice and 1 tablespoon of butter. Season with salt and pepper. Close and pleat edge with small folds to close. Continue with other five portions. Brush paper with melted butter. Bake 10 minutes on cookie sheet. Bring to table puffed and snip open for each guest. Aroma is incredible!

Serve with Pumpkin soup, Couscous, Vegetable Medley, Banana Foster and a white burgundy (i.e. Laforet).

Quick poached fish: *Poach fish in can of Buitino or Pregresso White Clam Sauce. Sprinkle with basil. Serve.*

BBQ SALMON FANCY FREE

Preparation time: 10 minutes   *Chef: Nancy Thorne*
Marinating time: 1 hour   *Yacht: Fancy Free*
Cooking time: 10 minutes
Serves: 6

Fancy Marinade: **2 salmon filets**
   1/2 cup dark soy   **2 Tblsp. cold butter**
   2 Tblsp. bourbon
   2 Tblsp. sesame oil   **Garnish: julienne scallions**
   1/4 cup rice vinegar   **blanched orange zest**
   1 tsp. minced garlic
   1 tsp. minced ginger
   zest of 1 orange
   tabasco to taste

Fancy Marinade: Mix all ingredients together, and marinate salmon one hour at room temperature.

Get barbecue going with lots of mesquite chips. While salmon is barbecuing (about 4 minutes per side) heat marinade and reduce by half. Whisk in butter and drizzle over salmon. Garnish with julienne scallions and blanched orange zest.

Begin meal with a hearts of palm, orange and avocado salad with raspberry vinaigrette.

Serve salmon accompanied by chinese noodles with slivered vegetables and end with Gratineed Pineapple with noncream. A good wine choice would be an oaky chardonnay (Seeward, Jordan) to stand up to the mesquite.

Alternative: Rockfish

SALMON-CRAB CASSEROLE IN PASTRY SHELLS

Preparation time: 10 minutes   *Chef: Karen Day*
Cooking time: 30 minutes   *Yacht: Schooner Windsong*
Serves: 4-6

pastry shells, frozen
1/2 stick butter
3 Tblsp. flour
1 cup cream
1 (10 oz.) can cream of
  shrimp soup*

1/2 cup shredded cheddar
  cheese
1 lb. salmon, (fresh or
  canned)
1 lb. imitation crabmeat
  (sea legs)
1 cup frozen peas

Bake frozen pastry shells in oven, according to directions on package. Make a roux by melting 1/2 stick butter and adding the flour a little at a time, stirring rapidly. Whisk in the cream slowly, stirring quickly to avoid lumps. Add the cream of shrimp soup. (* If not available, substitute 1 cup tomato juice, 2 tablespoons cooking sherry, 1 teaspoon celery salt, and a splash of half-and-half or milk.) Do not boil this mixture. Melt cheese into the pot. If mixture is too thick add a little half-and-half. Add salmon, (boned carefully), crabmeat and the peas. *Serve over the pastry shells.*

SIMPLE SALMON STEAKS WITH SESAME SEEDS

Preparation time: 10 minutes   *Chef: Jan Robinson*
Cooking time: 10 minutes   *Yacht: Vanity*
Serves: 6

1/3 cup margarine
Juice of 1 lemon
2 Tblsp. sesame seeds, toasted
black pepper, to taste

6 (6 oz.) salmon steaks
  3/4-inch thick
1/4 chopped parsley
Garnish: lemon wedges and
  sprigs of parsley

Preheat broiler: In a small saucepan, melt margarine. Add lemon juice, sesame seeds, pepper and parsley. Brush steaks with melted margarine. Broil about 4 minutes on each side, or until fish flakes easily. Brush occasionally with remaining mixture. Garnish with lemon wedges and parsley. *Serve with new boiled potatoes and broccoli, followed by Better Than Sex Cake (see recipe in SHIP TO SHORE I)*

CONFETTI SALMON MOUSSE

Preparation time: 20 minutes   *Chef: Gisela Huffman*
Chilling time: 2-4 hours   *Yacht: Nighthawk*
Serves: 4

1 (1/4 oz.) envelope plain
  gelatin
1/2 cup boiling water
2 Tblsp. fresh lemon juice
1/2 cup onions, chopped
1/4 tsp. paprika
1 tsp. dried dill
cayenne pepper, to taste

1 cup non-fat yogurt
1 (16 oz.) can pink salmon
  drained, bones removed
1/4 cup diced red and green
  bell pepper

Garnish: Romaine lettuce
  leaves and alfalfa spouts

Pour gelatin powder into food processor and add boiling water, lemon juice, onion, paprika, dill and cayenne pepper and puree for 1 minute. Add yogurt and mix. Mash salmon and stir into yogurt mixture. Sprinkle the mixed red and green peppers around the bottom of a ring mold and pour salmon mixture into mold. Chill at least 2-4 hours. To unmold, place form in a hot water bath for 1 minute. Serve on a platter lined with greens. Place alfalfa sprouts in center. *Serve with sliced cucumbers, tomatoes, and crackers or fresh French bread.*

SAUCES

BASIC WHITE SAUCE

Preparation time: 15 minutes   *Chef: Jan Robinson*
Cooking time: 5 - 10 minutes   *Yacht: Vanity*
Makes: about 1 cup

Equal amounts of butter and flour, salt and pepper, to taste milk

Roux Method: Melt the butter in a saucepan, blend in the flour and cook over low heat for 2-3 minutes, stirring constantly so that the roux bubbles but does not brown. Gradually add the warm or cold liquid to the roux, which will at first thicken to a nearly solid mass. Beat vigorously until the mixture leaves the sides of the pan clean, then add a little more milk. Allow the mixture to thicken and boil between each addition of milk. Continuous beating is essential to obtain a smooth sauce. When all the milk has been added, bring the sauce to a boil. Let it simmer for about 5 minutes and add the seasoning.

Note: *To make a richer sauce:* Use 1 egg yolk, add 2 Tblsp. cream, or milk and beat with a whisk until blended. Then add a ladle of the hot sauce and continue whisking for a minute until the egg is blended. Turn into the rest of the sauce and heat, still over low heat and stirring all the time, till sauce is hot and thick.

CREAM SAUCE

Preparation time: 2 minutes   *Chef: Jan Robinson*
Cooking time: 5 minutes   *Yacht: Vanity*
Makes: 1 cup

1 cup basic white sauce   **salt and pepper, to taste**
1/2 cup heavy cream   **1 tsp. lemon juice**
       1 Tblsp. unsalted butter

Add 1/4 cup heavy cream to the hot white sauce and reduce over low heat to 1 cup. Add another 1/4 cup heavy cream and heat. Season to taste, add 1 teaspoon lemon juice and swirl in 1 tablespoon unsalted butter.

HOLLANDAISE SAUCE

Preparation time: 10 minutes   *Chef: Jan Robinson*
Cooking time: 10 minutes   *Yacht: Vanity*
Makes: 1 cup

3 Tblsp. white wine vinegar   3 egg yolks
1 Tblsp. water   12 Tblsp. (6 oz.) butter,
6 black peppercorns   softened
1 bay leaf   salt
                                       freshly ground black pepper

Boil the vinegar and water with the black peppercorns and the bay leaf in a small saucepan, until the mixture has reduced to 1 tablespoon. Leave to cool. Cream the egg yolks with 1 tablespoon butter and a pinch of salt. Strain the vinegar into the egg yolks and set the bowl over a pan of simmering water. Turn off the heat. With a wire whisk, beat in the remaining butter, 1 tablespoon at a time, until the sauce is shiny and has the consistency of thick cream. Season with salt and pepper. *Hollandaise may be served immediately or kept warm in a warm water bath for an hour or so.*

Note: A Hollandaise sauce may curdle because the heat is too sudden or too high, or because the butter has been added too quickly. If the sauce separates, it can often be saved by removing from the heat and beating in 1 tablespoon of cold water.
Hollandaise sauce is similar to a Bearnaise sauce, but has a milder flavor.

CREME FRAICHE

Preparation time: 2 minutes   *Chef: Jan Robinson*
Standing time: 8 hours   *Yacht: Vanity*
Makes: 1 cup

1 cup heavy cream   2 tsp. buttermilk, yogurt, or
                                    sour cream

Put the heavy cream in a jar. Add the buttermilk, yogurt, or commercial sour cream. Shake to mix. Cover loosely and place in an oven with a pilot light for 8 hours or overnight, or let stand at a room temperature of 85 degrees F. (At a lower temperature, the cream mixture must stand from 24 to 36 hours). Stir, cover, and refrigerate. When cold, the creme will be thick and ready to use.

Note: Use in cooking as a substitute for sour cream. Unlike sour cream, creme fraiche will not curdle when boiled.

SCALLOPS

The name "scallop" describes the fluted edges of the fan-shaped scallop shell. The shells of young scallops, in particular are beautiful; the outside is delicately colored, sometimes having pink and white or other darker color variations. The inside of the shell is pearly-white and has a satiny luster.

Throughout the centuries many romantic and historical events have evolved with the beautiful scallop shell as a symbol. Buildings in ancient Pompeii were ornamented with scallop shell designs and during the Crusades scallop shells were the symbol of the holy pilgrimages. Poets have written about their beauty and artists admired their symmetry and grace so much that they were often used in paintings. Today the shells are eagerly sought by collectors. The larger shells are frequently used as practical, individual containers for cooking and serving fish mixtures.

Inside the scallop shell is another work of art that is also a source of eating pleasure to all people who love good food from the sea. Scallops, like clams and oysters, are mollusks having two shells. They differ, however, from those shellfish in that they are active swimmers. The scallop swims freely through the waters and over the ocean floor by snapping its shells together. This action results in the development of an oversized adductor muscle called the "eye" and this sweet-flavored muscle is the only part of the scallop eaten. <u>Scallops are an excellent source of protein, very little fat and have many essential vitamins and minerals. They contain only 23 calories per ounce.</u>

There are two varieties of scallops commonly used for food in the United States:

The Sea Scallop is the most commercially important scallop in the United States. It has a saucer-shaped shell and grows as large as six inches in diameter with the muscle or "eye" sometimes reaching up to two inches across.

The Bay Scallop is much less plentiful but greatly desired by scallop fanciers. It reaches a maximum size of about three inches in diameter with the muscle or "eye" about 1/2 inch across. The bay scallop shell is similar to that of the sea scallop except that it is smaller, more grooved, and the edges are more serrated or scalloped.

HOW TO BUY SCALLOPS:

Scallops cannot close their shells tightly and die soon after being taken from the water. Because of this, they are opened at sea and the meats are iced down or frozen immediately to insure freshness. Fresh or frozen scallops, when thawed should have a sweetish odor and very little liquid should be present.

TIPS:

Before cooking frozen scallops, thaw them until they can be separated from one another. Always dry them very carefully if they are to be panfried or sauteed.

Allow 1/3 pound sea scallops, or 1/4 pound bay scallops per serving for sauteing or broiling. When scallops are prepared in a sauce, a pound will serve 6.

Allow 1/3 pound sea scallops, or 1/4 pound bay scallops per serving for sauteing or broiling. When scallops are prepared in a sauce, a pound will serve 6.

Because they are somewhat difficult to procure in quantity, commercial distributors often put scallop through a process of "soaking" which depletes the delicate flavor of a fresh bivalve. The small cream-colored eye, or adductor muscle, which is the part that goes to the market, is placed in freshwater for several hours until the meat has absorbed enough water to increase the bulk by about one-third. Actually this improves the appearance of the scallop in that it becomes very white, but the flavor is inferior. When you see scallops drastically reducing in size during cooking you know they have been "soaked".

Makes a great seviche when marinated in a citric acid (lemon juice, lime juice, or vinegar).

It is much better to undercook rather than overcook scallops. Being perfectly edible raw, prolonged heating will only shrink and toughen an already tender meat. If you saute them in butter or oil, allow only 3 minutes for bay scallops and no more than 5 minutes for the larger sea scallops if cooked without cubing.

SCALLOP AND CUCUMBER SALAD WITH LIME CORIANDER DRESSING

Preparation time: 10 minutes　　　　*Chef: Helen Bromley*
Cooking time: 1 minute　　　　　　　*Yacht: Golden Rule*
Marinate: overnight
Serves: 6

1 lb. scallops
4 cucumbers, peeled
　and sliced
2 tomatoes, peeled
　and chopped
1 large onion, chopped

Lime Coriander Dressing:
　1/4 cup lime juice
　1/4 cup dry white wine
　1 tsp. sugar
　1/4 cup oil
　1 Tblsp. chopped fresh
　coriander

Trim scallops, combine with cucumbers, tomatoes and onions. Add hot dressing. Cover. Marinate overnight in refrigerator before serving.

Lime Coriander Dressing: Combine lime juice, wine and sugar in pan. Bring to boil, remove from heat. Whisk in oil and coriander. Use immediately.

SEAFOOD NEWBURG

Preparation time: 30 minutes　　　　*Chef: Beth Avore*
Cooking time: 30 minutes　　　　　　*Yacht: Perfection*
Serves: 6

1 lb. medium shrimp
1 lb. scallops
1 lb. crab meat or crab blend
2 (10 oz.) lobster tails
any other fresh fish
butter

butter and flour
milk
sherry
paprika
Garnish: lemon spirals

Peel shrimp and lobster tails. Cut all fish into bite size pieces. Saute each item separately in small amounts of butter. Make a roux of butter and flour. Add milk to make a thick sauce. Flavor with a small amount of sherry. Color with paprika. Add all seafood to sauce. Cover and simmer about 5 minutes. Serve in shells or individual dishes. Garnish with 2-3 lemon spirals on top.

SEAFOOD ITALIENNE

Preparation time: 20 minutes　　　　*Chef: Sue Bushnell*
Cooking time: 5 minutes　　　　*Yacht: Emily Morgan*
Chilling time: 30 minutes
Serves: 4-6

1/2 cup dry white wine
1 parsley sprig
1 strip lemon rind
1/2 small onion, finely
　chopped
1 lb. sea scallops, sliced
8 oz. cooked shrimp or
　lobster

8 oz. button mushrooms,
　sliced
6 Tblsp. olive oil
2 Tblsp. lime juice
1 clove garlic, crushed
1 Tblsp. chopped parsley
Garnish: lettuce leaves,
　parsley sprigs, lime slices

Put wine, parsley sprig, lemon rind and onion into a pan, add scallops and cook for 3 minutes. Drain, remove parsley and lemon rind. Add shrimp or lobster, set aside. Put mushrooms in another bowl and add olive oil, lime juice, garlic and parsley. Toss and leave to stand for 30 minutes. Season to taste, add to fish and stir well. Chill until required.
Serve on a bed of lettuce leaves, garnish with lime slices and parsley sprigs. Great with pasta salad and French bread.

SCALLOP FETTUCINE WITH DILL

Preparation time: 10 minutes　　　　*Chef: Ann Gracie*
Cooking time: 20 minutes　　　　*Yacht: Sandcastle*
Serves: 6

1 lb. fettucine noodles
1-1/2 sticks (6 oz.) butter
6 cloves garlic
1 lb. scallops
1-1/2 cups heavy cream

1/3 cup minced fresh dill
8 oz. Parmesan, grated
1/2 cup dry white wine
salt and pepper, to taste
Garnish: lemon wedges,
　dill sprigs

Cook pasta until barely tender, drain, rinse and set aside. In a heavy skillet saute garlic briefly in butter. Add scallops and saute 1 minute more. Set scallops aside and use the liquid to complete the sauce: add cream, dill, grated Parmesan, wine. Cook for 2 minutes, stirring continuously. Add scallops and pasta. Season with salt and pepper to taste. Garnish with lemon and dill sprigs.

Note: If sauce becomes too thick, whisk in a little milk.

SEAFOOD CREPES WITH TARRAGON BEARNAISE

Preparation time: 30 minutes
Cooking time: 30 minutes
Serves: 6

Chef: Ann Gracie
Yacht: Sandcastle

12 crepes (your favorite
  or mix)
Tarragon Sauce:
  5 scallions, chopped
  1 Tblsp. tarragon
  12 crushed peppercorns
  1/2 tarragon vinegar
  5 egg yolks
  1/4 cup hot water
  2 sticks (8 oz.) butter in
    1" cubes

Filling:
  1/2 cup fish stock
  1/2 cup white wine
  1/2 lb. scallops
  1/2 lb. white fish fillets
  1/2 lb. shrimp, peeled
    and deveined
Garnish: parsley sprigs,
    lemon wedges or wheels

Tarragon Sauce: Boil vinegar, scallions, peppercorns and tarragon over medium heat until vinegar is reduced to 3 tablespoons. Strain, reserving liquid. In a double boiler over high heat, beat in eggs yolks, one at a time, then water, then butter. Beat continuously during additions and reduce heat if necessary. Set sauce aside and keep warm.

Poach seafood in stock and wine until just cooked. Roll filling in crepes, pour sauce over and garnish to serve.

Hint: Add 1 tablespoon of vinegar to the fat in which you are going to deep fry. It will keep the food from absorbing too much fat and elimate the greasy taste.

NANCY'S 'FANCY FREE' SEAFOOD TORTELLINI WITH CHARDONNAY SAUCE

Preparation time: 15 minutes
Cooking time: 10 minutes
Serves: 6

Chef: Nancy Thorne
Yacht: Fancy Free

1 lb. scallops
1/2 lb. crabmeat
1 lb. large shrimp,
    shelled and deveined
1 red pepper, julienne
1 can artichoke hearts,
    halved
1 Tblsp. garlic, minced
2 Tblsp. butter

2 cups Chardonnay wine
2 cups cream
1 cup fresh basil, shredded
1 cup freshly grated
    Parmesan
salt and pepper to taste
12 oz. cheese stuffed fresh
    tortellini, freshly cooked
Garnish: fresh basil

Lightly saute seafood with butter and vegetables. Reserve. Reduce wine by half. Add cream and reduce by 1/4. Stir in basil. Add sauce and seafood-vegetable mixture to hot freshly cooked tortellini and toss with Parmesan. Garnish with fresh basil.

Precede this meal with prosciutto-endive-papaya salad, hot French bread and serve with a good oaky chardonnay (like cakebread). Finish with Chocolate Decadence. (See SHIP TO SHORE II)

PASTA CHANTAL

Preparation time: 10 minutes   *Chef: Christine Davies*
Cooking time: 20 minutes   *Yacht: Ceo Na Mara*
Serves: 6-8

1 lb. spaghetti
2 oz. butter
8 oz. mushrooms, sliced
salt and pepper
3 Tblsp. plain flour
1/2 cup dry white wine
1 lb. baby scallops

1/2 lb. prawns or shrimps
5 Tblsp. Parmesan cheese
4 oz. grated ementhal cheese
1/2 cup cream (half and
   half)
Garnish: chopped parsley
   and lemon wedges

Cook spaghetti al dente. Meanwhile, melt butter and add sliced mushrooms with salt and pepper. Add scallops, prawns and cheeses.   Simmer for 2 minutes then add cream. ' Serve immediately on spaghetti. Sprinkle with chopped parsley and lemon slices.

Note: Don't be put off by the number of ingredients, it all comes together very quickly. This is best served with a crisp green salad and garlic bread.

SHRIMP AND SCALLOPS ST. GERMAINE

Preparation time: 30 minutes   *Chef: Joy Smith*
Cooking time: 15 minutes   *Yacht: Falcon*
Serves: 6

2 lbs shrimp (about 36)
   cooked, peeled and
   deveined
2 lbs. sea scallops, sauteed
3 Tblsp. butter
3 Tblsp. flour

1 (14 oz) can condensed
   milk
Small amount of milk
1-2 tsp. Pernod
Garnish: parsley

Prepare shrimp and scallops. Melt butter and add flour. Cook over medium heat until bubbly. Remove from heat and slowly stir in can of condensed milk. Cook over medium-low heat until thickened, stirring constantly.   Adjust consistency with regular milk. Add Pernod to taste. Add shrimp and scallops. Heat. *Serve over white rice with dilled carrots and spinach salad.* Garnish with parsley.

BLUEBERRY SCALLOPS

Preparation time: 10 minutes   *Chef: Jennifer Dudley*
Cooking time: 3 minutes   *Yacht: September Morn*
Marinating time: 25 minutes
Chilling time: 1 hour
Serves: 4-6

1 1/2 lbs. sea scallops
Garnish: Fresh blueberries,
    fresh mint leaves, lemon wheels

Blueberry Mayonnaise:
    1 whole egg   **1/4 cup blueberry vinegar**
    2 egg yolks   **salt, fresh pepper**
    1 Tblsp. Dijon mustard   **2 cups light salad oil**

Blueberry Mayonnaise: In a blender combine all ingredients
except oil. Blend 1 minute. With motor on, dribble in oil in a slow
steady stream. When all is incorporated, taste and correct for
seasoning. Makes 2 1/2 cups. Cover and refrigerate.

For Scallops: Rinse scallops and place in saucepan. Cover with
lightly salted water. Bring water to simmer. Cook for 1 minute.
Remove saucepan from heat and let scallops cool to room
temperature in their poaching liquid. Drain scallops and arrange
on a small plate. Spoon blueberry mayonnaise over and around
scallops but do not mask them completely. Garnish with
blueberries, mint sprigs and lemon wheels. *Serve immediately!*

Note: This is a super and refreshing first course or an elegant lunch
item with crusty hot bread.

SCALLOPS IN TARRAGON WINE SAUCE

Preparation time: 10 minutes   *Chef: Ann Cupelli Brown*
Cooking time: 20 minutes   *Yacht: Antipodes*
Serves: 8

4 Tblsp. butter   3 lbs. bay scallops,
3 Tblsp. onion, minced   well rinsed, drained
1/2 bottle dry white wine   dash celery salt
3 Tblsp. dried tarragon   Garnish: thin lemon
dash white pepper   wheels and parsley

In a large skillet saute the onion in butter until softened. Add the wine and tarragon and boil until reduced by half. Stir in scallops, pepper and celery salt. Cook until scallops are just opaque, about 4-5 minutes. *Serve immediately over rice.*

Note: While planning a cook's night out, we discovered at 7:00 p.m. that every restaurant on Virgin Gorda was booked solid! I grabbed the scallops out of the freezer and put them in water for a quick thaw. Dinner was served at 7:30, right on time. *The menu:* Melon with Prosciutto, Scallops in Tarragon Wine Sauce, Brown Rice Almondine, Saute of Summer Squash, Bananas Flambe'. The ultimate quickie and everyone loved it!

SEVICHE

Preparation time: 10 minutes   *Chef: Carole Watkins Manto*
Marinating time: 2-6 hours   *Yacht: Drumbeat*
Serves: 4

1-1/2 lbs. bay scallops   1 clove garlic, minced
1 cup lemon juice   1/4 cup cilantro, freshly
1 cup lime juice   chopped
1/4 tsp. dried red pepper
   flakes   Garnish: red and green
1 red onion, sliced very thin   pepper slices, black olives

Mix ingredients together and marinate 2 - 6 hours. Set scallops in the center of serving platter. Surround with red pepper, green pepper and black olives. Put olives at each end of platter and stick frilled toothpicks in them.

SEAFOOD ST. JACQUES

Preparation time: 20 minutes
Cooking time: 1 hour
Serves: 6

Chef: Martha Purinton
Yacht: Iskareen

1 lb. sea scallops, defrosted
1 (6-1/2 oz.) can small
  shrimp,   drained
1/2 lb. fresh mushrooms or
  1 (3 oz.) can drained
5 Tblsp. butter
Juice of 1 lemon
1 cup dry white wine
1/4 tsp. thyme

1 bay leaf
1/2 tsp salt
1/8 tsp. pepper
3 Tblsp. flour
1 cup milk
Buttered breadcrumbs
grated Parmesan cheese
Garnish: lemon wedges
  and parsley

Cut scallops in quarters if large. Slice mushrooms and saute in 2 tablespoons butter and lemon juice until golden; reserve. Add wine and seasonings to scallops in small saucepan. Cook 10 minutes. Drain scallops, reserving 1 cup broth.

Make white sauce with remaining 3 tablespoons butter, flour, broth and milk. Add scallops, shrimp and mushrooms. Spoon into scallop shells, top with crumbs and cheese. Place under broiler until brown.

Note: This may be made with just scallops or a combination of scallops, shrimp and lobster. This recipe may be made ahead and reheated at mealtime. *I serve it for lunch with a small salad and French bread or as an appetizer for dinner.*

TIMBALE OF BAY SCALLOPS IN SPINACH

Preparation time: 25 minutes   *Chef: Gisela Huffman*
Marinate: several hours   *Yacht: Nighthawk*
Cooking time: 10 minutes
Serves: 4

1 lb. bay scallops	1 medium red bell pepper
1 Tblsp. minced jalapeno	3/4 lb. trimmed leaf
pepper	spinach,
(no seeds, only skin)	blanched, drained,
2 Tblsp. minced orange rind	and squeezed dry
2 oz. minced shallots	Garnish:Top carefully with
1 clove garlic, minced	any type tomato-style
1/3 cup orange juice	sauce

Place the scallops in a bowl with the jalapeno pepper, orange rind, shallots and garlic and orange juice. Let them marinate several hours or overnight in the refrigerator.

Peel and cut the bell pepper in half, discarding core and seeds. Cut out 4 even rounds about 1 inch in diameter (place quarter coin on top and cut around). Place each in the center of the bottom of a 1 cup souffle dish. Arrange 5 scallops in an even circle around the pepper in each dish.

Divide half the spinach among the dishes, pressing it down. Top with remaining scallops and remaining spinach. Wrap twice with good plastic wrap. Cook for 10 minutes on the steamer rack of a skames. Remove, loosening each one by running a knife around the inside edge. Tip to pour out any liquid that has accumulated.

ORANGE SCALLOP KABOBS

Preparation time: 20 minutes   *Chef: Jennifer Dudley*
Marinating time: 1 hour   *Yacht: Chaparral*
Cooking time: 15 minutes
Serves: 4

Orange Marinade:
   grated peel of 1/2 fresh
      orange
   1/3 cup fresh squeezed
      orange juice
   1/4 cup corn oil
   1/4 cup minced onion
   1/4 tsp. rosemary leaves

2 lbs. scallops
1 orange, unpeeled, cut in
12 wedges
12 cherry tomatoes
12 fresh mushrooms

Garnish: lemon curl with
   fresh flower

Orange Marinade: Combine ingredients for marinade.
Add scallops and marinate for 1 hour, stirring occasionally.
Arrange orange wedges, scallops, cherry tomatoes and
mushrooms alternately on 4 skewers. Place on broiler pan and
broil 4 inches from heat for 12-14 minutes. (May use outdoor
grill). *Serve with wild brown rice and steamed green beans.*
Note: All the colors - orange, red, green and yellow make for an
eye appealing meal! This is a beautiful, colorful dish. I garnish
with lemon curl with a piece of fresh flower tucked inside.

GINGER SCALLOPS

Preparation time: 15 minutes   *Chef: Jacqueline Cheetham*
Cooking time: 10 minutes   *Yacht: Rajada*
Serves: 4

2 lbs. scallops
salt and pepper
4 Tblsp. chopped shallots
2 oz. butter
2 tsp. grated fresh ginger
4 oz. fish stock

4 oz. white wine
1 tsp. lime juice
6 oz. heavy cream
2 medium tomatoes, skinned,
   seeded and chopped

Halve the scallops if large. Rinse, pat dry and season. Saute the
chopped shallots in butter making sure they do not brown. Add the
grated ginger, fish stock, white wine and lime juice to the pan.
When heated gently poach the scallops several minutes until just
opaque. Remove scallops and keep warm. Reduce the pan juices,
add cream and further reduce until required consistency. Add
chopped tomato. Season to taste. Pour sauce over scallops. *Serve
immediately with rice and Mange Tout.*

SCALLOPS EN PAPILLOTE

Preparation time: 20 minutes
Cooking time: 30 minutes
Serves: 2

Chef: Jennifer Dudley
Yacht: Chaparral

2 pieces parchment paper,
  24 x 16 (or aluminum foil)
3 small new red potatoes,
  sliced
salt, to taste
1 lb. bay Scallops
1 cup julienned asparagus
  strips

1/2 cup red and yellow
  pepper, diced
2 tsp. minced fresh ginger
2 scallions, thinly sliced
1/4 cup fresh lemon juice
1 tsp. grated lemon peel
1 Tblsp. vegetable oil

Preheat oven to 350 degrees F.   Fold parchment paper in half so each measures 16 x 12. Cut half heart from folded piece to make full heart when unfolded. Place potatoes in saucepan. Add salt and water to cover. Heat to boiling, then cook over medium heat 3 minutes. Drain thoroughly. Open hearts and place potatoes in center. Combine remaining ingredients and spoon over potatoes. Fold paper over and double fold edges to seal tightly. Place on baking sheet and bake 30 minutes. Transfer to plate and open. To complete the meal, *serve with warm bread, and a fruit sorbet.*

Note: This is super for guests who are watching their weight, yet still want a gourmet meal.

SCALLOPS MORNAY

Preparation time: 20 minutes *Chef: Evelyn Flanagan*
Cooking time: 20 minutes *Yacht: Vanity*
Serves: 4

2 lbs. scallops	Sauce:
2 oz. butter	2 oz. butter
4 cloves garlic, crushed	2 oz. flour
1 cup onions, finely chopped	1/4 pint milk
2 cups sliced mushrooms	salt and black pepper
1 cup white wine	
1/4 cup cream	
4 potatoes, boiled and	
creamed	

Saute scallops in butter and garlic for 10 minutes. Remove from pan and keep warm in oven. Saute onions and mushrooms in pan, add more butter if required. **To make sauce:** In a separate pot, melt butter and sprinkle in flour, stirring continuously in a separate pot. Cook for 3 minutes. Add milk, gently stirring all the time. Bring to boil and leave until thickened. Add salt and black pepper. Add to vegetables in pan and mix well. Add wine and cook for 2 minutes. Add scallops and heat. Finally add cream. *Serve on scallop shells with piped potatoes around sides.*

SAUTEED SCALLOPS EASY

Preparation time: 5 minutes *Chef: Jan Robinson*
Cooking time: 5 minutes *Yacht: Vanity*
Serves: 4

1-1/2 lbs. scallops	3 cloves garlic, crushed
flour	pepper, to taste
2 oz. butter	1/2 cup freshly chopped
2 Tblsp. peanut or olive oil	parsley

Dust scallops with flour. Shake off excess. Melt butter and oil in a large skillet. Add garlic and cook about 1 minute (Do not brown). Add scallops and cook quickly, for about 3 minutes. Do NOT overcook. Add pepper and parsley, stir for 1 minute more and remove to a heated plate. *Serve immediately.*

Note: It is much better to undercook rather than overcook scallops.

SCALLOPS WITH PLANTAINS AND ALMONDS

Preparation time: 15 minutes   *Chef: Gregor Rohlsson*
Cooking time: 5 minutes   *Yacht: Sea Cloud*
Serves: 4

1 oz. clarified butter
16 large sea scallops
flour, for dredging
1 plantain (peeled and sliced)
2 oz. banana liqueur
1/4 lb. whole unsalted butter

3 oz. sliced toasted almonds
chopped fresh parsley
salt, to taste
white pepper, to taste

Garnish: watercress

Heat clarified butter in saucepan, lightly dredge scallops in flour and sear on both sides. Remove from pan. Add peeled, sliced plantains and saute for 1 minute. Add banana liqueur and flambe. When flame dies out, add butter and swirl until sauce emulsifies and thickens. Add sliced toasted almonds, parsley, salt and white pepper. *Garnish with watercress.*

Note: Plantains need to be well cooked as they should not be eaten raw and the scallops should be medium rare when served; flavor will be lost if overcooked.

To clarify butter: place butter in saucepan over low heat. When butter has melted, a milky substance will rise in small bubbles to the surface. Skim this off as it foams. Remove clarified butter from heat and refrigerate. The foam can be used for seasoning vegetables.

PASTA SHELLS
STUFFED WITH SCALLOP SEVICHE

Preparation time: 45 minutes   *Chef: Carol Owens*
Marinating time: 5 hours   *Yacht: Iemanja*
Serves: 10-15 as appetizer; 8 as first course

12 oz. sea scallops, cut into
  very small pieces
1 cup (or more) freshly
  squeezed lime juice

1/2 cup finely chopped red
  onion
1 small ripe tomato, chopped
2-3 fresh hot chili peppers
1/4 cup vegetable oil
2 Tblsp. white vinegar

1/4-1/2 cup Grand Marnier
1 tsp. granulated sugar
1/2 cup fresh coriander,
  chopped or 2-3 Tblsp.
  dry
salt and pepper, to taste
12 oz. large (not jumbo)
  pasta shells

Garnish: fresh coriander
  (cilantro) sprigs

An easy alternative to stuffing, toss one pound cooked tiny shell pasta with seviche and the accumulated juices and serve as a salad or first course.

To make seviche, place scallop pieces in a ceramic or glass container and add just enough lime juice to cover. Refrigerate at least 5 hours, but no more than 24 hours, stirring several times. After marinating, add onion, tomato, chilies (use gloves to finely chop these characters), vegetable oil, vinegar, Grand Marnier, sugar, chopped corianders, salt and pepper to scallops. Toss gently, cover, and refrigerate until assembly time, as long as overnight.

Drop shells into 4 quarts boiling water, stirring gently to prevent sticking. Reduce heat to medium and cook, uncovered, stirring frequently but gently, until shells are very al dente, about 10-12 minutes after it returns to a boil. Drain, place in a large bowl of cold water to cool for about 5 minutes. Discard any that tore during cooking, and place the good ones in a bowl. Cover with damp paper toweling and refrigerate about 30 minutes.

Drain seviche, spoon into pasta shells and arrange on a tray. Garnish with coriander sprigs and let stand a few minutes before serving.

Note: Always cook more shells than you think you'll need, since some will tear or lose their shape. Carefully follow the cooking and cooling instructions, which differ slightly from those for other dried pastas. The trick seems to be not to cook shells as long as other pastas. Cooling in water, resting in the refrigerator and the absorption of the filling juices further soften the shells.

GRILLED SCALLOPS WITH RED PEPPER SAUCE

Preparation time: 10 minutes   *Chef: Jan Robinson*
Cooking time: 20 minutes   *Yacht: Vanity*
Serves: 4

1 Tblsp. peanut oil
24 fresh medium sea
  scallops
pepper, to taste

Red Pepper Sauce:
  2 Tblsp. peanut oil
  3 medium red peppers,*
    roasted and cut into
    chunks
 1 pear, cut into chunks

1 red jalapeno pepper,
  chopped, with seeds
  removed
4 shallots, chopped
2 cloves garlic, chopped
1/4 cup white wine
1/4 cup chicken broth
1/4 cup light cream
Freshly ground pepper

To saute or grill scallops. Heat oil over medium heat in a large skillet, or heat grill. Brush scallops with oil. Season with pepper, add to pan or grill. Cook 1 minute each side. *Serve on a pool of Red Pepper Sauce.*

Red Pepper Sauce: *Place red peppers under a preheated broiler, broil 2 -3 minutes per side or until charred. Cool and peel off charred skin. Heat oil in a large skillet over medium heat. Add roasted red peppers, pear, jalapeno, shallots and garlic. Saute until soft, about 5 - 7 minutes. Add wine and broth. Cook until reduced by half, about 10 minutes. Remove from heat and place in a blender or food processor. Process until smooth. With machine running, add cream and process until thoroughly combined. Season with pepper.

This is a great spicy dish, I serve it with steamed pea pods. For effect, criss-cross red pepper on each scallop.

SEA URCHIN

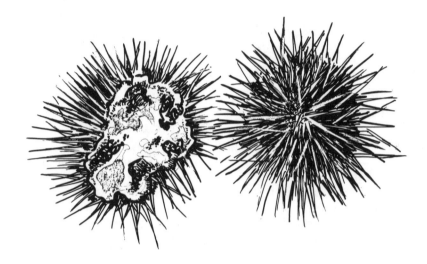

Description: The Sea Urchin is a spiny delicacy that looks like a large pin cushion, which can cause painful injury if stepped on with a bare foot. They are some 500 species of this black, green, brown, or purple sea animal depending on the species. The roe, which is sought as the prime food, is cream-to-orange colored.

Size: They are 1-1/2 to 10 inches in diameter including the spines.

Habitat: They are found worldwide, with the most widely distributed species being the Green Urchin found in both the Atlantic and Pacific oceans.

Flavor: The part of the Sea Urchin that is edible is the "roe". Depending on the species and maturity, it may require 6 to 12 urchins to gather enough roe for one portion. The female portion is more egglike while the male portion has a finer texture. Heaped on crusty French bread and squirted with lemon, the only other accompaniment might be a cold glass of white wine.

Preparation: Eating Urchin is simple. You merely cut around the bottom or "mouth" side of the shell with scissors or break a circular section loose with a knife and shake out the viscera; underneath and firmly attached to the top side of the shell you will find the 5-branched roe, which can be scooped out with a spoon.

SEA URCHIN DELICACY

Preparation time: 15 minutes   *Chef: Jan Robinson*
Cooking time: none   *Yacht: Vanity*
Serves: 4

**24 - 30 sea urchins, fresh   pepper, to taste
crusty French bread   Lemon wedges**

Cut around the bottom of "mouth" side of the shell with a pair of
scissors, or break a circular section loose with a knife and shake out
the internal organs. Underneath you will find the roe, which can
be scooped out with a spoon. The male gonads have a finer texture
than the female ovaries, which are more egglike. Heap on crusty
French bread, or melba toast.   Sprinkle with pepper and squeeze
lemon juice over. A true delicacy!

*There are seven ways to warm your feet in
February. Dipping them in the Caribbean is one.
If you can afford that forget the other six.*

SHARK

Description: There are many types of Shark. The most widely available and most desirable is the Thresher Shark. It is dark gray with a white belly and has an extremely long, flat-like tail. Also common is the Leopard Shark, which is light gray with black bars and stripes, and the Soupfin Shark, dark gray fading to white. Mako, Blue, Brown and Hammerhead sharks are also commercially used.

Size: The average weight for a Thresher Shark is about 100 pounds, while the Soupfin Shark is about 30 - 50 pounds. The Leopard Shark is even smaller at 4 to 15 pounds.

Habitat: The Thresher Shark is found worldwide while the Leopard Shark is only found from Central Mexico to Oregon. The Soupfin Shark is found in the temperate waters of the Pacific.

Flavor: The flesh is firm with a mild to moderate flavor. Because of their unique metabolism, all sharks tend to develop an aroma of ammonia. This can be neutralized by soaking the meat in a mild solution of vinegar or lemon juice, or in milk.

Preparation: The tough skin should always be removed, as it shrinks considerably in cooking, distorting the meat. Since shark meat has very little oil, to prevent drying out in grilling or broiling use an oil-based marinade or baste with a compound butter. Small sharks, like Leopard, are easily filleted, but the larger varieties are generally used as steaks. They can also be used in soups and stews, and cold, poached shark may be used like Tuna in salads.

FISH 'N' CHIPS

Preparation time: 30 minutes   *Chef: Jan Robinson*
Cooking time: 30 minutes   *Yacht: Vanity*
Serves: 4

2 lbs. fresh, firm white fish   **Seasoned flour**
    fillets shark, haddock or   **Oil for frying**
    cod
Beer Batter for fish: **Chips:**
    1 cup all purpose flour   **vegetable oil or shortening**
    1 egg   **2 lbs. baking potatoes**
    3/4 cup beer (flat is O.K.)
    1 Tblsp. oil

Chips: Slice potatoes lengthwise into strips 1/2-inch wide and 1/2-inch thick. Heat 4 to 5 inches of oil or shortening in a deep fryer to a temperature of 375 degrees F. on a frying thermometer. Preheat oven to 250 degrees F. Line a large shallow roasting pan with paper towels. Dry the potatoes thoroughly and deep fry them in 3 or 4 batches, until they are crisp and light brown. Transfer them to the lined pan to drain and place them in the oven to keep warm.

Beer Batter: Sift flour into a large mixing bowl. Make a well in the center. Separate egg. Beat egg yolk, beer and oil into flour to form a smooth batter. (Add a little more oil if necessary to get the right texture.) If possible, let the batter rest at room temperature for half an hour or so, although it may be used at once. Beat the egg white until stiff and fold into batter when ready to use.

Fish: Skin the fish and cut into 3 x 5-inch pieces. Wash the pieces of fish under cold running water and pat them completely dry with paper towels. Dust lightly with seasoned flour. Shake off surplus. Dip fish in the batter so that it is completely coated. Lift out, allowing fish to drain on the side of the bowl. Preheat oil to 375 degrees F. (185 degrees C.) Fry in deep oil. Drop 2 or 3 pieces of fish at a time into the hot oil, cook until golden and crisp. Occasionally turn with a spoon to prevent them sticking together or to the pan. Lift out with a perforated spoon on to absorbent paper to drain off the oil.

To serve: Heap the fish in the center of a large heated platter and arrange the chips around them. Traditionally, fish and chips are served sprinkled with malt vinegar and salt.

SHARK KEBOBS

Preparation time: 45 minutes
Marinating time: 2 hours
Cooking time: 15 minutes
Serves: 8-10

Chef: Lyn Tucker
Yacht: Impervious Cover

3 lbs. shark steak
8 oz. Hoisin sauce
1/4 cup honey
1/4 cup soy sauce
4 coins fresh ginger, chopped

2 Tblsp. chopped garlic
1 pint mushrooms
2 onions
cherry tomatoes
bell pepper

Preheat barbeque. Cut shark in bite size pieces. Mix Hoisin, honey, soy, ginger, and garlic. Marinate shark 2 hours. Clean and cut vegetables in bite size pieces. Marinate 5 minutes. Skewer meat and vegetables alternately. Lay on preheated barbeque, turn once or twice. *Good served with Mary's Favorite Oriental Rice.*

SHRIMP

Shrimp are considered to be the most popular shellfish in the United States. Shrimp have a distinctive flavor and the pink-white, cooked meat is tender, delicate and delicious. Shrimp is very versatile and can be prepared in hundreds of different ways. It is a ten-legged crustacean that acquired its name because of its small size. The word shrimp was derived from the middle English word "shrimpe" meaning puny person and the Swedish "skrympa" meaning to shrink. Like other crustaceans, the shrimp wears its skeleton on the outside of the body and in order to grow, casts off its shell and replaces it with a new one. They normally swim forward, but when frightened, with a flip of the abdomen, they can propel backward with great speed. <u>Shrimp are very high in nutrition. At only 35 calories per ounce, they contain large amounts of lean protein, vitamins A, B and D and are rich in minerals.</u>

There are three main varieties of shrimp harvested in the United States:

The Northern Shrimp is found in the offshore waters of Maine and Massachusetts. Northern shrimp are pink and are usually three to four inches in length. Some may reach six inches. Their body shape resembles a small lobster or crayfish without pinchers or claws. On the Atlantic coast, northern shrimp are found in muddy or sandy bottoms in water from 150 to 900 feet deep. These shrimp are also found off the coasts of Alaska and British Columbia. Northern shrimp may be used interchangeably with other varieties of shrimp in any recipe.

The North Pacific Shrimp is tiny shrimp which is found along the coastlines of California, Oregon, Washington, and Alaska.

The Southern Shrimp, is found in the waters of the Gulf and South Atlantic states. There are three species of the Southern shrimp which are commercially important. They are the common, or white shrimp, the brown shrimp, and the pink or brown-spotted shrimp.
A note should be made here about the lesser known Rock Shrimp. A Florida native, this succulent delight has a taste that hovers between lobster and shrimp.

HOW TO BUY:

Shrimp can be purchased fresh (known as "green" shrimp), frozen, canned, dried, with shells or without shells. They can be found year round, but are usually cheaper in season (November-April). Shrimp are usually bought according to size and are often referred to as jumbo, large, medium , and small.

When buying shrimp fresh, look for shrimp that are firm in texture and have a mild odor with no iodine smell. They should be almost translucent, with no discoloration. If they still have their heads, make sure they are attached firmly to their bodies.

If you are buying frozen shrimp, make sure they are solidly frozen, have little or no odor, no brown spots, and no sign of freezer burns (indicated by a very white, dry appearance around the edges).

Shrimp are priced according to the size or count , the larger ones being more expensive. The count ranges from 9 to 10 per pound to 50 to 60 per pound; both large and small are equally delicious. When buying fresh shrimp remember that 2 to 2-1/2 pounds of shrimp in the shell will yield one pound of cooked, deveined shrimp or 2 cups. Usually about 1/2 pound of fresh shrimp should be allowed per person.

PREPARATION FOR USE:

To clean shrimp, the heads are pinched off just behind the thorax and discarded. After heading the shrimp, they should be washed and placed in ice. Shrimp will shell and devein easier if they are chilled first.

To peel and devein, place your thumb on the stomach and you will feel a separation, work your thumb in the separation and peel off the skin. Use a paring knife to run down the back and remove the black sand vein. If you are using a deveining tool, place the pointed end of the tool in the cavity where the head was removed and run all the way down the back of the shrimp to the joint just before the tail and pull up. This will remove the shell and the vein at the same time.

Shrimp should be cooked within one to two days of purchase. If you are not going to cook them until later, it would be best to freeze them immediately after purchase.

To freeze shrimp, wash the shrimp well, rinse several times and seal in bags. If you are planning to store them for a long time, remove the heads. Frozen shrimp maintain their flavor for up to six months. It is better if you freeze only raw shrimp. When you are ready to cook them, simply add them to whatever dish you are making, you do not need to defrost before cooking.

TIPS:

To butterfly: after deveining, make a deep cut along the back, cutting almost but not completely through the body, and flatten to form a butterfly.

When purchasing fresh shrimp, look for good firm flesh, no odor or discoloration.

Frozen shrimp should not be thawed to room temperature.

Remember, never overcook shrimp. This makes them tough.

Cooking shrimp in their shells adds considerable flavor.

Usually about 1/2 pound of fresh shrimp in the shell should be allowed for each person.

Cooked shrimp can be stored in the refrigerator for up to three days.

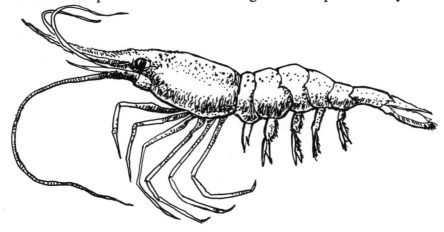

BARBEQUED SHRIMP

Preparation time: 30 minutes   *Chef: Jill Cooper*
Marinating time: 8 hours   *Yacht: Kestrel*
Cooking Time: 5 minutes on BBQ Grill
Serves: 6

1 cup orange juice   **Orange Rice:**
1 cup peanut oil   **1-1/2 cups white rice**
30 jumbo shrimp   **3 cups orange juice**
6 strips raw bacon   **Garnish: grilled pineapple**
barbeque sauce   **slices**

Shell and devein shrimp, then wrap each one in a small piece of bacon and secure by a toothpick. When all shrimp are prepared, place in a bowl and cover with orange juice and peanut oil. Let marinate for 8 hours. Before dinner time, drain marinade, and place shrimp on hot grill. Cover with barbeque sauce. Grill shrimp for 3 to 5 minutes. Do NOT overcook. Garnish with grilled pineapple slices.
Serve over **Orange Rice** *(white rice boiled in orange juice instead of water.)*

SUZI'S SISTER'S SHRIMP SPREAD

Preparation time: 10 minutes   *Chef: Suzi DuRant*
Cooking time: 10-15 minutes   *Yacht: Courvoisier*
Serves: 6

2 cups cheddar cheese,   **1 (6 oz.) can baby shrimp,**
**   shredded**   **   drained**
8 oz. cream cheese, softened   **lemon pepper**
4 Tblsp. mayonnaise   **Swiss cheese crackers**
2 Tblsp. chives

Preheat oven to 350 degrees F. Mix cheeses, mayonnaise and chives, then shrimp. Sprinkle with lemon pepper. Heat in oven-proof serving dish until bubbly. Serve with Swiss cheese crackers.

Note: If using fresh shrimp, be sure to squeeze as much moisture out as possible. Can also be prepared on stove top, stirring frequently over low heat.

BOILED SHRIMP

Preparation time: 20 minutes   *Chef: Ann Landry Cast*
Cooking time: 12 minutes   *Yacht: Sonrisa*
Chilling time: 2 hours
Serves: 6-8

3 quarts water
1 bag (Zatarains) crab and
   shrimp boil seasoning

2 lbs. shrimp, peeled and
   deveined
1 Tblsp. salt

Bring water to a boil. Add salt and shrimp boil seasoning. Boil for 10 minutes. Add shrimp and let water return to a boil. Cook 2 minutes. Drain shrimp, cool and chill. *Serve with Remoulade Sauce* (see recipe below) *for hors d'oeuvre or first course.*

Remoulade Sauce:
   1-1/2 cups chili sauce
   1/3 cup Creole mustard
   1/3 cup prepared
      horseradish
   1/4 cup yellow mustard
   1 Tblsp. lemon juice
   1 Tblsp. Worcestershire
      sauce
   1/2 tsp. finely chopped
      parsley
   1/2 tsp. Lea & Perrins

   4 dashes Tabasco sauce
   2 pinches cayenne
   1/2 tsp. paprika
   1 tsp. finely chopped red
      onions
   1 tsp. finely chopped green
      onion
   1 tsp. finely chopped
      celery

Combine all ingredients in mixing bowl. Whip briskly until well blended. Refrigerate to cool, then serve over shredded lettuce. Arrange shrimp over the remoulade sauce.

Is this what you call Boiled Shrimp?

SHRIMP AND SPINACH QUICHE

Preparation time: 15-20 minutes   *Chef: Fiona Baldrey*
Cooking time: 45 minutes   *Yacht: Promenade*
Serves: 6

Pastry:
6 oz. all-purpose flour   1-1/2 oz. margarine
1-1/2 oz. vegetable shortening   2-3 Tblsp. water

Filling:
2 eggs, beaten   2 Tblsp. light cream
4 oz. cottage cheese   1 (7 oz.) can shrimp, drained
1 (9 oz.) can spinach, drained   Salt and pepper
1/4 tsp. nutmeg, ground

Preheat oven to 400 degrees F. Make up the pastry and line an 8-inch pie tin. Prick and line base with a round of foil. Bake shell for 15 minutes. Remove foil. Mix the filling ingredients. Fill the pastry shell and bake for 25-30 minutes at 350 degrees F. until the filling has set. *Serve hot or cold with a tossed salad.*

SHRIMP PATE

Preparation time: 15 minutes   *Chef: Jane Dixon*
Chilling time: 3 hours   *Yacht: Verano Sin Final*
Serves: 12

4 (7 1/2 oz.) cans shrimp,   Sauce:
   rinsed and drained   2 Tblsp. horseradish
2 Tblsp. fresh lemon juice   2 tsp. lemon juice
1 small onion, minced   1 cup catsup
1/2 cup butter, softened   Garnish: lemon slices
1/3 cup mayonnaise   and parsley
Salt and pepper, to taste
Dash of Tabasco sauce

Mash shrimp and add lemon juice. Mix. Add onion and mix. Add butter and mix. Add mayonnaise, salt, pepper, Tabasco sauce and mix well. Pack into a decorative mold and chill well (I usually prepare this at lunch time). Mix and chill sauce ingredients. At serving time, unmold on platter. Pour sauce over and garnish with lemon slices and parsley. *Serve with crackers.*
Note:: This recipe make 2-1/2 cups and can be cut in half to serve six.

SHRIMP CRUZAN

Preparation time: 10 minutes   *Chef: Jan Robinson*
Cooking time: 10 minutes   *Yacht: Vanity*
Serves: 4

1 lb. large or jumbo shrimp,   3 oz. cream cheese,
   peeled and deveined   softened
pepper   1 oz. Roquefort, or other
juice of 1 lime   blue cheese, softened
4 oz. butter, melted   Garnish: paprika and
                     fresh sprigs of parsley

Preheat oven to 400 degrees F. Wash shrimp, pat dry. Place in a shallow baking dish. Sprinkle with pepper and lime juice. Blend butter and both cheeses together. Spread over shrimps. Cover with aluminum foil. Bake at 400 degrees F. for 10 minutes. *Serve over pasta or rice.* Sprinkle with a little paprika. Garnish with parsley.

This makes a great easy meal. I also serve steamed or sauteed pea pods. The whole meal only takes 20 minutes, and always receives rave reviews!!

SHRIMP AND SPAGHETTI

Preparation Time: 10 minutes   *Chef: Rip Collins*
Cooking Time: 15 minutes   *Yacht: Firefly*
Sitting Time: Several hours
Serves: 4

1 lb. spaghetti   1 tsp. basil (fresh if possible)
1 lb. cooked shelled shrimp   1 tsp. oregano
1 lb. Feta cheese, crumbled   pepper to taste
6 scallions, sliced (use green   2 Tblsp. olive oil (optional)
   part too!)
2 tomatoes, peeled, diced,
   and seeded

Cook 1 lb. spaghetti. Toss with the above ingredients several hours before serving time. Refrigerate for several hours before serving. Accompany with green salad. May be served at room temperature or hot.

FANCY SCAMPI AND FETTUCINE

Preparation time: 30 minutes
Cooking time: 10-15 minutes
Serves: 6

Chef: Mary Woods
Yacht: Silent Joy

30 large shrimp, peeled and deveined
flour for dredging
3 Tblsp. butter
2 Tblsp. oil
1/4 cup minced shallots
1 cup sliced mushrooms
2 tomatoes, peeled, seeded and chopped

minced garlic (lot's - to taste)
4 oz. butter, softened
1 cup dry white wine
1/4 - 1/2 cup light cream
1 lb. fettucine noodles, cooked
Garnish: 1/4 cup chopped parsley, grated Parmesan cheese

Quickly and very lightly dredge shrimp in flour, saute in heavy large skillet with 1/3 butter and oil. When shrimp starts to change color, push to one side. Add 1/3 more butter, then shallots, mushrooms, tomatoes and garlic. Saute all, mix into shrimp. Add wine to deglaze, remaining butter, making a sauce. Add cream while stirring. All should be cooked by now. If needed, add more butter, wine and or cream. Add parsley. Place hot fettucine on plates, top with 5 shrimp each, spoon sauce on top. Sprinkle with Parmesan cheese.

Note: Have all ingredients ready and work quickly to avoid overcooking shrimp. A combination of regular and spinach fettucine is lovely with this dish. *Serve with Honeyed Carrots.*

Hint: To devin shrimp, make a shallow cut lengthwise down the back of each shrimp; remove sand vein with point of knife.

FETTUCCINE WITH BAY SHRIMP

Preparation time: 15 minutes   *Chef: Debbie Ulrey*
Cooking time: 50 minutes   *Yacht: Dream Merchant*
Serves: 6

6 Tblsp. butter
2 Tblsp. minced garlic
  cloves
6 cups whipping cream
6 Tblsp. dry Marsala
1 tsp. salt
1/2 tsp. pepper

8 oz. Parmesan cheese,
  freshly grated
1-1/2 lbs. spinach
  fettucine
10 oz. cooked bay or small
  shrimp
Garnish: parsley sprigs

Melt butter in heavy skillet, add garlic and saute cooking 4-5 minutes. Stir in cream, Marsala, salt and pepper and bring to a boil. Cook stirring frequently until liquid is reduced to 3-1/2 cups (about 40-45 minutes). Remove from heat and add grated Parmesan cheese. Stir until melted. Meanwhile bring a large pot of water to boil. Add fettucine and cook until just done. DO NOT OVERCOOK. Drain well, return to pot, add sauce and shrimp - toss well. Serve on heated platter. Top with more Parmesan cheese and garnish with parsley sprigs. *Great served with Caesar salad and piping hot French bread to dip up all the sauce with.*

SHRIMP A LA CYNTHIA

Preparation time: 30 minutes   *Chef: Annie Scholl*
Cooking time: 10 minutes   *Yacht: Bon Vivant*
Serves: 6

3 lbs. medium shrimp
1 lb. spaghetti
2 cups dry white wine
1-1/2 cups butter or margarine

1 Tblsp. garlic, minced
1 cup parsley, chopped
Salt and pepper

Peel and devein shrimp. Saute the garlic in butter and add wine and parsley. Simmer for 3 minutes. Meanwhile, have a pot of boiling water to prepare spaghetti. When spaghetti is half done, cook shrimp in wine and butter sauce until pink. Drain spaghetti and place immediately on a large platter. Pour the shrimp on top and put remaining sauce in a small dish to be used for dipping.

Note: This recipe was given to me by a lovely lady we met cruising in Port O'Connor, Texas.

SCRUMPTIOUS SHRIMP SCAMPI

Preparation time: 30 minutes   *Chef: Sharon Strong*
Cooking time: 15 minutes   *Yacht: Promises*
Serves: 6

30 jumbo shrimp (15-20 count)
1/3 cup melted butter
1/3 cup olive oil
3 Tblsp. lemon juice
5 garlic cloves, crushed
pepper, to taste
1/4 cup chopped fresh parsley

3 cups hot pre-made white fettuchini Alfredo
3 cups hot cooked green angel hair pasta
grated Parmesan cheese
6 tomato flowers

Shell, devein and remove the feet from the shrimp. Butterfly the shrimp by cutting all the way back to the last segment before the tail. Rinse throughly and pat dry. Divide the butter and oil equally between the 2 saute pans. (Oil keeps the butter from burning.) Divide up garlic and lemon juice. Add the shrimp when the pans are hot. Lay shrimp cut side down on the pan first, then turn over to cook evenly. Be careful not to overcook - about 5 minutes, or until they turn a delicate shade of pink. Sprinkle with parsley.

To Serve: Place 1/2 cup pre-made white fettuchini alfredo in the center of each plate. Add about 1/2 cup cooked green angel hair pasta tossed with butter and Parmesan cheese around perimeter extending the circle 1-1/2 inches or more in width. Place a tomato flower in the middle, and add 5 jumbo shrimp, evenly spaced on the pasta.

Serve with steamed baby pods and baby peas with red pepper strips. Pina Colada Souffle for dessert. (See SHIP TO SHORE II for recipe.)

Hint: To get rid of the "canned taste" in canned shrimp; soak them in a little sherry and 2 tablespoons of vinegar for about 15 minutes.

DONNA'S SHRIMP SCAMPI

Preparation time: 30 minutes   *Chef: Donna Keller*
Cooking time: 30 minutes   *Yacht: Adela*
Serves: 6

8 oz. butter or margarine   **30 jumbo shrimp - peeled,**
8 cloves garlic, minced   **with tails left on**
oregano, to taste   **2 cups cooked white rice**
parsley, dash or two   **Garnish: lemon twists and**
2 lemons   **fresh parsley**

Melt 4 ounces butter and saute 4 cloves minced garlic, oregano, parsley and juice of half lemon for about 5 minutes. When hot, place peeled shrimp in pan, try to keep them in a curled position. Saute on first side adding more oregano, parsley, and lemon juice. Turn until all shrimp are cooked on both sides (about 3 minutes). Arrange rice on large circular tray, place shrimp on top of rice attractively and garnish with remains in pan. Add lemon twists sprinkled with parsley.

Serve with hot dark bread and cold green bean, tomato, pepper and onion salad.

TAHITIAN SKILLET SHRIMP

Preparation time: 20 minutes   *Chef: Ronnie Hochman*
Cooking time: 5 minutes   *Yacht: Illusion II*
Serves: 6

1 (lb. 4 oz.) can pineapple   **4 Tblsp. soy sauce**
**   chunks**   **2 Tblsp. cornstarch**
2 Tblsp. oil   **1 Tblsp. fresh ginger,**
1 cup celery, chopped   **   minced**
2 medium green peppers,   **2 cloves garlic, crushed**
**   cubed**   **10 cherry tomatoes, cut**
2 lbs. large shrimp, parboiled   **   in halves**
1/2 cup green onion, chopped

Drain pineapple reserving syrup. Heat oil in skillet. Add celery and pepper, saute until pepper turns bright green; do not overcook. Add shrimp, and toss with vegetables until heated through. Add pineapple chunks and green onions. Combine syrup, soy sauce, cornstarch, ginger and garlic. Stir into shrimp mixture and heat until thickened and bubbly. Add cherry tomatoes and *serve at once over rice or noodles.*

MARINATED SHRIMP

Preparation time: 10 minutes   *Chef: Ann Landry Cast*
Chilling time: 4 hours   *Yacht: Sonrisa*
Serves: 6-8

1-1/2 cups olive oil   2-3 dash Tabasco sauce
3/4 cups white vine vinegar   1 medium red onion, sliced
1-1/2 tsp. salt   3 Tblsp. capers
1/2 cup dried celery   2 lbs.medium shrimp,
         boiled

Prepare marinade by combining the first 7 ingredients. Add shrimp and marinate in refrigerator at least 4 hours to overnight. *Serve as hors d' oeuvre or first course.*

GALATOIRE'S SHRIMP POUPON

Preparation time: 20 minutes   *Chef: Cass Stewart*
Cooking time: 3 minutes   *Yacht: Morning Star*
Marinating time: 6 hours
Serves: 6-8

1 bunch green onions   Salt and pepper
1 stalk celery   1/3 cup wine vinegar
2 cloves garlic   Pinch of sugar
1 sprig parsley   1/3 cup vegetable oil
5 Tblsp. Poupon mustard   1/3 cup olive oil
2 Tblsp. paprika   2-1/2 to 3 lbs. shrimp
1/2 tsp. basil   Garnish: parsley

Chop vegetables until very fine. Put in a bowl and add: mustard, paprika, basil, salt and pepper. Add vinegar and sugar, mix thoroughly. Gradually add oils. Let marinade mix stand for a few hours.

Drop shrimp in boiling water 3-4 minutes only. Shell and devein shrimp. Marinate shrimp in marinade mix at least 3 hours. To serve:*Arrange shrimp on a bed of lettuce.*

Note: It is best to start early in the day for this recipe.

BAYOU SHRIMP

Preparation time: 5 minutes   *Chef: Linda Green*
Cooking time: 10 minutes   *Yacht: Elysee*
Serves: 6

1 lb. raw shrimp in shells,   2 Tblsp. barbeque sauce
   (20-24 count)   1 bay leaf, crumbled
1/4 cup margarine or butter   2 garlic cloves, crushed
1/4 cup vegetable oil   1/2 tsp. each dried rosemary,
2 Tblsp. lemon juice   paprika, basil leaves
1/4 tsp. salt   (crushed)
1/4 tsp. pepper   dried red peppers

Butterfly shrimp by cutting lengthwise down back thru shell, but not cutting all the way through. Don't remove shells. In large skillet melt butter. Add shrimp and saute 3 to 4 minutes till shrimp begins to turn pink. Add all the remaining ingredients. Cook over low heat 4 more minutes, stirring frequently. Cover and let stand 5 minutes. Spoon shrimp and sauce into large serving dish. This is quick and easy and very tasty. *Serve with lots of napkins and a dish for discarded shells.*

INDIAN SHRIMP CURRY

Preparation time: 20 minutes   *Chef: Kathy Prentice*
Cooking time: 30 minutes   *Yacht: Point of Sail*
Serves: 4

1 bouillon cube   1- 1/2 tsp. sugar
1 cup boiling water   1/2 tsp. ginger
5 Tblsp. butter   2 cups milk
1/2 cup minced onions   4 cups cooked shrimp
6 Tblsp. flour   1 tsp. lemon juice
1 Tblsp. or more curry
   powder   Garnish: coconut,
1-1/4 tsp. salt   chutney, etc.

Dissolve bouillon cube in water. In a large skillet, melt butter and add onions, saute until tender. Stir in flour, curry, salt, sugar, ginger and cook until bubbly. Gradually stir in bouillon and milk. Add shrimp, lemon juice and heat shrimp through. Garnish. *Serve with rice and crusty bread.*

SHRIMP DILEAS

Preparation time: 20 minutes
Cooking time: 30 minutes
Serves: 6

Chef: Jean Crook
Yacht: Dileas

1(13-3/4 oz.) can cut up
   artichoke hearts
1-1/2 lbs. medium shrimp,
   cooked, shelled, deveined
2 Tblsp. butter
1/2 lb. fresh mushrooms,
   sliced

1 Tblsp. Worcestershire
   sauce
1/4 cup sherry
2 cups medium Cream
   Sauce
1/4 cup Parmesan cheese

Garnish: paprika & parsley

Preheat oven to 375 degrees F. Grease 1-1/2 quart casserole. Arrange artichokes in casserole. Place shrimp on them. Melt butter in skillet, and saute mushrooms for 6 minutes. Add to casserole. Combine Worcestershire, sherry and cream sauce. Pour into casserole. Sprinkle with cheese and paprika. Bake 30-40 minutes till bubbly. Garnish with parsley.

I serve this with baby peas and mushrooms, Uncle Ben's Long Grain & Wild Rice with Apples and Raisins.

Hint: When you burn yourself in the kitchen vanilla will help ease the pain. (Apply it, don't drink it!)

SHRIMP EL GRECO

Preparation time: 20 minutes   *Chef: Marita Tasse*
Cooking time: 20 minutes   *Yacht: Flower of the Storm*
Serves: 4-6

1/4 cup olive oil
1/2 cup chopped onion
2 garlic cloves, crushed
4 medium tomatoes or 1
  (16 oz.) can tomatoes,
  drained and chopped
1/2 cup dry red or white wine

1/4 tsp. sugar
1/2 tsp. each oregano, basil
  and thyme
1-1/2 lb. shrimp, shelled
1/4 lb. feta cheese, 1/4 inch
  cubes
12 (approx.) black olives

Saute onions and garlic in oil until soft. Add tomatoes, wine, sugar, and herbs. Cook over medium-high heat 3-5 minutes until sauce is reduced slightly. Reduce heat and add shrimp, cooking 3-5 minutes until shrimp are pink. Remove skillet from heat and stir in cheese and olives. Season with salt and pepper. Garnish with parsley. *Serve over rice - or as is!*

SHRIMP FIJI

Preparation time: 15 minutes   *Chef: Ronnie Hochman*
Cooking time: 5 minutes   *Yacht: Illusion II*
Serves: 6

3 Tblsp. butter
2 cloves garlic, crushed
2 lbs. large shrimp, cleaned
  and parboiled
1-1/2 Tblsp. fresh ginger,
  grated

1/2 cup slivered almonds
1 cup fresh orange juice
1 cup dry white wine
1/2 cup honey
1-1/2 Tblsp. cornstarch

Heat butter and garlic in skillet. Saute shrimp, 1 Tblsp. ginger and almonds for 3 minutes. Remove from skillet and drain off butter. Combine orange juice, wine, honey, 1/2 Tblsp. ginger and cornstarch. Add to skillet and bring to boil. Add shrimp. Cook until mixture becomes glossy, about 2 minutes. Season to taste with salt and pepper. *Serve over rice.*

SHRIMP FLORENTINE

Preparation time: 20 minutes
Cooking time: 35 minutes
Serves: 4

Chef: Liz Tuson
Yacht: Possible Dream

2 (10 oz.) packages frozen spinach, chopped
1 lb. shrimp, cooked, shelled deveined
1/4 cup margarine or butter
1/4 cup flour
1-1/2 cups milk

1/2 cup dry white wine
1/4 cup green onion, chopped
1/2 tsp. salt
1/4 tsp. pepper
1 cup Swiss cheese, shredded
Paprika

Preheat oven to 350 degrees F. Thaw spinach and squeeze dry. Spread spinach in 9-inch pie plate; top with shrimp. In saucepan melt margarine and stir in flour. Gradually add milk, wine and green onion. Cook, stirring constantly over low heat until sauce bubbles and thickens. Add salt, pepper, and cheese. Cook until cheese melts. Pour sauce over shrimp. Sprinkle with paprika. Bake in 350 degrees F. oven for 35 minutes or until bubbly.

SHRIMP LOUISIANA

Preparation time: 10 minutes
Cooking time: 10 minutes
Serves: 6

Chef: Louise Brendlinger
Yacht: Ring-Andersen

1 onion, finely chopped
1-1/2 oz. butter
2 oz. flour
2 cups milk
1 tsp. chili powder

3 Tblsp. ketchup
1 Tblsp. Worcestershire sauce
2 Tblsp. sherry
3 cups cooked shrimp

Saute the onions in the butter until soft. Add flour and stir well. Add the milk and stir until boiling. Then add chili powder, ketchup, Worcestershire sauce, and sherry. Taste and adjust seasoning. Add the cooked shrimp and bring back to a boil. Just heat shrimp. Do NOT overcook. *Serve at once with rice.*

SHRIMP NEWBURG

Preparation time: 10 minutes   *Chef: Kate Young*
Cooking time: 20 minutes   *Yacht Alize'*
Serves: 6

4 Tblsp. butter   1 1/2 lbs. cooked shrimp
4 Tblsp. flour   1/4 cup sherry
salt and pepper, to taste
2 cups milk   **Garnish: parsley sprig**
2 egg yolks, slightly beaten   **and lemon wedge**

Melt butter over low heat, slowly add flour, salt and pepper, stirring constantly until smooth. Slowly add milk, stirring constantly until thickened. Add a little of hot milk mixture to egg yolks, stir and return it to milk mixture. Stir and cook for two minutes. Add shrimp and heat thoroughly being careful not to boil. Remove from heat, add sherry and stir well. *May be served in individual seafood dishes or over rice.*

SHRIMP AND VEGETABLE COGNAC

Preparation time: 45 minutes   *Chef: Carol Lowe*
Cooking time: 10 minutes   *Yacht: Natasha*
Serves: 4

1-1/2 lbs. shrimp, raw   1 cup sweet pepper,
5 Tblsp. butter   (red or green) julienned
Salt and freshly ground   2 cups mushrooms, thinly
   pepper   sliced
3 Tblsp. shallots, finely   3 Tblsp. cognac
   chopped   1/2 cup heavy cream
1 cup celery, finely chopped

Peel and devein the shrimp. Rinse well in cold water and pat dry. Melt 2 Tblsp. butter in skillet and add shrimp. Add salt and pepper to taste. Cook, stirring shrimp over high heat so they cook evenly, for about 2 minutes. Cook only until shrimp turns pink, and lose their raw look. Using a slotted spoon, remove shrimp, and put into a bowl. Add 1 more Tblsp. butter to skillet and add shallots. Cook briefly, stirring. Add celery, pepper strips, and mushrooms. Cook about 2 minutes. Sprinkle with cognac and add cream. Bring to a boil. Add any liquid that has accumulated from the shrimp. Cook for about 30 minutes and add shrimp. Cook until shrimp are thoroughly heated. Stir in remaining 2 Tblsp. butter. *Serve with Red Onion and Endive Salad, Rice with Parsley, Broiled Tomatoes, and Pineapple Surprise.*

ARTICHOKE AND HEARTS OF PALM SALAD

Preparation time: 10 minutes　　　*Chef: Patricia Bryant*
Marinating time: 24 hours　　　　　*Yacht: Skylark*
Serves: 6

1 pkg. Good Seasons Italian
　Dressing
1 (13-3/4 oz.) can of heart
　of palm
1 (13-3/4 oz.) can artichoke
　hearts

1 small jar mushroom,
　pieces
1 (4-1/2 oz.) can med.
　shrimp
shredded carrots
Romaine lettuce

Mix dressing as directed on package. Chop up drained heart of palm and artichoke hearts. Add drained mushrooms and shrimp. Toss with dressing. Marinate 24 hours. *Serve on romaine lettuce.*

For variety, add macaroni twists to above. *Serve with gazpacho soup and hot crusty French bread.*

DEEP SEA AVOCADO SALAD

Preparation time: 25 minutes　　　*Chef: Elizabeth Tuson*
Marinating time: 30 minutes　　　　*Yacht: Possible Dream*
Serves: 4

1 grapefruit, peeled and
　sectioned
1 (11 oz.) can Mandarin
　oranges
1/2 cup bay shrimp, shelled,
　cooked
2 avocados, halved
1 small red onion, sliced in
　rings

Vinaigrette Dressing:
　1/2 cup salad oil
　2 Tblsp. red wine vinegar
　1/2 tsp. salt
　 dash of pepper
　1/2 tsp. prepared
　　mustard
　1 tsp. dried chives
Garnish: salad greens

Vinaigrette Dressing: Mix all ingredients together and shake well.

Marinate fruits and shrimp in dressing for 30 minutes. Spoon mixture into avocado halves. *Serve on greens as a luncheon salad with soup and homemade hot muffins.*

SHRIMP, MANDARIN SALAD

Preparation time: 10 minutes   *Chef: Louise Maloney*
Chilling time: 1 hour   *Yacht: Angel Eyes*
Serves: 4

1 (11 oz.) can mandarin   pepper
    oranges   1/4 to 1/3 cup Italian
1 (6 oz.) can medium shrimp   vinaigrette dressing
3-4 green onions

Drain mandarin oranges and shrimp. Combine in bowl, add finely sliced green onion and pepper. Marinate and chill one hour in Italian Dressing (or a vinaigrette of your choice). *Serve on lettuce leaves.*

TROPICAL FRUIT, PRAWN AND PASTA SALAD

Preparation time: 30 minutes   *Chef: Helen Bromley*
Cooking time: 10 minutes   *Yacht: Golden Rule*
Serves: 6

3 lbs. cooked prawns   Tropical Dressing:
    (or shrimp)   1/2 cup whipping cream
7 oz. pasta   2 Tblsp. coconut cream
1 mango, chunks   1 Tblsp. mayonnaise
1 papaya, chunks   1 Tblsp. grated fresh
1 lb. can unsweetened   ginger
    pineapple pieces   1 Tblsp. lime juice
1 (10 oz.) can mandarin
    segments, drained
3 green shallots, sliced

Add pasta to large pan of boiling water. Boil rapidly, uncovered, for about 10 minutes or until tender. Drain, cool.

Tropical Dressing: Combine all ingredients thoroughly.

Shell and devein prawns. Combine prawns, mango, papaya, pineapple, and mandarins with dressing in a bowl. Combine pasta and shallots and place on serving plates; top with salad dressing mixture.

AVOCADOS WITH SHRIMP STUFFING

Preparation time: 20 minutes　　　　*Chef Kimberly Foote*
Serves: 6　　　　　　　　　　*Yacht: Oklahoma Crude II*

1/4 cup water
1-1/2 cups Pepperidge Farm
　stuffing mix
3 ripe avocados, cut in halves
　and stones removed

1 (6-1/2 oz.) can broken
　shrimp
2 tsp. curry powder
fresh ground pepper
1 tsp. paprika
1 tsp. parsley

Mix approximately 1/4 cup water with stuffing. Add drained shrimp and spices. Place dollop of mixture in the center of avocado halves. Sprinkle with parsley and paprika. *Serve immediately with salad and chips for a cool, light lunch.*

STUFFED SHRIMP SUPREME

Preparation time: 30 minutes　　　　*Chef: Lee Ann La Cesa*
Cooking time: 10 minutes　　　　　　*Yacht: Flute*
Serves: 6

2-1/2 lbs. jumbo shrimp
1 (1 lb.) package crabmeat
　stuffing
6 oz. butter
3/4 cup sour cream

3 cloves garlic, crushed
Parmesan cheese

Garnish: 6 lemon slices
　and 6 sprigs parsley

Peel, devein, and butterfly shrimp. Arrange on cookie sheet with tails upward. On each shrimp, put approximately 1 tsp. of stuffing. In saucepan, melt butter, and add garlic. Spoon butter over shrimp. Top each shrimp with 3/4-1 tsp. sour cream. Sprinkle with Parmesan cheese over all. Broil for 8-10 minutes or until shrimp are pink and lightly browned. *Serve with a garden salad, rice pilaf, glazed carrots and bananas flambe . Along with a chilled bottle of white wine.*

SHRIMP WITH A DILL MUSTARD MAYONNAISE

Preparation time: 25 minutes   *Chef: Sharon Strong*
Chilling time: 30 minutes   *Yacht: Promises*
Serves: 6

6 firm, large tomatoes
1 medium cucumber, peeled
    seeded and cut into
    1/3-inch cubes
3-1/2 cups medium shrimp,
    shelled, deveined, cooked,
    coarsely chopped
6 reserved shrimp, whole and
    cooked for garnish.
1/4 cup celery, minced
1/4 cup scallions, finely
chopped

Dill Mustard Mayonnaise:
1 egg
1/2 tsp. dry mustard
1/2 tsp. Dijon mustard
1/4 tsp. salt
4 tsp. white wine vinegar
1 cup olive oil
1/4 cup fresh dill, minced

Cut the tops off the tomatoes 1/3 the way down. Cut the stem ends out in a circle. Seed and save the tops. Scoop out the pulp from the tomatoes. Seed and chop the flesh. Save. Turn the tomato shell upside down on a towel. Chill for 1/2 hour along with the coarsely chopped shrimp, cucumber, celery, and scallions. When chilled, fill the tomato shells with the chopped shrimp mixture, and place on tomato tops. There should be a 1/2-inch gap between tomato base and lid to show chopped shrimp. Garnish with one shrimp (whole) sticking through the lid with a sprig of dill. *Serve on a bed of lettuce with carrot curls, hard boiled egg flower, and a lemon wheel.*

Note: It is also nice to add fresh fruit for garnish with a cold salad instead of vegetables. Try adding a 1/2 slice of fresh pineapple with rind and an orange circle with kiwi slice on a lettuce base. Serve with Avocado Gazpacho Soup.

Dill Mustard Mayonnaise: Combine egg, mustards, and salt in a blender. Turn to high. Add vinegar and blend for a few seconds. Add olive oil in a thin stream. Transfer to a small bowl and stir in dill. NOTE: If in a hurry, here's an easy dill -mustard recipe. Add 1 cup mayonnaise with 2 Tblsp. Dijon mustard and blend. Stir in dill.

CIOPPINO

Preparation time: 45 minutes   *Chef: Jan Robinson*
Cooking time: 40 minutes   *Yacht: Vanity*
Serves: 6

l lb. large shrimp in shells
1-1/2 lbs. rockfish, halibut,
    bass or other white fish
    fillets
1 lb. clams or mussels in shells
2 medium size crabs
2 (14 -1/2 oz.) cans no-salt
    tomatoes, undrained
    and chopped
1 green bell pepper, chopped
1/2 cup olive oil

1 large onion, chopped
4 cloves garlic, minced
3 Tblsp. chopped parsley
1 tsp. each of basil, oregano,
    rosemary and majoram
fresh ground pepper, to
    taste
1/2 tsp. red pepper flakes
1-1/2 cups red Burgundy
    or other dry red wine

Shell shrimp, leaving the tails intact. Cut raw fish into serving pieces. Clean clams or mussels with stiff brush under cold water. If using mussels, debeard them. Put clams or mussels in a heavy pot, add about 1/2 inch of water and steam them until they open. Save the liquid. Break the crab apart, cut into several pieces. Place olive oil in a Dutch oven or a large pot with lid. When hot, add the onion, garlic, parsley, green pepper and other spices. Cook about 5 minutes over medium heat. Next add the tomatoes, wine and liquid from clams. Cover and simmer 30 minutes.

Add shrimp, cut-up fish and crab. Cook over low heat about 7 minutes or until fish fillets flake easily when tested with a fork. Add the clams or mussels to reheat them for a minute. *Serve in large heated bowls, accompanied with red wine and crusty garlic bread.*

Note: Frozen rock lobster tails may be used in place of crabs; frozen shrimps may be substituted for fresh; canned clams (two 10-1/2 oz. can) may be used when fresh clams are not available.

Cioppino (prounced cho-PEE-no), is quite a lot of work, but well worth the effort. Also great for a party, just double or triple the ingredients.

PRAWNS A LA PLAKA

Preparation time: 10 minutes   *Chef: Page Hanson*
Marinating time: 1- 4 hours   *Yacht: Rampant*
Cooking time: 20 minutes
Serves: 6-8

2-1/2 lbs. large shrimp   1/4 cup dried oregano
   with shells   4 garlic cloves, chopped
1 cup olive oil   Juice of 1 lemon
1 cup sherry   Salt and pepper
1/2 cup parsley, chopped

                               Richmond "Tree" Salad

Preheat oven to 450 degrees F. Mix together the olive oil, sherry, parsley, oregano, garlic, lemon juice, salt and pepper, in a glass dish that can go right from the hot oven to the table. Add the shrimp and marinate for at least an hour (more if possible.) Make sure the oven is 450 degrees F. to cook the shrimp quickly. When they turn pink they are ready to serve. This is a "peel-your-own" night. *Serve with plenty of crusty bread to dunk in sauce. I serve this the first night of most charters with a fresh broccoli salad, Richmond "Tree" Salad (recipe below). I also usually double the recipe and use whatever is uneaten for salads the next day.*

Note: When chartering in the Mediterranean, use the whole shrimp with the head for added flavor. I serve this the first night of most charters with a fresh broccoli salad.

Richmond "Tree" Salad: Trim 3 bunches of broccoli into bite-size florets, cutting off most of the stem. Make sauce of 10 slices of bacon (cooked and crumbled), 1/2 cup onions (chopped), 2/3 cup raisins, 2 Tblsp. peanuts (chopped), 1 cup mayonnaise and 3 Tblsp. vinegar. Mix broccoli with sauce and chill or serve immediately.

BAKED JUMBO SHRIMP

Preparation time: 25 minutes *Chef: Susan David*
Cooking time: 15 minutes *Yacht: Wishing Star*
Serves: 6

2-1/2 lbs. large raw shrimp 1/3 cups chopped parsley
1/2 cups butter or margarine 3 tsp. grated lemon peel
1 tsp. salt 3 Tblsp. lemon juice
6 cloves garlic, minced Garnish: lemon wedges
  and parsley

Preheat overn to 400 degrees F. Shell shrimp, devein, wash and drain on paper towel. Melt butter or margarine in 13x9x2-inch baking dish. Add salt, garlic and half of parsley. Arrange shrimp in a single layer in the baking dish. Bake uncovered for 5 minutes. Turn shrimp and sprinkle with lemon peel, lemon juice and rest of parsley. Bake 8-10 minutes more, or just until they turn pink. Arrange on a platter, pour garlic butter overall. Garnish.

I found this recipe in a country innkeepers cookbook - it always turns out great!

RED SNAPPER

Description: The Red Snapper is the most valuable of all the edible reef fishes and of course very easily recognized by its basically rose - red color that fades to pink when removed from the water. The iris of the eye is also bright red.

Size: The Red Snapper found in the market is usually between 4 to 8 pounds in size.

Habitat: The Red Snapper is found from North Carolina to Brazil. It is very abundant around Florida and the Gulf of Mexico and is found among reefs and outcroping rocks along the ocean shelf.

Flavor: The meat is white and flaky with a delicious sweet taste that makes it a favorite.

Preparation: Red Snapper is marketed whole, dressed, as fillets, fresh and frozen. This white meat fish may be cooked by any method, especially baked and stuffed. As Snappers are very boney, it is a good procedure to cut the fish in half and remove as many bones as possible. And remember to scale this fish as soon as possible after removal from the water.

WEST INDIAN FISH (ROATAN STYLE)

Preparation time: 30 minutes
Cooking time: 40 minutes
Serves: 6

Chef: Karen S. Day
Yacht: Schooner Windsong

1/4 cup oil
2 cloves garlic, minced
1 small head of cabbage, cut into 1-inch strips
1 large onion, sliced
2 large green peppers, sliced
1 (16 oz.) can whole tomatoes
1 (6 oz.) can tomato paste
1-1/2 cups water
6 fillets, red snapper
velvetta or muenster cheese

Seasonings:
1/2 tsp. thyme
1/2 tsp. oregano
2 bay leaves, whole
1 tsp. salt
3/4 tsp. black pepper, coarse
1/2 tsp. sugar
2 tsp. lemon juice
1/2 tsp. Tabasco
Garnish: orange and lime slices, fresh toasted coconut

Note: This takes a while to prepare and cook, but it's well worth it.

In a large pot, saute cabbage, in oil and garlic. Add onion and peppers, "cook down" considerably. Add whole tomatoes plus their juice and the tomato paste. Stir until blended and bubbling. Add the seasonings and stir well, continue cooking. Skin fillets if necessary. Fasten with a toothpick. Place fish on top of sauce, then add cheese. Spoon bubbling liquid over, cook about 10 minutes or until cheese melts.

Serve *on a bed of rice garnished with slices of orange and lime, and fresh toasted coconut.*

Note: Leftover sauce makes a superb sailing lunch for the next day. To make **Red Chowder:** simply heat sauce, add 1 can condensed tomato soup, and an extra fillet of fish that you reserved. Incongruous as it sounds, breakfast sausage in chunks is a great addition to Red Chowder. Serve in mugs with Sea Rounds or Pilot crackers. Garnish with a slab of cheese atop the chowder.

Alternatives: Dolphin, Grouper, Halibut

STUFFED SNAPPER FILLETS

Preparation time: 20 minutes
Cooking time: 20 minutes
Serves: 6

Chef: Kate Hinrichs
Yacht: Mystique

1 (7-1/2 oz.) can crab, drained
6 snapper fillets
mayonnaise

1/4 cup chives
1/2 cup white wine
Hollandaise sauce

Preheat oven to 350 degrees F. Prepare crab with mayonnaise and chives. Spread over one side of fillets. Roll jelly roll fashion, securing with toothpick. Stand in pan and pour 1/2 cup wine around. Cover with foil. Bake at 325 degrees F. for 20 minutes until fish is firm to the touch.

Serve on bed of fresh steamed spinach with Hollandaise sauce. Serve with rice.

FILET OF BAKED SNAPPER IN WINE SAUCE

Preparation time: 15 minutes
Cooking time: 15 minutes
Serves: 4

Chef: Bonnie Ratrie
Yacht: Tara

"A" list :
  1 stick butter
  1 cup finely minced
    onion
  2 garlic cloves, finely
    minced
  1 (8 oz.) can mushrooms,
    drained

2 lbs. red snapper fillets *
salt, pepper and accent, to
  taste
1 cup white wine
1 cup chicken stock
3 tsp. soft butter, 3 tsp. flour
1/2 cup cream
2 tsp. chives
Garnish: parsley sprigs

Place all "A" ingredients in 12 inch skillet in exact order. Cut fish in 4 serving pieces. Next, place fish fillets in pan. Cover with fish seasonings, wine and stock. Cover pan - bring to boil. Simmer 5-7 minutes, remove fish fillets and keep warm. Blend flour and butter into a paste. Add slowly in small pieces to boiling sauce, whip smooth and thick. Add cream and chives. Whip smooth. Pour sauce over fish and serve or place fish back into sauce and hold warm until needed. Garnish with parsley sprigs. *Great served with rice pilaf.*

* Any type of fish may be used.

SNAPPER WITH CURRIED RICE

Preparation time: 10 minutes   *Chef: Gunilla Lundgren*
Cooking time: 20 minutes   *Yacht: Bambi*
Serves: 4

2 Tblsp. butter	4 snapper fillets
1 Tblsp. curry	1 egg, beaten
1 big onion, chopped	1 cup bread crumbs
1 apple, chopped	salt, to taste
4 cups water	2 bananas, or plaintains
2 bouillon cubes	Garnish: lemon wedges,
2 cups rice	paprika and parsley

Melt butter in frying pan and fry curry. Add onion and apple and fry for 1 minute, then add water and bouillon cubes. Boil. Add rice, cover and simmer about 18 minutes.

Dip fish first in egg then in bread crumbs and salt. Fry them in butter. Peel and halve bananas lengthwise and fry them for a short time in butter. Put rice on individual plates. Make a frame of bananas and put the fish in the middle. Garnish with lemon wedges, half dipped in paprika and half in chopped parsley. *Serve with boiled christophene or zucchini.*

Alternatives: Rockfish, Black Sea Bass

SNAPPER ALMONDINE

Preparation time: 10 minutes   *Chef: Ann Landry Cast*
Marinating time: 30 minutes   *Yacht: Sonrisa*
Cooking time: 10 minutes
Serves: 4

1-1/2 lbs. snapper, fillets   **Sauce:**
milk   **3/4 stick butter**
1/2 tsp. salt   **1/4 cup sliced almonds**
2-3 dashes tabasco   **2 Tblsp. lemon juice**
flour seasoned with salt   **1/4 tsp.Worcestershire**
   and pepper   **sauce**
2 Tblsp. safflower oil   **2 Tblsp. chopped parsley**
4 Tblsp. butter

Soak fillets in milk seasoned with salt and tabasco for 30 minutes. Drain fillets and pat dry. Dust with seasoned flour and cook in oil and butter. Keep warm in oven while preparing sauce.

Sauce: Melt butter and saute almonds. Add other ingredients. Mix and pour over fish.

Hint: Try soaking fish in vinegar and water before cooking it for a sweet tender taste.

HOT AND SPICY FISH CHOWDER

Preparation time: 30 minutes   *Chef: Holly Carr*
Cooking time: 15 minutes   *Yacht: Skeets*
Serves: 6-8

1/2 stick butter, (2 oz.)
1 inch piece of ginger, peeled
   and minced finely
2 cloves garlic, minced finely
1 small hot, red pepper,
   minced finely
1 Tblsp. basil
1 medium onion, chopped
1/2 red bell pepper, chopped
1/2 green bell pepper,
   chopped
2 stalks celery, chopped

2 large potatoes, peeled and
   chopped into cubes
3 lbs. red snapper or grouper
2 (12 oz.) cans evaporated
   milk
1 (10-1/2 oz.) can tomato
   soup
   or cheddar cheese soup
3 Tblsp. sherry

Garnish: sprig fresh basil
   and dollop of sour
   cream

Melt butter in large pot over low heat. Add first five ingredients. Saute until onions are transparent. Don't burn garlic. Add bell peppers and celery, saute 2 minutes. Set pan aside. Simmer potatoes in 2 cups water until al dente. Add potatoes with reserved water to pot of sauteed vegetables. Steam fish until just white. Remove fish from steaming water and add to vegetable pot. Put pot back on very low heat. Add 2 cans evaporated milk. Stir to mix. Add canned soup. Stir again to blend liquids. Bring to simmer. Do not boil. Add more milk or water if too thick. Just before serving stir in 3 tablespoons sherry. Serve with dollop of sour cream and sprig of basil.

Note: First four ingredients can be chopped together with metal blade in food processor. Also use less hot pepper and ginger if you don't like it too hot and spicy.

Alternatives: Grouper, Sole, Black Sea Bass, Tilefish

POISSON CRU

Preparation time: 40 minutes   *Chef: Holly Carr*
Marinating time: overnight   *Yacht: Skeets*
Serves: 8

2 lbs. fresh fish fillets
  (snapper, grouper,
  mahimahi, tuna)
1-1/2 cup fresh lime juice
1 tsp. salt
1/4 cup white wine vinegar
3/4 cup salad oil
1-1/2 tsp. dry mustard
1 tsp. sugar
1 tsp. pepper
3 cloves garlic minced

1 cup chopped onions or
  scallions
1 cup peeled, chopped
  cucumber (seeds removed)
3 Tblsp. chopped parsley
1/2 cup shredded coconut
chopped tomatoes
1 cup coconut cream (pressed
  out liquid of fresh grated
  coconut meat)

Marinate the fish in the lime juice and salt for 6 hours at room temperature. Drain. Combine the rest of the ingredients and toss gently but thoroughly. Add the fish, tossing lightly and chill overnight. When serving, garnish with ripe chopped tomatoes.

Coconut Cream: Grate enough fresh coconut to make 2 cups. Pour 1 cup boiling water over this. Let stand 1 hour. Strain all thru cheesecloth to reserve liquid. (If a fresh coconut is not available, substitute with 1/2 cup canned cream of coconut.)

Note: Chopped red and/or green peppers and celery may be added if serving as a salad. You may also add finely minced hot pepper for more zip.

Alternatives: Dolphin, Grouper, Tuna

SOLE

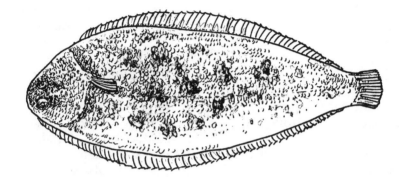

Description: The true Sole is not found in North American waters, but is imported from England, the Netherlands, Belgium and Denmark.   North American "Sole" is actually a variety of Flounder. The color of the skin on the underside of the fish varies according to the bottom surface of the ocean where they are caught. They are usually olive green to dark brown on top.

Size: Sole weighs between 1 to 5 pounds and measures around 12 to 20 inches long.

Habitat: North American "Sole" is found from central California to Alaska. "True" sole is imported from Europe as stated above. They are found year round but more abundantly in the winter.

Flavor: Some say "Sole doesn't taste like fish" which pleases people who are not fish fanciers. The whiter the skin the better the texture and flavor. It has a very delicate smooth taste.

Preparation: Most Sole is either poached or sauteed; however, with practice and careful timing they may be grilled with excellent results. Its texture and flavor are ideally suited to the elaborate use of sauces, herbs, spices, fruit and vegetables, as well as contrasting seafoods. Few fish can tolerate this without losing their identity.

Other names: Petrale Sole, Brill

GOLDEN GOUJONS

Preparation time: 15 minutes   Chef: Anne Evans
Cooking time: 20 minutes   Yacht: Golden Skye
Serves: 8

2 lbs. sole fillets	oil for frying
flour for dredging	Garnish: lemon wedges
2 eggs, beaten	tartar sauce
bread crumbs (Progresso)	

Trim the sole into strips 3-inch x 1-inch, removing any remaining bones. Dredge with flour making sure they are well coated. Dip each strip in the egg wash in a large flat bowl and then coat with bread crumbs. Fry in batches until golden, about five minutes, drain on paper towels and keep warm in a low oven. *Serve garnished with lemon wedges accompanied by a bowl of tartar sauce.*

DISHWASHER SAFE FISH

Preparation time: 10 minutes   Chef: Jan Robinson
Cooking time: 20 minutes   Yacht: Vanity
Serves: 4

4 fillets of sole, flounder, or salmon	freshly ground black pepper
1 lemon, thinly sliced	2 Tblsp. melted butter
1 lime, thinly sliced	Garnish: lemon and lime wedges and parsley

Place fillets on a large double piece of aluminum foil. Arrange alternate lemon and lime slices on top. Sprinkle with black pepper and pour over melted butter. The aluminum foil should be big enough to wrap over the fish. Close foil edges and ends tightly. Place in the top basket of the dishwasher. DO NOT ADD SOAP. Close machine.Turn on to a full cycle. This really works. This method of cooking keeps the fish nice and moist.

Alternatives: Tilefish, Orange Roughy

SOLE GRENOBLOISE WITH LEMON AND CAPERS*

Preparation time: 20 minutes
Cooking time: 10 minutes
Serves: 4

Chef: Sylvia Dabney
Yacht: Native Sun

1-1/4 lb. sole
1/4 cup milk
salt and pepper
1 small lemon
1 Tblsp. parsley, chopped

1/2 cup peanut oil
1 Tblsp. capers, drained
1/2 cup flour
1/4 cup butter

Place sole in dish in single layer. Pour milk over then sprinkle with salt and pepper. Turn fish to coat with milk on both sides. Let stand while you peel lemon, removing all skin and white pulp, cube remaining lemon. Scatter flour over large pan, add more salt and pepper. In separate large skillet, heat oil and 1 tablespoon butter. Remove fish from milk and coat with flour. When oil is quite hot (not smoking) add fish. Cook till brown on both sides, 4-5 minutes total. Transfer to warm platter. Heat remaining butter in small skillet and cook until foamy and brown. Remove skillet and add lemon cubes and capers. Stir and pour evenly over fish. Sprinkle with parsley and serve.

Note: This takes a few pots and pans, but the raves are worth the time and water doing the dishes.

* *Always made with love for Stanley.*

Alternative: Flounder

COLD SOLE WITH A DELICIOUS SAUCE

Preparation time: 10 minutes　　　　*Chef: Gunilla Lundgren*
Cooking time: 10 minutes　　　　　　　　　　*Yacht: Bambi*
Chilling time: 30 minutes
Serves: 4

1-1/2 lb. fresh or frozen Sole　　**Delicious Sauce:**
lemon juice　　　　　　　　　　**1 1/2 cup sour cream**
1 cup water　　　　　　　　　　**1/2 cup whipped cream**
salt　　　　　　　　　　　　　**curry powder, to taste**
4 peppercorns　　　　　　　　　**mustard, dijon type**
1 bay leaf　　　　　　　　　　**pinch of tarragon**
　　　　　　　　　　　　　　　　Garnish: cooked shrimp,
　　　　　　　　　　　　　　　　　　black caviar and
　　　　　　　　　　　　　　　　　　lemon wedges

Sprinkle sole fillets with lemon juice and roll them up. Put them in a large skillet. Add water and spices. Simmer covered for about 10 minutes. Let fillets cool in their own sauce, then place on a dish and   refrigerate.

Delicious Sauce: Mix sour cream with whipped cream, curry, mustard, and tarragon. Put the cold fillets on a serving platter and pour the sauce over. Garnish with shrimps, caviar and lemon wedges.

Cook fish the day before and you will have an easy and very appreciated lunch. Serve with a tossed green salad.

Alternative: Flounder

STOCKS:

COURT BOUILLON OR NAGE

Preparation time: 20 minutes　　　　*Chef: Sylvia Schihs*
Cooking time: 30 minutes　　　　　　*Yacht: Kea 1*
Serves: 4

2 medium carrots	1 small bouquet garni
white part of a leek	1 tsp. peppercorns
1/2 celery stalk	2 Tblsp. white wine vinegar
1/2 fennel stalk (optional)	13 fl. oz. dry white wine
4 shallots	1 oz. butter
4 butter onions	12 oz. water
1 garlic clove	1 oz. coarse salt

Nage Court Bouillon is used for cooking many kinds of shellfish. It can be prepared in advance and kept for 2 or 3 days in the refrigerator.

Peel and wash carrots, leek, celery, fennel, shallots and onions. Slice them into very thin rounds, 1/10-inch thick. Place butter and vegetables in a saucepan, cover it. Sweat the vegetables for 10 minutes. Pour in the vinegar, wine and water; add the salt, bouquet garni and the unpeeled garlic clove. As soon as the mixture comes to a boil, lower the heat and simmer it for 20 minutes. Crush the peppercorns and tie them in a small muslin. Add them to the liquid after 15 minutes.

Jan Robinson from Vanity omits the vinegar, leek, fennel, butter onions, and adds 2 large onions, chopped, 1/4 cup chopped parsley and stems, 2 Tablespoons lemon juice

Note: Court Bouillon is a seasoned liquid used for poaching fish, meats or vegetables. The liquid should be cooled before it is poured over the fish or before the fish is lowered into it, so that the fish skin is not torn or the flesh broken apart. After being used to poach fish, the liquid is a good base for a *fumet* made with the remaining bones or trimmings.

STOCKS:(cont'd)

FUMET (FISH STOCK)

Preparation time: 10 minutes
Cooking time: 2 hours
Makes: about 2 quarts

Chef: Jan Robinson
Yacht: Vanity

2-3 lbs. fish and/or shellfish
   heads bones and trimmings
1/4 cup olive oil
1/2 cup diced celery
1/2 cup sliced carrots
1/2 cup chopped onions
6 cups white wine

6 cups water
1/4 cup chopped parsley
thyme, fennel, oregano, or
   other dried herbs
2 bay leaves
salt and pepper, to taste

Heat oil in large saucepan. Add vegetables and cook until they just begin to soften. Add wine, water and fish parts. Bring to a boil. Skim any foam from the surface. Add dried herbs, parsley, bay leaves, pepper and salt. Simmer for 2 hours. Strain and reserve the stock.

Note: <u>Storing Fumet/Stock:</u> Stock may be stored in the refrigerator after the fat has been removed. Pour the cooled stock into a container and cover tightly. It will keep for a couple of days. The stock may also be frozen. Pour into a container, or plastic ice cube trays. Seal or cover it well. Freeze quickly. Transfer the stock cubes to plastic bags. Keeps about 2 months. <u>To use Fumet/Stock:</u> Let it thaw at room temperature or simply turn it into a saucepan and heat over low heat, stirring occasionally. Add a little water.

STRIPED BASS

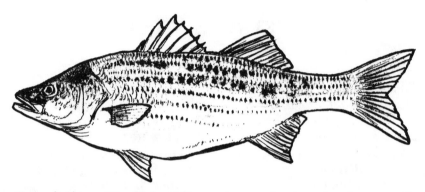

Description: The Striped Bass often varies in color, but usually it is a dark olive-green to steel blue on top, becoming silvery on the sides and white on the belly. The most distinguishing features are the stripes. Seven to eight rows longitudinally and very prominent. This identifies the Striped Bass from all other fish.

Size: The typical Striped Bass is usually about 6 to 8 pounds when it reaches a peak in taste and texture. The larger fish (up to 50 pounds) tend to have coarse meat.

Habitat: The Atlantic coast from the Gulf of St. Lawrence to Northern Florida. The Gulf of Mexico from Western Florida to Louisiana. And from the Columbia River in Washington to Los Angeles, California.

Flavor: A very delicate, firm and moderately sweet taste which peaks with freshness. The Northern (Cold Water) Striped Bass are often used for the oriental dish "Sashimi" because of its firm meat and sweet taste.

Preparation: It is marketed fresh, frozen, canned, in steaks, fillets and whole. Grilling, broiling, poaching and steaming are all appropriate cooking methods. While Striped Bass is one of the few fish that does not require prompt cleaning and icing, however, **the fresher the better the taste.** Remember, when testing for freshness the Striped Bass should always be silvery and sparkling in appearance.

Other names: Striper, Rockfish(Chesapeake Bay area)

SWEET AND SOUR FISH

Preparation time: 15 minutes   *Chef: Peggy Curren*
Cooking time: 10 minutes   *Yacht: Scatteree*
Serves: 4-6

2 carrots, thinly sliced
1/2 cup water
1-1/2 lb. fish fillets (striped
   red bass, drum, shark)
1/2 cup packed brown sugar
1/3 cup vinegar
2 Tblsp. cornstarch
2 Tblsp. soy sauce
1 can (13-1/2 oz.) pineapple
   chunks

1 green pepper, cut into 1-
   inch pieces
vegetable oil

Batter: (mix together)
   3/4 cup water
   2/3 cup flour
   1-1/4 tsp. salt
   1/2 tsp. baking powder

Heat carrots and water to boiling. Cover and cook until crisp and tender (8-10 minutes). Cut fish into 1-inch pieces. Pat fish dry with paper towels. Mix brown sugar, vinegar, cornstarch and soy sauce in a sauce pan. Stir in carrots with liquid, pineapple with syrup and green pepper. Heat to boiling, stirring constantly. Boil and stir 1 minute. Keep warm. In a deep saucepan heat 1 to 1-1/2 inches of oil. Prepare batter. Dip fish in batter. Fry until golden brown (1 minute on each side). Drain on paper towels. Arrange fish on platter over white rice. Pour sauce over fish.

Serve with Egg Drop Soup as an appetizer.

Alternatives: Red Drum, Shark, Rockfish

SQUID

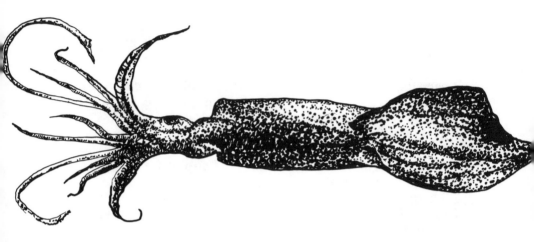

Description: Squids are characterized by a large head and eyes, beaklike jaws, have 10 arms and a long cigar - shaped body with fins at the end. There is no "backbone" as in fish. The color cells in the skin are able to change quickly and may range from red, pink, brown, blue, or yellow.

Size: Smaller squids that are an inch long travel in large schools, while the giant squid, which may exceed 6 feet, are more solitary.

Habitat: They are found throughout all parts of the world and are widely used as bait and food for other species such as Tuna, Marlin, Swordfish and certain whales.

Flavor: The firm flesh of a squid, which turns yellow after cooking, is delicately flavored. Its lean meat contains about 18% protein which makes it highly nutritious.

Preparation: Squids can be used either fresh, salted, dried, candied, smoked, canned or frozen. They can also be poached and used in salads, sauteed, fried, stuffed and baked, braised or grilled. Japanese species are eaten raw.

Other names: Market Squid, Common Squid, Calamari

SQUID SLICES

Preparation time: 15 minutes   *Chef: Gilhian Bethell*
Cooking time: 30 minutes   *Yacht: SS PAJ*
Serves: 4

8 squid (defrosted or   **salt and pepper**
    fresh cleaned)   **2 medium onions**
4 rashers bacon   **sesame seeds**
1 cup breadcrumbs   **1 egg**
mixed herbs   **sherry (optional)**

Cut the tentacles from the squid and chop finely. Chop bacon and onions finely. Fry bacon and onions until soft, add tentacles and fry quickly together. Remove from heat and mix all other ingredients together and add the fried mixture after draining off all excess fat.

Stuff into the squid and bake for 20 minutes or until squid are white and tender on a lightly buttered tray. Remove when cooked. Slice into round or serve whole with a wine or sherry sauce.

Alternatives: Octopus

CALAMARI RINGS

Preparation time: 10 minutes   *Chef: Jan Robinson*
Cooking time: 3-5 minutes   *Yacht: Vanity*
Serves: 4

3 lbs. squid, cleaned and   **1 tsp. black pepper**
    cut into rings   **peanut oil for frying**
2 cups flour   **Garnish: lemon wedges**
                                       fresh parsley

Dry the squid with absorbent towels. Combine flour and pepper. Coat squid with flour mixture. Heat peanut oil to 365 degrees F. Deep fry a few rings at a time until golden brown, about 3 minutes. Do not overcook. Drain on absorbent towels. *Serve hot with horseradish, sweet and sour sauce or a teriyaki sauce. Or, squeeze fresh lemon juice over.*

SWORDFISH

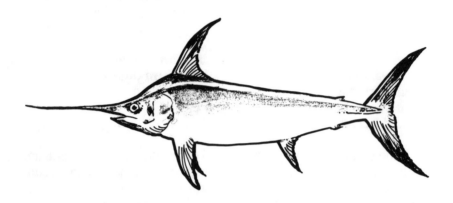

Description: The Swordfish gets its name from his long flattened bill which is in the shape of a sword. He uses this to slash and impail his prey. Swordfish have been known to attack boats as well as other floating objects. The color varies from dark brown or bronzy to grayish - blue or black above and whitish below.

Size: The average size of the Swordfish is between 150 to 250 pounds with the worlds record of over 1,100 pounds.

Habitat: The Swordfish is found worldwide in the temperate and tropical areas of the oceans.

Flavor: The meat of the Swordfish is very firm and has a distinctive flavor of its own. The flavor is enhanced by marinating in herbs, spices and oils due to the meat being lean and dry.

Preparation: Swordfish are marketed fresh or frozen as steaks. Grilling over charcoal and oven - broiling are the two best methods of preparing this fish. However, baking is beginning to be popular.

SEAFOOD KABOBS

Preparation time: 15 minutes   *Chef: Laurie Carloni*
Marinating time: 1 hour   *Yacht: Kreiss Collection*
Cooking time: 10 minutes
Serves: 4

1-2 red peppers, depending   16 medium-size shrimp
  on size   16 scallops
1-2 green peppers, depending   1/2 cup olive oil
  on size   2 cloves garlic, chopped
1 large red onion   fresh parsley
2 tomatoes   salt and pepper, to taste
2 swordfish steaks

Cut all vegetables into 2-inch chunks. Peel and devein shrimp. Cut swordfish into 2-inch chunks. Alternate vegetables and fish on 4 skewers. Marinate in olive oil, garlic and fresh parsley for 1 hour. Broil for 10 minutes - remove skewers keeping shape. *Serve over Saffron Rice. For more color - add finely chopped red pepper or pimento to rice.*

Alternatives: Shark

MARINATED SWORDFISH

Preparation time: 10 minutes   *Chef: Jacqueline Cheetham*
Marinating time: 2 hours   *Yacht: Rajada*
Cooking time: 10 minutes
Serves: 8

2 Tblsp. olive oil   2 tsp. scallions, chopped
5 Tblsp. soy sauce   1/2 tsp. marjoram
1 Tblsp. dry white wine   1 tsp. ground black pepper
4 Tblsp. fresh orange juice   8 (6 oz.) pieces of swordfish,
1 Tblsp. fresh lemon juice   3/4 -inch thick
2 Tblsp. tomato puree   Garnish: Lemon slices and
2 Tblsp. parsley, chopped   chopped parsley
3 garlic clove, crushed

Mix together the olive oil, soy sauce, white wine, orange and lemon juice, tomato puree, parsley, garlic, scallions and marjoram until well blended. Sprinkle the swordfish with black pepper and marinate covered for 2 hours, basting occasionally. Remove swordfish from the marinade and cook under a preheated grill for approximately 5 minutes on each side. This is also delicious barbecued! Garnish.

SIMPLY WONDERFUL SWORDFISH STEAKS

Preparation time: 10 minutes   *Chef: Ann Glenn*
Cooking time: 9 minutes   *Yacht: Encore*
Serves: 6

6 swordfish steaks, 1-inch   **salt, to taste**
   thick (about 3 lbs.)   **freshly ground black pepper**
white wine   **Garnish: herb butter**

Preheat oven to 375 degrees F. Arrange swordfish steaks in a single layer in 1 or 2 baking dishes just large enough to hold them comfortably. Pour wine around the fish, to a depth of 1/2 the thickness of the steak. Season lightly with salt and pepper.

Set the dish or dishes on the middle level of the oven and bake for 9 minutes. Check the fish for doneness with a fork, remembering that residual heat will continue to cook the fish. Garnish with herb butter. *Serve immediately.*

Note: It's quick. Simple preparation; quick, simple cooking - simply delicious, always wonderfully moist and absolutely delicious!

Alternative: Mako Shark

GRILLED SWORDFISH

Preparation time: 10 minutes
Cooking time: 20 minutes
Marinating time: 1 hour
Serves: 4

Chef: Nora Frei
Yacht: Memories

4 Swordfish steaks
olive oil
4 Tblsp. dried parsley
4 Tblsp. chives
2 Tblsp. & 2 tsp. basil

2 Tblsp. & 2 tsp. oregano
1 Tblsp. teriyaki
paprika, to taste
Garnish: red leaf lettuce
**   and radish flowers**

Rinse steaks with water, pat dry. Moisten both sides with olive oil, cover each side with parsley followed by chives, basil and oregano. Then sprinkle with teriyaki and make sure all herbs are moist by pressing with your fingertips. Add a few dashes of paprika and marinate 30 minutes - 1 hour. Grill over hot coals 10 minutes on each side. Flip when you see white spots around skin. Baste second side with leftover marinade. Serve on a bed of red leaf with 2 radish flowers.

You can use this recipe for tuna, but instead of using olive oil, substitute mustard. I serve this with hot red pepper, linguine and honey glazed carrots, preceded by hearts of palm salad with poppy seed dressing.

Alternatives: Tuna, Swordfish

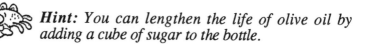

Hint: You can lengthen the life of olive oil by adding a cube of sugar to the bottle.

GRILLED SWORDFISH STEAKS WITH ALMOND BUTTER

Preparation time: 15 minutes
Cooking time: 20 minutes
Marinating time: 2 hours
Serves: 6

Chef: Jennifer Dudley
Yacht: Chaparral

Marinade:
  1/2 cup soy sauce
  2 cloves garlic, pressed
  2 tsp. fresh lemon juice
  1/2 cup orange juice
  1/2 tsp. each lemon rind
  and orange rind

6 large swordfish steaks,
  cut 3/4-inch thick
Butter: 1/2 cup softened
  butter,
1/3 cup almonds, chopped
Garnish: whole almonds,
  lemon slice and
  orange slice

Combine soy sauce, garlic, lemon juice, orange juice, lemon and orange rind. Pour over fish in glass dish and marinate several hours, turning once. While fish is marinating, combine butter and chopped almonds. Pour into shell butter molds and chill until serving time. Prepare grill. Grill fish turning once and basting often for 20 minutes or until fish flakes easily with fork. Put fish on plate, add 2 butter molds and sprinkle with whole almonds.

Garnish: I use a lemon wedge and cut outer rind almost all the way down, add orange slice. Do same for orange and add lemon slice. Makes a colorful garnish.

Alternative: Pompano

GRILLED SWORDFISH SONORA WITH AVOCADO HOLLANDAISE

Preparation time: 15 minutes
Marinating time: 2 hours
Cooking time: 10 minutes
Serves: 6

Chef: Nancy Thorne
Yacht: Fancy Free

Marinade:
6 (8 oz.) swordfish steaks
1/2 cup olive oil
1/4 cup gold tequila
1/4 cup fresh lime juice
1 tsp. minced garlic
1 jalepeno pepper, minced
2 Tblsp. cilantro minced
sliver of red pepper &
    cilantro

Avocado Hollandaise Sauce:
3 egg yolks
1 lime, squeezed
1 dash Tabasco sauce
2 Tblsp. cilantro, chopped
1/2 lb. butter, melted
1/2 avocado, cubed
salt and pepper

Combine all marinade ingredients and pour over swordfish. Marinate for two hours, turning once. For best flavor, prepare grill with mesquite chips.   Grill fish about 5 minutes on each side, basting frequently.   Top with avocado hollandaise.

Avocado Hollandaise Sauce: Blend egg yolks, lime juice, Tabasco and cilantro in blender. Slowly add hot melted butter. When thickened add avocado, salt and pepper; blend 30 seconds.

Serve with Seafood Gumbo, Southwestern Rice, Stuffed Zucchini and Mango Flan. Serve with a good Chardonnay, i.e. Iron Horse or Leeward.

TILEFISH

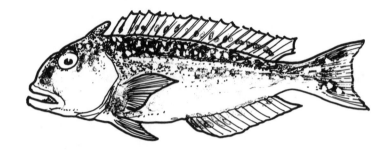

Description: The common Tilefish is a gaily colored, stout - bodied fish with a bluish to olive - green back that fades into a yellow - gold and rose on its sides and belly. It has moderately large scales.

Size: Tilefish grow up to 50 pounds but are usually marketed at 6 to 8 pounds

Habitat: Tilefish live from Nova Scotia to southern Florida and in the Gulf of Mexico. It is a deep water fish that is found along the outer limits of the continental shelf at a depth of about 300 to 1000 feet.

Flavor: Tilefish have an unusually firm yet tender flesh which is best compared to the lobster or scallop.

Preparation: Tilefish can be cooked by a variety of methods including poaching, baking, broiling, deep - frying, smoking and cut into cubes to make chowders.

Other names: Tile Bass

FRUIT SALAD WITH TILEFISH

Preparation time: 15 minutes   *Chef: Jan Robinson*
Cooking time: 10 minutes   *Yacht: Vanity*
Serves: 6

1-1/2 lbs. tilefish fillets   **1/2 cup slivered almonds,**
1 avocado, peeled and sliced   **blanched and toasted**
1 Tblsp. lemon juice   **1/2 cup mayonnaise, or**
2 cups orange sections   **salad dressing**
1-1/2 cups chopped celery   **Romaine lettuce**

Place fillets in boiling salted water. Cover and simmer for about 10 minutes, or until fish flakes easily when tested with a fork. Drain and cool. Break fish into large pieces. Sprinkle avocado with lemon juice to prevent discoloration. Reserve 6 avocado slices and 6 orange sections for garnish. Cut remaining avocado and orange into 1-inch pieces. Combine all ingredients, except salad greens. Chill. Shape the salad mixture into a mound on salad greens and garnish with alternative slices of avocado and orange.

Alternatives: Rockfish, Striped bass

Hint: Lemon cups are great filled with tartar sauce, fruit sherbet, pickle chips or relish and provide a colorful garnish to a fish platter. To make lemon cups, cut lemons crosswise, ream out juice carefully and scoop out pulp lining. Cut a slice from the bottom so that cups will stand upright. (Scallop or notch edges as you cut)

TROUT

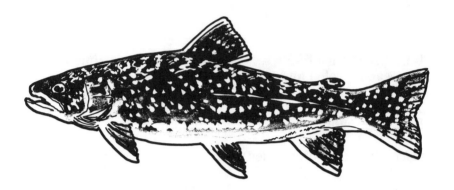

Description: The Spotted Seatrout is prized as a game and food fish. It has a relatively long, slender body. The upper jaw possesses two large, curved canine teeth. The back is usually a dark silvery gray with a bluish tint; the sides are silvery. Round black spots are distributed on the back, upper sides, and the second dorsal fin.

Size: They may live as long as 10 years and weigh as much as 10 pounds. However, the average catch weighs 1 to 5 pounds and measures 8 to 30 inches.

Habitat: It is found year-round on the Atlantic and Gulf coasts from New York to the northern part of Mexico. However, populations north of North Carolina tend to leave in early winter and return the next spring.

Flavor: The meat spoils rapidly so extra care should be taken to chill it at all times and to prepare it as soon as possible. The white flesh is fine and delicately flavored with a moderate fat content.

Preparation: It may be fried, baked, or broiled after stuffing with crabmeat.

Other names: Speckled trout, sea trout, weakfish

GYPSY FISH

Preparation time: 20 minutes
Cooking time: 20-25 minutes
* (or microwave 5-8 minutes)*
Serves: 4

Chef: Suzan Salisbury
Yacht: Gypsy

2 lbs. white fish (trout)
salt and pepper, to taste
aluminum foil *
1 medium tomato, thinly
** sliced circles**
1 green bell pepper, thinly
** sliced circles**

1 medium onion, thinly sliced
4-8 mushrooms, sliced
4 Tblsp. lemon juice
2 cloves garlic, minced
4 Tblsp. margarine

Garnish: lemon wheels

Peheat oven to 350 degrees F. Wash fish and pat dry. Salt and pepper to taste. Place in baking dish lined with enough aluminum foil to wrap and seal fish and ingredients. Arrange tomato, bell pepper, onion and mushrooms on top of fish. Pour lemon juice over. Sprinkle with garlic and dot with margarine. Carefully fold together the foil to seal the contents for baking. Bake at 350 degrees F. for 20-25 minutes.

*To microwave: use a one gallon ziplock plastic bag, instead of foil.

Your order Sir

RAINBOW TROUT WITH SAUCE LOUIS

Preparation time: 20 minutes   *Chef: Jan Robinson*
Cooking time: 14 minutes (microwave)   *Yacht: Vanity*
Chilling time: 1 hour 30 minutes
Serves: 2

Sauce Louis:
1/4 cup mayonnaise
3 Tblsp. chili sauce
2 Tblsp. sliced scallion
1/2 tsp. grated lemon peel
1 tsp. lemon juice
pepper
1/4 cup heavy cream,
  whipped

1 Tblsp. chopped fresh
  parsley
1 tsp. grated orange peel
1/4 tsp. salt
6 peppercorns
1 bay leaf, broken in half
2 drawn rainbow trout,
  1/2 lb. each

1/4 cup water
1/4 cup dry white wine
1 small onion, sliced
1 carrot, thinly sliced

Garnish: sieved egg yolks,
  chopped scallions, spinach
  leaves and tomato wedges

For Sauce Louis, combine the first 6 ingredients; fold in whipped cream. Cover with plastic wrap; refrigerate 1 hour. Combine next 9 ingredients in 12x8x2-inch microwave-safe baking dish. Cover with plastic wrap, turning back one edge to vent. Microwave on HIGH (100%) power 4 to 6 minutes. Uncover; place trout in dish and re-cover with plastic wrap, turning back one edge to vent. Microwave on HIGH (100%) power 6 to 8 minutes per pound or until fish flakes easily, rotating dish once. Remove cooked fish to platter. Remove skin from top side of fish; leave head and tail skin attached. Cool 30 minutes. Carefully cut down back of fish and lift off top portion; remove bones. Place 1/4 of sauce on each fish; spread evenly. Replace top portions; frost with remaining sauce. Decorate with rows of egg yolk and scallion strips to make a striped design. Surround the trout with spinach leaves; outline with tomato wedges.

TROUT IN BANANA CURRY SAUCE

Preparation time: 20 minutes
Cooking time: 20 minutes
Serves: 4

Chef: Jan Robinson
Yacht: Vanity

4 whole trout, 12 oz. each, dressed
1 cup evaporated milk
1 cup cornflake crumbs
melted butter
2 cups boiled rice

Garnish: fresh or dried grated coconut, 2 hard cooked eggs, mashed

Banana Curry Sauce:
4 Tblsp. butter
4 Tblsp. flour
2 cups milk, room temperature
1/2 tsp. onion juice
2 Tblsp. curry powder
1/2 ground ginger
1 egg yolk
2 firm bananas

Preheat oven to 350 degrees F. Dip trout in evaporated milk and dust with cornflake crumbs. Place fish belly down on foil in an oven pan. Drizzle with melted butter and cook at 350 degrees F. for about 20 minutes, or until nicely browned. Arrange fish over a bed of rice in "swimming" position. Pour hot Banana Curry Sauce over each portion. Ring with grated coconut and sprinkle mashed egg over sauce.

Banana Curry Sauce:
Melt butter in saucepan. The instant it is melted, remove from heat, then sprinkle with flour, spoon by spoon, and stir in until well blended. Slowly add the milk and onion juice, stirring constantly. Sauce will become smooth and faintly yellow. Combine curry powder and ginger in a cup. Add several spoons of the warmed milk and stir to make a paste. When smooth, add paste to the sauce. Put pan back over heat and continue stirring over low heat until sauce starts to thicken. Have egg yolk in a cup. Pour several spoons of now hot sauce on yolk, blend, and stir into the rest of the sauce. Quarter bananas and cut in fingers. Add bananas to sauce and stir until thick. Makes 3 cups.

Note: If you prefer to use trout fillets, buy 4 trout 12 oz. each, dressed, boned and butterflied.

Alternative: Grouper fillets

TUNA

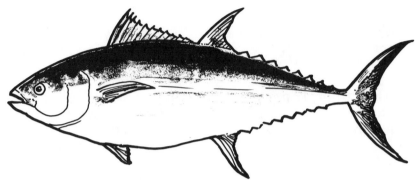

Description: From the Albacore to the Yellowfin, the Tuna has been around since the beginning of recorded time. Today it's still popular throughout the world, from the small Skipjack and Blackfin to the giant Bluefin. These smooth blue-gray torpedo shaped fish, with long pectoral fins, move around the oceans in schools, covering long distances.

Size: Depending on the Tuna species the average sizes can run from a small 10 - 20 pounds to the great Bluefins of 400 - 600 pounds.

Habitat: While each variety has a particular area it habitats, generally there is some species in every ocean and sea of the world.

Flavor: Tuna is a very unusual fish in that the taste undergoes considerable change when cooked. When eaten raw it doesn't have a fish flavor. Its more like a soft-textured thin sliced fillet of aged beef. But when its cooked, it becomes firm and changes its flavor to a mild fish-like taste.

Preparation: The Tuna is marketed fresh, frozen or canned. It comes as fillets or steaks and can be baked, broiled or prepared as tuna salad. In some areas of the world the Tuna is cooked, then refrigerated overnight and served the next day either as a hot or cold dish.
Sashimi, the japanese style of preparing and eating raw fish is very popular with Tuna. However, it would be wise to use only "cold-water" Tuna for that dish.

Other names: Albacore, Bigeye, Blackfin, Bluefin, Bonito, Little Tunny, Skipjack and Yellowfin

FISH FONDU

Preparation time: 20 minutes   *Chef: Mary Usmar*
Cooking time: varies   *Yacht: Voyager*
Serves: 4

2 lbs. tuna, or any red-fleshed fish
oil

Cut fish into bite-size pieces and proceed as with meat fondu.
Invent dips. Chutney - Seafood Cocktail Sauce - tartar sauce -
curry in yogurt - lemon butter - chili sauce - sweet mustard sauce.
Serve with fluffy rice and a tossed green salad

Note: a shrimp fondu is also good.

TUNA AND PEA SALAD IN SHELLS

Preparation time: 10 minutes   *Chef: Nancy May*
Cooking time: 20 minutes   *Yacht: Oh Be Joyful*
Serves: 6

1 box jumbo pasta shells   **1 tsp. lemon juice**
1 (9 oz.) pkg. frozen sweet peas **1/2 tsp. dill weed**
1/2 cup celery, chopped   **1/2 cup sour cream**
2 Tblsp. green onion, chopped   **1/4 cup mayonnaise**
2 cans tuna, drained   **Garnish: bibb lettuce**

Cook shells and chill. Blanch the peas and chill. Combine
remaining ingredients, add to peas and chill. Stuff shells with tuna
mixture and place on bibb lettuce.

Great way to serve tuna salad. Serve with a fruit salad.

TUNA GLAZED WITH GINGER AND LIME

Preparation time: 15 minutes
Cooking time: 7 minutes
Chilling time: 1 hour
Serves: 6

Chef: Jan Robinson
Yacht: Vanity

6 1-inch thick tuna steaks
(about 6 oz. each)
3 Tblsp. fresh lime juice
2 Tblsp. low-sodium soy
sauce
3 garlic cloves, crushed
3 tsp. grated fresh ginger

3 tsp. oriental sesame oil
1 tsp. minced seeded fresh
hot chili (such as jalapeno)
or pinch of dried red
pepper flakes (optional)
1 tsp. sugar

Arrange fish in shallow ceramic or glass baking dish. Whisk remaining ingredients together in small bowl. Pour marinade over fish and turn to coat. Cover with plastic and let marinate 30 minutes at room temperature or 1 hour in refrigerator, turning fish once or twice and spooning marinade over.

Preheat broiler. Transfer fish to broiler pan or ridged foil pan and spoon some marinade over. Broil 4 inches from heat source until glazed and golden, basting twice with marinade, about 3 minutes. Carefully turn fish over and spoon remaining marinade over. Broil until glazed and just cooked through, basting once with marinade in pan, about 3 minutes; do not overcook. Transfer to plates. Spoon pan juices over and serve.

Alternatives: Dolphin

INDIVIDUAL TUNA FISH PIES

Preparation time: 25 minutes
Cooking time: 20-25 minutes
Serves: 4

Chef: Ann Glenn
Yacht: Encore

2 slices white bread, torn in
   pieces
1 cup tuna, drained and
   flaked (cooked or canned)
1/2 cup shredded sharp
   cheddar cheese
1/4 cup milk

1 Tblsp. cider vinegar
1 tsp. grated onion
1/4 tsp. salt
1/8 tsp. pepper
2 eggs
pie crust mix for 2 - 9 inch
   crusts

For filling: Combine bread, tuna, cheese, milk, vinegar, onion, salt, pepper and 1 egg. Stir and set aside. Prepare piecrust mix as label directs. Roll out half of pastry. With knife, cut pastry into four fish shapes, 8 x 4. Place on large cookie sheet. Spoon 1/4 of tuna mixture onto center of each pastry fish. Roll out remaining pastry to make four more fish shapes for top crusts.

Preheat oven to 400 degrees F. Moisten edges of bottom pastry shape. Gently place top pastry shape over tuna filling. With fork, press edges together, all around to seal. Beat remaining egg and brush surfaces of fish. Bake 20-25 minutes until lightly browned. *Serve hot, room temperature or cold - especially nice for picnic fare.*

 *Hint: Freeze fresh fish or shimp in cold water to retain freshness and lessen ordor when cooking.*

ELEGANT TUNA

Preparation time: 15 minutes   *Chef: Jan Robinson*
Cooking time: 35 minutes   *Yacht: Vanity*
Serves: 6

2 (6-1/2 oz.) cans tuna, drained 1/4 cup finely chopped
1 (10 oz.) pkg. frozen   onion
   asparagus, defrosted, or 1/2 cup sour cream
   1 bunch fresh   1/4 cup sliced black olives
1 (10-3/4 oz.) mushroom soup   2 Tblsp. melted butter
1 pint cottage cheese   1/2 cup bread crumbs

Preheat oven to 350 degrees F. Drain and flake tuna. Reserve six asparagus spears. Cut remainder into 1/4-inch pieces. Mix tuna, asparagus, soup, cottage cheese, onion, sour cream and olives. Pour into a greased two-quart casserole. Add bread crumbs to melted butter and sprinkle over top. Bake at 350 degrees F.for 30 minutes, or until browned on top. During last 10 minutes of baking time, steam asparagus spears. When casserole is done, garnish with asparagus spears. *Serve with a crisp green salad and and chilled white or rose wine.*

GOLDEN TUNA COCKTAIL DIP

Preparation time: 5 minutes   *Chef: Anne Evans*
Chilling time: 3 hours   *Yacht: Golden Skye*
Serves: 6-8

2 (7-1/2 oz.) cans tuna,   1/2 small tin pineapple
   drained well   chunks, drained
3 Tblsp. mayonnaise   1/2 small tin mandarin
3 Tblsp. cream cheese,   oranges, drained
   softened

Combine tuna with mayonnaise and cream cheese, flaking the tuna but not breaking it up completely. Add the fruit, stirring gently. Chill for three hours. *Serve garnished with the extra fruit and with the crackers of your choice.*

CREAMY TUNA GARDEN "PIZZA'

Preparation time: 20 minutes   *Chef: Ann Glenn*
Cooking time: 10 minutes   *Yacht: Encore*
Chilling time: 1 hour 10 minutes
Serves: 6-8

2 cups Bisquick
1/2 cup cold water
8 oz. pkg. cream cheese,
    softened
1/2 cup mayonnaise
1/2 cup green onions,
    chopped
2 tsp. prepared horseradish
1/8 tsp. hot sauce

1 (6-1/2 oz.) can tuna,
    drained
assorted fresh vegetables:
    (sliced mushrooms,
    cherry tomatoes,
    broccoli florets, zucchini
    rounds, celery slices,
    chopped onion, etc.)
cheese, grated

Heat oven to 450 degrees F.   Combine Bisquick and water, mix until soft dough forms. Beat vigorously, 20 strokes. Pat dough in 12-inch ungreased pizza pan, with floured hands, forming 1/2-inch rim. Bake about 10 minutes. Cool 10 minutes.

Combine next six ingredients and spread evenly over the crust. Top with vegetables in decorative pattern to simulate "pizza". Finish with grated cheese. Cover and refrigerate at least an hour. Serve. Refrigerate any remaining.

Can be a luncheon dish, or an appetizer, presented whole, with guests cutting their own bite-sized pieces.

Hint: *Sprinkle a little salt into the frying pan to prevent spattering.*

GRILLED FRESH TUNA
WITH HERBS

Preparation time: 10 minutes   *Chef: Jan Robinson*
Marinating time: 15 minutes   *Yacht: Vanity*
Cooking time: 6 minutes
Serves: 4 - 6

2 lbs. fresh tuna, preferably   **3 Tblsp. freshly squeezed**
  from the belly portion   **lemon juice**
freshly ground black pepper   **4 strips lemon rind**
1/3 cup olive oil   **1/4 tsp. red pepper flakes**
6 sprigs fresh thyme   **2 Tblsp. melted butter**
4 cloves garlic, crushed   **Garnish: lemon wedges**
                                  and parsley flakes

Heat charcoal, gas grill or broiler to high. Sprinkle tuna with pepper on both sides. Place oil in a flat dish and add thyme, garlic, lemon juice, lemon rind and hot red pepper flakes. Add tuna and coat on both sides. Marinate for about 15 minutes. Remove tuna from the marinade. Add butter to marinade and place the dish in a warm place.

If the tuna is to be cooked on a charcoal or gas grill, place it directly on the grill, fatty side down, and cook, turning often, 5 to 6 minutes. If it is to be cooked under a broiler, arrange tuna on a rack, fatty side up. Broil about 2 inches from heat, leaving broiler door partly open. Cook 3 minutes and turn; continue cooking 2 minutes. Transfer tuna to marinade. Turn tuna to coat on both sides. Cut into thin slices and serve. Garnish.

Serve with *Maitre d' hotel Butter and new small red boiled potatoes, along with a tomato and onion salad.

*Maitre d'hotel Butter: Blend 2 ounces of softened butter with 1 Tablespoon finely chopped parsley. Then add a squeeze of lemon juice and freshly ground black pepper. Roll butter into a tube shape, wrap tightly in wax paper, chill or freeze. Slice off as needed.

TROPICAL ALBACORE SALAD

Preparation time: 25 minutes   *Chef: Jan Robinson*
Cooking time: 8 minutes   *Yacht: Vanity*
Serves: 4

1-1/2 lbs albacore (tuna), loin cuts or steaks
water

Tropical Dressing:
  6 Tblsp. low-fat plain yogurt
  2 Tblsp. sour cream
  2 Tblsp. chutney
  2 tsp. grated ginger root
  3 tsp. lime juice

1 lemon sliced
1 medium onion, sliced
1 bay leaf
peppercorns, to taste
1/4 cup diced celery
1/2 tsp. grated lime rind
1/2 cup sliced grapes
1/4 cup chopped green onion

Garnish: Lettuce leaves and 2 Tblsp. sliced roasted almonds

Rinse albacore with cold water. Pat dry. Place albacore in large skillet in just enough water to cover. Season water with lemon and onion slices, bay leaf and black peppercorns to taste. Cover and simmer. Cook 8 minutes per inch of fish measured at its thickest point. Do NOT overcook. Albacore should be pink in center when removed from heat. Drain, cool and break into large chunks. While albacore is cooling make dressing (see recipe below). Toss albacore and grapes with dressing. *Serve on bed of lettuce and garnish with almonds.*

Tropical Dressing: Combine yogurt, sour cream, chutney, ginger root, lime juice, green onion, celery and lime rind. Blend well.

Alternatives: Tilefish

TURBOT

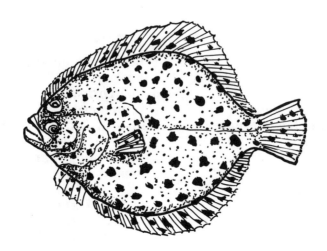

Description: The Turbot is markedly diamond - shaped in outline and when they are fresh caught the upper or left side is brownish - gray with speckles,the right side is opaque white.

Size: Turbot grow up to 30 pounds, but the average sold at the market in Europe is in the 10 to 14 pound size. In the United States they are sold as fillets and therefore are much smaller in size.

Habitat: The Turbot is very abundant in Europe from the Black Sea around through the Mediterranean and into the east Atlantic north to the Baltic.

Flavor: This European delicacy is prized for its firm white flesh with a delicate and moist taste.

Preparation: While they are sold fresh in Europe they are usually filleted and frozen when shipped to the United States. It is best when baked and or stuffed and baked. Sauces blend well with this fish.

SMOTHERED TURBOT GRATIN

Preparation time: 15 minutes
Cooking time: 25 minutes
Serves: 4-6

Chef: Jean Crook
Yacht: Dileas

2 Tblsp. butter
1/2 cup onion, finely chopped
1/2 cup celery, finely chopped
1/3 cup mushrooms,
    finely chopped

2 Tblsp. pimiento, chopped
1/2 tsp. grated lemon rind
1-1/2 lb. turbot fillets
gratin topping
Lemon egg cream sauce*

Preheat oven to 375 degrees F. In skillet melt butter, cook onions, celery and mushrooms over low heat for five minutes or until tender. Increase heat to evaporate moisture. Remove vegetables with slotted spoon. Transfer to a greased 6 cup gratin dish. Sprinkle pimento and lemon rind over vegetables. Add more butter to skillet if necessary. Saute fillets till outer edge is firm. Arrange on vegetables. Sprinkle with gratin topping. Bake 375 degrees F. for 20 minutes until topping is crisp.

*Sauce: Take 2 cups beurre manie and 1/2 cup heavy cream and reduce over low heat to 2 cups. Add one tablespoon lemon juice. Swirl in 1 tablespoon butter.

Serve with tossed salad or crispy cooked green beans.

Alternative: Flounder, Sole

TURBANS FLORENTINE

Preparation time: 25 minutes   *Chef: Jan Robinson*
Cooking time: 20-25 minutes   *Yacht: Vanity*
Serves: 4 -6

4 to 6 skinless Turbot fillets,   **1/8 tsp. salt & pepper**
  6 to 8 inches long   **1/4 cup melted margarine**
1 box (6-1/2 oz.) seasoned   **1 beaten egg**
  bread crumbs   **1/4 tsp. thyme**
1 pkg. (1 oz.) frozen, chopped   **1/8 tsp. pepper**
  spinach, well drained   **pimento for garnish**
1/2 cup chopped celery   **shrimp sauce**

Preheat oven to 350 degrees F.   Rinse fillets and pat dry. Place fillets on a work counter. Sprinkle with salt and pepper. In a large mixing bowl, combine breadcrumbs, spinach and remaining ingredients except pimento and sauce. Place a scoopful of stuffing on each fillet. With thin end of fillet on top, skewer ends of fish together with wooden picks.   Stand turbans on end in lightly greased baking dish. Bake at 350 degrees F. for 20 to 25 minutes or until fish is opaque and flakes.   Extra stuffing can be baked separately or used in another meal.

Shrimp Sauce: Combine one can (10-1/2 oz) cream of shrimp soup, 1/2 cup chopped shrimp and 1/4 cup milk. Heat and pour over turbans. Garnish with pimento strips.

Alternatives: Snapper, Flounder, Halibut

TURBOT STUFFED AND BAKED

Preparation time: 15 minutes
Cooking time: 20 minutes
Serves: 6 - 8

Chef: Jan Robinson
Yacht: Vanity

3 lbs. Turbot fillets
1/2 - 1/3 lb. Monterey Jack
   cheese
1 lb. any moist stuffing
1 (7-1/2 oz.) can crabmeat

real mayonnaise
2 cloves garlic, crushed
paprika

Garnish: Orange twists and
   parsley sprigs

Preheat oven to 375 degrees F. Slice cheese approximately 1/4-inch thick. Mix stuffing with crab meat and garlic. Lay each fillet flat. Place one slice of cheese on each fillet. Divide the stuffing mixture into eight and spread on each fillet. Wrap the turbot fillet around the stuffing and cheese. Secure with toothpicks. Spread mayonnaise liberally over top of stuffed turbot. Sprinkle with paprika. Bake about 20 minutes. *Serve with fresh buttered steamed spinach, boiled baby carrots and rice.*

Note: Sometimes I double the crabmeat and omit the mayonnaise and cheese.

Alternatives: Flounder, Sole, Halibut

WEST INDIAN WHALE

Preparation time: 4 weeks   *Chef: Jan Robinson*
Cooking time: 5 weeks   *Yacht: Vanity*
Serves: 3,500

1 whale, large
1 truckload potatoes,
   chopped
1 truckload carrots, chopped

2 wheel barrow loads of
   onions, thinly sliced
Sea salt and pepper

Garnish: Sea grape leaves

Peel whale and cut into 1-inch squares, this should take about 4 weeks. Place in a 500 gallon pot. Add potatoes, carrots and onions. Salt and pepper to taste. Cook 5 weeks over a kerosene stove at 650 degrees F.
Garnish. Drain oil and blubber!!!

Note: This may be cooked in a microwave oven, if there is one available. Cooking time can then be cut to two weeks if cooked on HIGH.

TABLE OF EQUIVALENTS
UNITED STATES AND METRIC

U.S.	EQUIVALENTS	METRIC *volume-milliliters*
Dash	Less than 1/8 tsp.	
1 teaspoon	60 drops	5 ml
1 Tablespoon	3 teaspoons	15 ml.
2 Tablespoons	1 fluid ounce	30 ml.
4 Tablespoons	1/4 cup	60 ml.
5-1/3 Tablespoons	1/3 cup	80 ml.
6 Tablespoons	3/8 cup	90 ml.
8 Tablespoons	1/2 cup	120 ml.
10-2/3 Tablespoons	2/3 cup	160 ml.
12 Tablespoons	3/4 cup	180 ml.
16 Tablespoons	1 cup or 8 oz.	240 ml.
1 cup	1/2 pint or 8 oz.	240 ml.
2 cups	1 pint	480 ml.
1 pint	16 oz.	480 ml.
1 quart	2 pints	960 ml.
2.1 pints	1.05 quarts	1 liter
2 quarts	1/2 gallon	1.9 liter
4 quarts	1 gallon	3.8 liters

		weight-grams
1 ounce	16 drams	28 grams
1 pound	16 ounces	454 grams
1 pound	2 cups liquid	
1 kilogram	2.20 pounds	

A

Abalone, 29
  Abalone in Chili Sauce, 30
  Abalone "Paua" Fritters, 31
  Bahamian Crack Conch, 62
  Battered Conch with Red Sauce, 63
  Goombay Conch Chowder, 69
  Cornmeal Conch Fritters, 71
Angler (see Goosefish)
Appetizers
  Battered Conch with Red Sauce,63
  Bayou Shrimp, 215
  Beer Crab Puffs, 81
  Boiled Shrimp, 207
  Calamari Rings, 243
  Caviar Pie, 45
  Caviar Souffle, 43
  Chaparral Crab Cakes, 82
  Cheese Crab Dip, 78
  Clam Stuffed Mushrooms, 52
  Crabbies A La Scamp, 85
  Crab Dip, 79
  Freezer Crab Puffs, 83
  Golden Goujons, 235
  Golden Tuna Cocktail Dip, 260
  Hot Crab Meat Canapes, 86
  Marinated Shrimp, 214
  Native Sun's Canapes, 169
  Oyster Hors d'oeuvre, 156
  Pasta Shells Stuffed with Scallop
    Seviche, 196
  Seviche, 189
  Shrimp Pate, 208
  Smoked Salmon Canapes, 168
  Suzi's Sister's Shrimp Spread, 206
  Swiss Crab Bites, 87
Atlantic Butterfish
  Use any Mackerel recipe
Available Market Forms, 12
Avocado Hollandaise Sauce, 247

B

Butters:
  Almond Butter, 262
  Maitre d' hotel Butter,262

Banana Curry Sauce, 255
Basic White Sauce, 178
Bass, Channel (see Red Drum)
Bass, Red (see Red Drum)
Bass, Striped (see Striped Bass)
Bass, Tile (see Tilefish)
Beer Batter, 201
Black Sea Bass
  Broiled Catfish, 40
  Hot and Spicy Chowder, 232
  Indonesian Fish, 145
  Snapper with Curried Rice,230
BBQ Marinade, 175
Blueberry Mayonnaise, 188
Bluefish, 32
  Breakfast Bluefish, 33
  Greek Style Bluefish, 33
Bonefish, 34
  Caribbean Bonefish, 35
Bone Structure, 19
Braising, 26
Breakfasts:
  Breakfast Bluefish, 3
  Clam Corn Griddle Cakes, 56
  Golden Caviar Crepes, 46
  Tomatoes Stuffed with Cod, 59

C

Calamari, (see Squid)
Carp, 36
  Caribbean Carp, 37
Catfish, 38
  Broiled Catfish Steaks, 40
  Catfish Caribbean, 39
Caviar, 41
  Caviar Pie, 45
  Caviar Potato Salad, 42
  Caviar Souffle, 43
  Golden Caviar Crepes, 46
  Potato Cakes with Caviar, 44
  Russian Egg, 42
Champagne Dressing, 117
Champagne Sauce, 165

Channel Bass (see Red Drum)
Chardonnay Sauce, 186
Clams, 47 -49
  Baby Clams China Cloud, 51
  Basic Clam Chowder, 55
  Clam Corn Griddle Cakes, 56
  Clams Linguine, 53
  Clam Stuffed Mushrooms, 52
  Elegant Cream Clam Chowder, 54
  Quick 'n' Easy Clam Chowder, 56
  Spicy Clams in Oyster Sauce, 50
  Spinach Soup with Clams and
      Plenty of Garlic, 57
  Steamed Shellfish Platter, 135
Coconut Cream Mayonnaise, 148
Cod, 58
  Golden Sea Food Pastries, 59
  Fish 'n' Chips, 201
  Tomatoes Stuffed with Cod, 59
  Virgin Island Red Cod, 60
Conch, 61
  Abalone in Chilli Sauce, 30
  Abalone "Paua" Fritters, 31
  Bahamian Crack Conch, 62
  Battered Conch with Red Sauce, 63
  Carib Conch Salad, 64
  Cayman Conch Fritters, 72
  Clams Linguine, 53
  Conch and Egg Salad, 65
  Conch Chowder, 68
  Conch Curry, 66
  Conch Fusion, 64
  Conch Marinara, 68
  Conch Salad, 65
  Cornmeal Conch Fritters, 71
  Crisp Conch, 62
  Goombay Conch Chowder, 69
  Italian Conch Salad, 67
  Manhattan Conch Chowder, 67
  Paella Caribiana, 134
  Star Conch Fritters, 71
  Sweet and Sour Conch over Rice, 66
  West Indian Stewed Conch, 70

Cooking Methods: 22,23
  Baking, 22
  Braising, 26
  Broiling, 24
  Deep Frying, 24
  Grilling, 23
  Planking, 26
  Poaching, 25
  Sauteing, 24
  Steaming, 25
Cookware, 18
Court Bouillon, 238
Crab, 73 -75
  Acorn Crabs, 77
  Aubergines with Crab, 89
  Bahamian Stuffed Crab, 91
  Beer Crab Puffs, 81
  Chaparral Crab Cakes, 82
  Cheese Crab Dip, 78
  Cioppino, 224
  Crab and Asparagus Mousse, 78
  Crab, Avocado and Tomato Soup, 91
  Crabbies A La Scamp, 85
  Crab Crepes, 77
  Crab Dip, 79
  Crab Meat Gracie, 79
  Crab Meat 1000, 86
  Crab Shrimp Bake, 80
  Crab Stuffed Christophenes, 76
  Creamy Crab and Spinach, 87
  Daddy's Favorite Seattle Crab
      Souffle, 84
  Freezer Crab Puffs, 83
  Ginger Crab and Corn Soup, 90
  Hot Crab Avocado Salad, 85
  Hot Crab Meat Canapes, 88
  Lobster Aromatique, 122
  Mariners Crab Quiche Delight, 76
  Maryland Style Crab Salad, 83
  Nancy's "Fancy Free' Seafood
      Tortellini with Chardonnay
      Sauce, 186

Salmon Crab Casserole in Pastry
    Shells, 176
Stuffed Snapper Fillets, 229
Swiss Crab Bites, 87
Crawfish (see Crayfish)
Crayfish, 92
Boiled Crayfish, 93
Crayfish with Garlic, 93
Cajun Pasta Langostine, 94
Cream Sauce, 155 & 178
Creme Fraiche, 179
Crepes:
Crab Crepes, 77
Golden Caviar Crepes, 46
Seafood Crepes with
    Tarragon Bernaise, 185
Croaker (see Red Drum)
Cutting Steaks, 21

D

Dedication, 4
Delicious Sauce, 237
Dill Dressing, 173
Dill Mustard Mayonnaise, 223
Dolphin, 95
(this is not Flipper!)
Baked Dolphin (Mahimahi), 98
BBQ Mackerel, 126
Delicious Dolphin Dish, 97
Dolphin and Plantains, 98
Dolphin Delightful, 97
Orange Ginger Fish Steaks, 108
Poisson Cru, 233
The True Tahitian Marinated
    Dolphin, 96
*Tuna Glazed with Ginger and
    Lime, 258*
*West Indian Fish (Roatan
    Style), 228*

Dressings:
Champagne Dressing, 117
Dill Dressing, 173
Lime Coriander Dressing, 183
Orange Lemon Dressing, 172
Tropical Dressing, 263
Vinaigrette Dressing, 220
Vinaigrette Dressing, 129
Dressing & Cutting Techniques, 17-21
Dressing, 18
Filleting, 19 - 21
Pan Dressing, 19
Drum (see Red Drum)

E

Eel, 99
Eel Stewed in Red Burgundy, 100

F

Fancy Marinade, 175
Filleting, 19 - 21
Finfish Selection Guide, 9
Flounder, 101
Baked Flounder, 102
*Cold Sole with a Delicious
    Sauce, 237*
Dishwasher Safe Fish, 235
Drunken Flounder, 103
Fish Fillets with Spinach, 143
Fish Turbans Florentine, 266
Flounder with Apples, 103
Light White Fish Casserole, 102
North Carolina Fish Stew, 160
Smothered Turbot Gratin, 265
*Sole Grenboise with Lemon
    and Capers, 236*
Turbot Stuffed and Baked, 267

G

Galley Gadgets, 18
Garlic Mayonnaise, 170
Goosefish, 104
　Monkfish Brochettes, 105
　Baked Gorda Goosefish, 106
Grilling, 23
Grouper, 107
　Almondine Grouper, 111
　Baked West Indian Mackerel, 127
　Festive Grouper, 109
　Fettucine Al Pesco, 112
　Filet of Baked Snapper in
　　Wine Sauce, 229
　Fish Parmesan, 130
　Fish with Sour Cream, 144
　Golden Grouper, 110
　Grouper Almondine, 109
　Grouper West Indian Style, 112
　Hot and Spicy Chowder, 232
　Krokeatikos Rofus, 111
　Orange Ginger Fish Steaks, 108
　Orange Roughy Fillets in White
　　Wine, 141
　Poisson Cru, 233
　Trout in Banana Curry Sauce, 255
　West Indian Fish (Roatan Style), 228

H

Haddock (see Cod)
Hake (see Cod)
Halibut (see also Flounder and Sole)
　Cioppino, 224
　Light White Fish Casserole, 102
　Turbot Stuffed and Baked, 267
　Turbot Florentine, 266
　West Indian Fish(Roatan Style) 228
Hollandaise Sauce, 179
Hors d'oeuvres: (see Appetizers)
How to use **Sea to Shore**, 28

I

Introduction, 2

J

Jack, Pacific, (see Mackerel)

K

Kingfish: (also see Mackerel)
　Kingfish and Fungi, 125

L

Langouste (see Lobster)
Lemon Mayonnaise, 164
Lime Coriander Dressing, 183
Lobster, 113 -115
　Blanquette of Lobster, 120
　Langoustines in Porto, 118
　Lobster Aromatique, 122
　Lobster and Asparagus with Orange
　　Butter Sauce, 121
　Lobster and Pasta Salad with
　　Pesto Sauce, 116
　Lobster Medallions in Garlic
　　Butter, 121
　Lobster Supreme, 122
　Lobster Souffle, 119
　Paella Caribiana, 134
　Patti's Lobster Pasta, 123
　Seafood Italienne, 184
　Shrimp and Lobster Salad with
　　Champagne Dressing in Puff, 117
　Stuffed Lobster, 123
　　Pastry Fish, 11
Lunches:
　Avocados with Shrimp Stuffing, 222
　Blueberry Scallops, 188
　Cold Sole with a Delicious
　　Sauce, 237
　Crab Crepes, 77
　Creamy Tuna Garden "Pizza", 261
　Elegant Tuna, 260
　Mariners Crab Quiche Delight, 76
　Mussels Dingle Style, 136

North Carolina Fish Stew, 160
Octopus Stew, 139
Pasta with Smoked Salmon, 167
Salmon Asparagus Divan, 166
Salmon Salad Delight, 171
Seafood St. Jacques, 190
Steamed Shellfish Platter, 133
Tomatoes Stuffed with Cod, 59

M

Mackerel, 124
Baked West Indian Mackerel, 127
B.B.Q. Mackerel, 126
Broiled Spicy Mackerel, 127
Kingfish and Fungi, 125
Mackerel Vinaigrette, 128
Seafood Linguine, 128
Mahimahi (see Dolpin)
Marinades:
B.B.Q. Marinade, 175
Fancy Marinade, 175
Orange Marinade, 192
Shrimp Marinade, 214
Swordfish Marinade, 245 & 249
Tarragon Marinade, 171
Tequilla Fish Marinade, 245
Marlin, 129
Baked Sport Fish from the
    U.S.Virgin Islands, 130
Fish Parmesan, 130
Mayonnaise:
Blueberry Mayonnaise, 188
Coconut Cream Mayonnaise, 223
Garlic Mayonnaise, 170
Lemon Mayonnaise, 164
Mediterranean Sauce for Cold Fish, 149
Metric Table,
Monkfish (see Goosefish)
Mussels, 131 - 133
Cioppino, 224
Marinated Mussels, 136
Molly Malone Mussels, 135
Mussels Dingle Style, 136

Paella Caribiana, 134
Screaming Stuffed Mussels, 137
Steamed Shellfish Platter, 135

N

Nutrition, 6 - 7
Nutritive and Caloric Value, 8

O

Octopus, 138
Octopus Stew, 139
Squid Slices, 243
Ono, (see Wahoo)
Orange Ginger Sauce, 108
Orange Lemon Dressing, 172
Orange Marinade, 192
Orange Roughy, 140
Baked Fish Mozzarella, 146
Dishwasher Safe Fish, 235
Fillets Wellington, 145
Fish and Kraut Sandwiches, 146
Fish Fillets with Spinach, 143
Fish with Sour Cream, 144
Indonesian Fish, 142
Mild Fish Curry, 147
Orange Roughy Fillets in
    White Wine, 141
Orange Roughy with Fruit and
    Coconut Cream, 148
Orange Roughy Microwaved in
    Lemon Butter, 144
Pan Fried Orange Roughy, 141
Oyster, 150 - 152
Baby Clams China Cloud, 51
International Seafood Chowder, 169
Mama's Favorite Oyster Souffle, 153
Oyster Hors d'oeuvre, 156
Oyster Stew New England Style, 154
Poached Oysters in Cream Sauce, 155
Scalloped Oysters, 154

P

Pan Dressing, 19
Participating Yachts, 280
Pasta:
  Cajun Pasta Langostine, 94
  Clams Linguine, 53
  Creamy Crab and Spinach
    Fettucine, 87
  Donna's Shrimp Scampi, 213
  Fancy Scampi and Fettucine, 210
  Fettucine Al Pesco, 112
  Fettucine with Bay Shrimp, 211
  Nancy's 'Fancy Free' Seafood
    Tortellini with Chardonnay
    Sauce, 186
  Pasta Chantal, 187
  Pasta with Smoked Salmon, 167
  Pasta with Smoked Salmon in
    Dill Dressing, 173
  Pasta Shells Stuffed with Scallop
    Seviche, 196
  Patti's Lobster Pasta, 123
  Salmon Tetrazzini, 167
  Scallop Fettucine with Dill, 184
  Scrumptious Shrimp Scampi, 212
  Seafood Linguine, 128
  Shrimp A La Cynthia, 211
  Shrimp and Spaghetti, 209
  Tropical Fruit, Prawn and Pasta
    Salad, 221
Pesto sauce, 116
Petrale (see Sole and Flounder)
Planking, 26
Poaching, 25
Pompano, 157
  Mediterranean Pompano, 158
  Broiled Spicy Mackerel, 128
  Grilled Swordfish, 247
  *Grilled Swordfish with Almond
    Butter, 248*
Prawn (see shrimp)
Preparation Tips, 15
Pulpo (see Octopus)

Q

Quality Buying, 10 - 11

R

Red Drum, 159

  North Carolina Fish Stew, 160
  Sweet and Sour Fish, 241
Redfish (see Red Drum)
Red Pepper Sauce, 197
Red Sauce, 63
Remoulade Sauce, 207
Rockfish:
  B.B.Q. Salmon Fancy Free, 175
  Cioppino, 224
  Fruit Salad with Tilefish, 251
  *Orange Roughy Fillets in White
    Wine, 141*
  *Poached Salmon and Asparagus
    Spears, 168*
  Snapper with Curried Rice, 230
  Sweet and Sour Fish, 241
  Virgin Island Red Cod, 60
Round, 14
Round Bodied Fish, 19

S

Sailfish (see Marlin)
  *Baked Sport Fish From the U.S.
    Virgin Islands, 130*
  Fish Parmesan, 130
Salads:
  Artichoke and Hearts of Palm, 220
  Carib Conch Salad, 64
  Caviar Potato Salad, 42
  Conch and Egg Salad, 65
  Conch Salad, 65
  Deep Sea Avocado Salad, 220
  Fruit Salad with Tilefish, 251
  Hot Crab Avocado Salad, 85
  Italian Conch Salad, 67

Lobster and Pasta Salad with Pesto Sauce, 116
Maryland Style Crab Salad, 83
Prawns A La Plaka, 225
Russian Egg Salad, 42
Salmon and Avocado Salad, 170
Salmon Salad Delight, 171
Scallop and Cucumber Salad with Coriander Dressing, 183
Seafood Italienne, 184
Shrimp and Lobster Salad with Champagne Dressing, 117
Shrimp Mandarin Salad, 221
Smoked Salmon and Melon Salad,172
Tropical Albacore Salad, 263
Tropical Fruit and Prawn and Pasta Salad, 221
Tuna and Pea Salad in Shells, 257

Salmon, 161 - 162
B.B.Q. Salmon Fancy Free, 175
Confetti Salmon Mousse, 177
Dishwasher Safe Fish, 235
Fillet of Salmon with Zinfandel Sauce, 162
International Seafood Chowder, 169
Native Sun's Canapes, 169
Pasta with Smoked Salmon, 167
Pasta with Smoked Salmon in Dill Dressing, 173
Poached Salmon and Asparagus Spears, 168
Salmon Asparagus Divan, 166
Salmon and Avocado Salad, 170
Salmon, Crab Casserole in Pastry Shells, 176
Salmon en Papillote with Ginger Lime Butter, 174
Salmon with Pears, 166
Salmon Salad Delight, 171
Salmon Steaks with Champagne Sauce, 165
Salmon Supreme, 163
Salmon Tetrazzini, 167
Simple Salmon, 164

Simple Salmon Steaks with Sesame Seeds, 177
Smoked Salmon and Melon Salad, 172
Smoked Salmon Canapes, 168
Sanddab   (see Sole and Flounder)
Sauces:
Avocado Hollandaise Sauce, 249
Banana Curry Sauce, 255
Basic White Sauce, 178
Champagne Dressing, 117
Champagne Sauce, 165
Chardonnay Sauce, 186
Cream Sauce, 155 and 178
Creme Fraiche, 179
Delicious Sauce, 237
Hollandaise Sauce, 179
Mediterranean Sauce for Cold Fish, 149
Orange Ginger Sauce, 108
Pesto Sauce, 116
Red Pepper Sauce, 197
Red Sauce, 63
Remoulade Sauce, 207
Sauce Louis,254
Seafood Sauce, 71
Spicy Mustard Sauce, 110
Tarragon Bernaise Sauce, 185
Zinfandel Sauce, 162
Sauteing, 24
Scaling, 18

Scallops, 180 -182
Blueberry Scallops, 188
Ginger Scallops, 192
Grilled Scallops with Red Pepper Sauce, 197
Lobster Aromatique, 122
Nancy's Fancy Free Seafood Tortellini with Chardonnay Sauce, 186
Orange Roughy with Fruit and Coconut Cream, 148
Orange Scallop Kabobs, 192
Paella Caribiana, 134
Pasta Chantal, 187
Pasta Shells Stuffed with Scallop Seviche, 196

Sauteed Scallops Easy, 194

Scallop and Cucumber Salad with
   Coriander Dressing, 183

Scallop Fettucine with Dill, 184

Scallops Mornay, 194

Scallops en Papillote, 193

Scallops with Plaintains and
   Almonds, 195

Scallops in Tarragon Wine Sauce, 189

Seafood Crepes with Tarragon
   Bernaise, 185

Seafood Italienne, 184

Seafood Kebabs, 245

Seafood Newburg, 183

Seafood St. Jacques, 190

Seviche, 189

Shrimp and Scallops St.
   Germaine, 187

Timbale of Bay Scallops in
   Spinach, 191

Seafood Galley Gadgets and
   Cookware, 16

Seafood Sauce, 71

Seafood Serving Sizes, 14

Sea Trout:
   All recipes used for Salmon may be
      used for Sea Trout.
   *Fillet of Salmon with Crust and
      Zinfandel Sauce, 162*
   North Carolina Fish Stew, 160
   Salmon Supreme, 163
   Simple Salmon, 164

Sea Urchin, 198

Sea Urchin Delicacy, 199

Shark, 200

   Fish 'n' Chips, 201
   Marinated Swordfish, 245
   Seafood Kebobs, 245
   Shark Kebobs, 202
   *Simply Wonderful Swordfish
      Steaks, 246*

Shopping at the Market, 10 - 14

Shrimp, 203 - 205

   Artichokes and Hearts of Palm
      Salad, 220

Avocados with Shrimp Stuffing ,222

Baked Jumbo Shrimp, 226

Barbequed Shrimp, 206

Bayou Shrimp, 215

Boiled Shrimp, 207

Cioppino, 224

Crab Shrimp Bake, 80

Deep Sea Avocado Salad, 220

Donna's Shrimp Scampi, 213

Fancy Scampi and Fettucine, 210

Fettucine with Bay Shrimp, 211

Fish Fondu, 257

Galatoire's Shrimp Poupon, 214

Golden Seafood Pastries, 59

Indian Shrimp Curry, 215

International Seafood Chowder, 169

Marinated Shrimp, 214

Nancy's Fancy Free Seafood
   Tortellini with Chardonnay
   Sauce, 186

Paella Caribiana, 134

Pasta Chantal, 187

Prawns A La Plaka, 225

Scrumptious Shrimp Scampi, 212

Seafood Crepes with Tarragon
   Bernaise, 185

Seafood Italienne, 184

Seafood Kebabs, 245

Seafood St. Jacques, 190

Shrimp A La Cynthia, 211

Shrimp Cruzan, 209

Shrimp Dileas, 216

Shrimp with a Dill Mustard
   Mayonnaise, 223

Shrimp El Greco, 217

Shrimp Fiji, 217

Shrimp Florentine, 218

Shrimp and Lobster Salad with
   Champagne Dressing, 117

Shrimp Louisana, 218

Shrimp Mandarin Salad, 221

Shrimp Newburg, 219

Shrimp Pate, 208

Shrimp & Scallop St. Germaine, 187

Shrimp and Spaghetti, 209
Shrimp and Spinach Quiche, 208
Shrimp and Vegetable Cognac, 219
Stuffed Shrimp Supreme, 222
Suzi's Sister's Shrimp Spread, 206
Tahitian Skillet Shrimp, 213
Tropical Fruit Prawn and Pasta
    Salad, 221
Shrimp Sauce, 254
Spicy Mustard Sauce, 110
Skinning Fillets, 21
Snapper, 227
Filet of Baked Snapper in Wine
    Sauce, 229
Fish Fillets with Spinach, 143
Golden Grouper, 110
Greek Style Bluefish, 33
Hot and Spicy Fish Chowder, 232
Orange Ginger Fish Steaks, 108
Poisson Cru, 233
Snapper Almondine, 231
Snapper with Curried Rice, 230
Stuffed Snapper Fillets, 229
Turbot Turbans Florentine, 236
West Indian Fish (Roatan Style) 228
Sole, 234
Baked Flounder, 102
Cold Sole with a Delicious Sauce, 237
Dishwasher Safe Fish, 235
Golden Coujons, 235
Hot and Spicy Chowder, 232
Indonesian Fish, 145
Light White Fish Casserole, 102
Smothered Turbot Gratin, 265
Sole Grenboise with Lemon and
    Capers, 236
Turbot Stuffed and Baked, 267
Virgin Island Red Cod, 60
Soups and Chowders:
Baby Clams China Cloud, 51
Basic Clam Chowder, 55

Cioppino, 224
Conch Chowder, 68
Crab, Avocado and Tomato Soup, 91
Elegant Creamy Clam Chowder, 54
Ginger Crab and Corn Soup, 90
Goombay Conch Chowder, 69
Hot and Spicy Fish Chowder, 232
International Seafood Chowder, 169
Manhattan Conch Chowder, 67
Quick 'n' Easy Clam Chowder, 56
Red Chowder, 228
Spinach Soup with Clams and Plenty
    of Garlic, 57
Squid, 242
Calamari Rings, 243
Octopus Stew, 139
Squid Slices, 243
Steaming, 25
Stock:
    Court Bouillon, 238
    Fumet, 239
Striped Bass, 240
Fruit Salad with Tilefish, 251
Stuffed Snapper Fillets, 228
Sweet and Sour Fish, 241
Virgin Island Red Cod, 60
Sturgeon (see Caviar)
Suggested Seasonings, 27
Swordfish, 244
Baked Sport Fish from U.S.
Virgin Islands, 130
Fish Parmesan, 130
Grilled Swordfish, 247
Grilled Swordfish Steak with
    Almond Butter, 248
Grilled Swordfish Sonora, 249
Marinated Swordfish, 245
Seafood Kebabs, 245
Simply Wonderful Swordfish
    Steaks, 246
Swordfish Marinade, 245 and 249

T

Tarragon Marinade, 171
Tequila Fish Marinade, 249
Tilefish, 250
Dishwasher Safe Fish, 235
Filet of Baked Snapper in Wine Sauce, 229
Fruit Salad and Tilefish, 251
Hot and Spicy Chowder, 232
Snapper with Curried Rice, 230
Tropical Albacore Salad, 263
Tropical Dressing, 263
Trout, 252
Gypsy Fish, 253
Pan Fried Orange Roughy, 141
Rainbow Trout with Sauce Louis, 254
Trout in Banana Curry Sauce, 255
Tuna, 256
B.B.Q. Mackerel, 126
Creamy Tuna Garden "Pizza", 261
Elegant Tuna, 260
Fish Fondu, 257
Fish Parmesan, 130
Golden Tuna Cocktail Dip, 260
Grilled Fresh Tuna with Herbs, 262
Grilled Swordfish, 247
Individual Tuna Pies, 259
Poisson Cru, 233
Salmon Steaks with Champagne Sauce, 165
Tropical Albacore Salad, 263
The True Tahitian Marinated Dolphin, 96
Tuna Glazed with Ginger and Lime, 258
Tuna and Pea Salad in Shells, 257
Turbot, 264
Fish Turbans Florentine, 266
Smothered Turbot Gratin, 265
Turbot Stuffed and Baked, 267

W

Wahoo:
Dolphin and Plantains, 98
B.B.Q.\Mackerel, 126
Weakfish:
Mild Fish Curry, 148
North Carolina Fish Stew, 160
Whale
West Indian Whale, 268
Whelk:
Abalone in Chilli Sauce, 30
Abalone "Paua" Fritters, 31
Battered Conch with Red Sauce, 63

Z

Zinfandel Sauce, 162

PARTICIPATING YACHTS

Adaro: *Captain Bill Burnes, Chef Jan Burnes*
Adaro is a luxurious 53' Sloop offering 3 identical full-sized double cabins, all with en suite bathrooms. Captain Bill has 3 decades of sailing experience and wife Jan, your hostess, is a trained Cordon Bleu cook who also enjoys Asian and Mediterranean cuisine. Join Adaro for a Gourmet's Cruise.

Adela: *Captain Jerry Keller, Chef Donna Keller*
Adela is a 50' sailing yacht comfortably equipped for a cruising vacation you'll never forget. Come sail crystal clear waters, walk on white sandy beaches and enjoy enchanting tropical nights. Donna and Jerry look forward to making you their freinds.

Alize': *Captain Guy Pyck, Chef Kate Young*
Alize', not just another charter yacht! She's a 55' cutter, customer built in France, fast, spacious, comfortable and oh so pretty. Enjoy fine cuisine, a multitude of watersports and lots of fun in the sun. Kate and Guy, a fun loving couple, welcome you to share this paradise. Won't you join us?

Angel Eyes: *Captain Michael Maloney, Chef Louise Maloney*
Come to paradise and relax on our 41 foot Morgan while we make a video movie of your vacation.

Antipodes: *Captains Manfred &Dieter Zerbe, Chef Ann C. Brown*
Antipodes, an Ocean 60' Schooner accommodates up to 8 guests in 4 equal staterooms. Captains Manfred and Dieter Zerbe have chartered successfully in the Virgin Islands since 1973. Chef Annie Brown holds a bachelor's degree in Food Service Management and has experience as a restauranteur, caterer, and yacht chef.

Bambi: *Captain Bjorn Lundgren, Chef Gunilla Lundgren*
Bambi, a Gulfstar 37' is very spacious for her size. Three separate cabins with two heads. She is owned and operated by Bjorn and Gunilla Lundgren, a Swedish couple with extensive traveling experience. Gunilla loves cooking. Try her Swedish recipes here.

Begone: *Captain and Chef Janet Jacobs*

Bon Vivant: *Captain Jon Reeves, Chef Annie Scholl*
Captain Michael Kelly, Chef Renie Mousek
Bon Vivant, besides being luxuriously appointed and immaculately maintained, is a unique charter boat. We have two crews that alternate every 3 months. This not only guarantees a fresh, lively crew, it enables our guests to pick the couple that best serves their wide range of interests and needs. Bon Vivant - for the best vacation you'll ever have.

Ceo Na Mara: *Captain Gareth Davies, Chef Christine Davies*
Christine and Gareth Davies welcome you aboard Ceo Na Mara, a well appointed Bowman 57 which gives excellent sailing performance and ample shaded deck space for relaxation. Enjoy the delights of Christine's Caribbean and European cuisine. We look forward to making your stay the holiday of your lifetime.

Chaparral: *Captain Jerry Dudley, Chef Jennifer Dudley*
Chaparral - Double XX rated - exciting and exhilarating! The "must see" of the year. A fine performance by Captain Jerry Dudley - he combines great humor with superb sailing skills. His co-star, Jennifer, will delight you with her award-winning culinary talents. Children welcome - parental guidance suggested. Bring your Kleenex, the ending is a real tearjerker!

China Cloud: *Captain Bob Ellmann, Chef Nancy Raye*
China Cloud, an 85 foot custom Ketch designed for superb comfort with four equal guest staterooms. Host Sharon and Bob Ellman assure guest that dining is outstanding on this fabulous yacht. China Cloud's cook Nancy Raye uses these two favorite recipes for lunches or as side dishes for dinners.

Courvoisier: *Captain Nelson DuRant, Chef Suzi DuRant*
Sail the tropic islands of the Caribbean aboard this Morgan 60', accommodating 6 guests in comfort in one queen-sized, 2 double cabins. Snorkeling on colorful reefs - boardsailing in secluded anchorages - relaxing surrounded by clear blue water and white sand beaches - the perfect ingredients for a long-remembered vacation. Join us for a holiday of barefoot elegance aboard the Courvoisier.

Dileas/Finesse: *Captain David Crook, Chef Jean Crook*
Dileas/Finesse is a 60' Gulfstar that takes six guest in comfort. Jean and David understand that for a holiday to be totally relaxing and enjoyable the mixture of people and places must be just right.

Dream Merchant: *Captain Russ Ulrey, Chef Debbie Ulrey*
Dream Merchant, a 60' steel Schooner built in Australia features two oversized queen berth cabins, two double cabins, and full sun awnings over her enormous flush deck. Snorkel the blue Caribbean, try windsurfing, fishing, beachcombing, or just relax.DreamMerchant's   crew specializes in helping you fulfill your "Dream" vacation.

Drumbeat: *Captain Richard Manto, Chef Carole Watkins Manto*
Drumbeat is an Irwin 65' designed just for charter. Four double cabins with their own heads and showers. Luxurious and spacious. Lots of toys, lots of attention, and lots of gourmet food!! "Drumbeat" - The Ultimate Caribbean Vacation!

Elsa Jane: *Captain Dan Castaldo, Chef Elsa Castaldo*
Great food - great sailing - loads of fun. That's what to expect aboard the Elsa Jane. Not sure it's so?? Try us, you'll like it!!!

Elysee': *Captain Craig Tracy, Chef Linda Green*
Elysee' is a 65' lancer motorsailer. She boasts king and queen size staterooms to accommodate four guests in total luxury. Let Craig and Linda teach you to windsurf or waterski, or just lay back, relax and let them pamper you. Come sail "Elysee'" for an unforgettable holiday.

Emerald Lady: *Captain Paul Array, Chef Mardy Array*
Enjoy a totally catered and uniquely tailored charter vacation in the capable hands of your captain and chef. Experience the ambience of an old world galleon filled with every modern convenience. Let us introduce you to the exciting world of sailing, your wants...your desires...your fantasies...are all aboard the "Lady!"

Emily Morgan: *Captain Peter Thomas, Chef Sue Bushnell*
Dreams come true on Emily Morgan. A sleek, sea kindly, well appointed 57 foot Bowman Ketch, accomodating two couples or a family of six. Her experienced, friendly crew may not find Atlantis, but promise you other realms of fantasy. A gourmet adventure, a hedonists delight!

Encore: *Captain Marvin Glenn, Chef Ann Glenn*
Encore's 50' long triple hulls provide spaciousness and privacy on deck and below for groups of 4-6 guests. Great stability under sail and at anchor. We carry the full range of "toys" for active groups. The owner/operators did an 8-year "round-the-world" cruise in a smaller trimaran before buying ENCORE for charter in 1977. They have been chartering in the Virgin Islands since that time.

Falcon: *Captain Ted Beaumont, Chef Joy Smith*

Fancy Free: *Captain John Wolff, Chef Nancy Thorne*
"Fancy Free" is a beautiful high-performance sailboat serving beautiful high-performance cuisine. Nancy is a California Culinary Academy graduate and John is a Marine Life Specialist. So come be wined and dined to your heart's desire on "Fancy Free".

Flower of the Storm: *Captain Skip Crooks, Marita Tasse*
Offering luxury and comfort usually found only on much larger yachts, this 41' Islander Freeport Ketch is yours in paradise! Captain-owner Skip enjoys sharing his sailing knowledge and, with Marita, a naturalist, will guide your explorationof the marine world. Relaxation, conviviality and delectable dining aboard "Flower"!

Chef: LeAnn LaCesa now owns Caribbean Pacific Yacht Charters.

Freight Train: *Captain George Banker, Chef Candice Carson*
A boat who sails as fast as her name
Operated by owners in the charter game
Escape the cold, the frazzles and the mundane
Let your body grow healthy, your mind grow sane
If you have gotten this far, you know poets we're not
But good cooks and fun people reside on this yacht.

Golden Rule: *Captain Shaun Jarvis, Chef Helen L. Bromley*
60 foot schooner designed by Dominique Presle and built by Tecimar of France. White hull and teak decks. 3 double guest cabins equipped with sinks and fans. Excellent family boiat or young party boat !!

Golden Skye: *Captain Winton Evans, Chef Anne Evans*
Golden Skye, a new name on the charter scene but a familiar boat. It is a 63' aluminium ketch designed especially for chartering in the Caribbean. Come and discuss the day's delights, her superb afterdeck over sunset cocktails before enjoying sumptious cuisine in her spacious saloon.

Gracious Lady: *Captain Al Romagnolo, Chef Maureen Romagnolo*
This is the Caribbean vacation you've only dreamt about until now: pampered aboard a 53 foot motor yacht with every conceivable amenity. "Gracious Lady" is a tropical dream vacation come true.

Green Norseman: *Captain Kirk Weick, Chef Sally Chalker*

Gypsy: *Captain Glen C. Allen, Chef Suzan Salisbury*
Custom 65' ketch with four private double cabins, accomodating up to 12 guests. USCG certification. Windsurfing, snorkeling, sailing, fishing, swimming. Cassette stereo, VCR TV, library and underwater camera. A truly amiable crew and delicious meals. Ideal sailing yacht for families and active people.

Iemanja: *Captain Seymour Owen, Chef Carol Owens*
Iemanja is a 68' Irwin. As **Sea to Shore** goes to print, Carol and Seymour go to Newport. They have opened "Carol's Gourmet Gallery".

Illusion II: *Captain Roger Perkins, Chef Ronnie Hochman*
Illusion II is a 55' custom Bruce Roberts design ketch. The large, spacious interior accommodates up to 6 guests comfortably in 3 double staterooms, 2 full baths. Flush deck and center cock pit leave lots of area for outdoor fun.

Impervious Cover: *Captain Scott Tucker, Chef Lyn Tucker*
Imprevious Cover is a 62' sloop waiting to take you away where no one can find you. Be spoiled by this brother and sister team eager to make 2-6 guests feel right at home. Featuring hermit crab racing, halyard swinging, and movie making.

Iskareen: *Captain Bill Bennett, Chef Martha Purinton*
Iskareen is 65' of traditional swan, (hull #4) accommodating up to 6 guests. Learn to windsurf, come snorkeling, enjoy the sun and sea!

Kea 1: *Chef Sylvia F. Schiltz*

Kestral: *Captain Scott Tucker, Chef Jill Cooper*
Kestral is a 57' Bowman Ketch. She has successfully been in the charter circuit for 9 years, and continues so, spending summers in New England and winters in the Caribbean and French West Indies.

Knightwind: *Captain Basil Kazitoris, Chef Julie Fridlington*
Knightwind is your fantasy come true. A 45' ketch designed to make your holiday the most memorable of a lifetime. Experience the unforgettable with Captain Basil and Chef Julie guiding you through the islands. Knightwind caters to up to 4 guests in solid teak comfort.

Kreiss Collection: *Captain Dowl Bond, Chef Laurie Carloni*
Relax and enjoy aboard the Kreiss Collection. The same 65 foot custom motor yacht featured in the movie "Day of the Dolphin". Whether it's diving, snorkeling, waterskiing and fishing or just swimming and sunbathing. You're sure to work up an appetite for the varied and delicious meals and treats from our galley.

Luna De Peponi: *Captain Larry Donahue, Chef Suzanne Leonfellner*

Memories: *Captain Ricky Morales, Chef Nora Frei*
Come to Memories for a taste of heaven on earth. A beautifully appointed yacht, sleek and fast, comfortable and accommodating, equipped with all the toys you'll require. For 1 couple only. Let Ricky and Nora share with you all the splendors of the Caribbean. Let Nora pamper you with her delicious menu tailored specifically to your taste.

Morning Star: *Captain Jim Stewart, Chef Cass Stewart*
The understated elegance of this 46' Kelly/Peterson is enhanced by the fact that she charters for 1 couple, giving you the space and comfort needed to relax and enjoy your vacation. Your experienced crew will serve you a variety of delicious cuisine while anchored at some of the finest beaches in the Caribbean.

Mystique: *Captain Ken Culbert, Chef Kate Hinrichs*
Come aboard Mystique a 50 foot ketch to enjoy a cruise throughout the Caribbean. Ken and Kate can show you private coves or busy harbors. Sail and snorkle the reefs of Anegada. Partake in gourmet meals. A relaxing unique vacation. Contact Ken and Kate, Yacht Mystique, Homeport Inc., St. Thomas, VI 00802.

Natasha: *Chef Carol Lowe*

Native Sun: *Captains and Chefs Stanley and Sylvia Dabney*
"Native Sun" is a Valiant 40' specializing in day charters, snorkeling, lunch and entertaining stories of 40,000 miles of offshore sailing and 13 years of living aboard. As St. Thomas' leading day sailing yacht, we welcome every guest as a friend and treat each new friend as family. We consider beautiful Honeymoon Bay on Water Island, our home in the islands, the place where our love affair with the Caribbean and sailing began 18 years ago.

Nighthawk: *Captain Dave Huffman, Chef Gisela Huffman*
86' Motorsailer, 3 guest cabins. Big, comfortable boat

Non Sequitur: *Captain John Sackett, Chef Vicki Sparks*
Non Sequitur, 56' Bristol sailing yacht has been built for your sailing comfort. "Non Sequitur" means "Does Not Follow". Your vacation aboard Non Sequitur will not follow any other.

Oh Be Joyful: *Captain Phillip May, Chef Nancy May*
Phil and Nancy are owner operators of "Oh Be Joyful", a Gulfstar 50 ketch. They take 2 or 4 guests. They are young and energetic and enjoy active people. Nancy and Phil offer great food, tropical drinks, and home baked goodies served with southern hospitality.

Oklahoma Crude II: *Captain Colin Rees, Chef Kimberly Foote*

Pelikan: *Captain Arlen Wheeler, Chef Marjorie Lallier*
Pelikan, a 46' Sloop captained by owner Arlen Wheeler, was designed specially for service in the Caribbean charter trade. The interior has been extensively customized to accommodate up to 4 guests with privacy and comfort in her new tri-cabin layout, featuring two complete heads with showers and one bathtub.

Perfection: *Captain Skip Lookabaugh, Chef Beth Avore*
Perfection is a Gulfstar 60' sloop. The first Mark II and Gulfstars show boat in 1986. With her roomy salon, deluxe master stateroom, two forward cabins and spacious cockpit, she's perfect for a leisurely cruise through the Virgins or a down-island charter, while providing the comforts of home.

Point of Sail: *Captain Jeff Prentice, Chef Kathryn Prentice*
Point of Sail, a 56' Bristol is available for charter year round in the Caribbean and the Virgin Islands. With a stow-away main, roller job, electric winches and a colorful spinaker (MPS) she is a lively and comfortable sailor under any conditions.

Possible Dream: *Captain Gene Pelland, Chef Elizabeth Tuson*
This 44' Kalik sloop with two double staterooms and private heads, comfortably accommodates 4 guests. Gene and Liz are an enthusiastic, fun duo who enjoy showing guests the Virgin Islands. So, whether your aim is swinging in a hammock (colada in hand), or island exploration, come make that dream vacation "Possible".

Promenade: *Captain David Dugdale, Chef Fiona Baldrey*
Magnificent 60' Trimaran taking up to 10 guests; "Fantastic trip, thoroughly enjoyed all the water activities especially the scuba diving. Great food and wonderful service." A quote from our guest book.

Promises: *Captain Ray Zanusso, Chef Joanne Van Alstine*
           Chef Sharon Strong
A luxurious 52' Irwin Ketch, is carefully maintained as a perfect   Caribbean charter yacht. for 3 couples. We strive to make each week unique and tailor made to our guests wishes. We enjoy serving a varied and flexible gourmet menu and are an enthusiastic but patient crew.

Rajada: *Captain Sol Davidson, Chef Jacqueline Cheetham*
Rajada is a unique 63 ft. wooden boat accommodating six people. She offers a comfortable, happy and relaxing vacation with good company and excellent cuisine. Sol Davidson is an experienced Australian captain, your cook/hostess English and the charming deck/hand, St. Lucian. We know the islands well.. and welcome you

Rampant: *Captain Ivan Seago and Chef Page Hanson*
The Bowman 57' "Rampant" has sailed the Atlantic, Mediterranean, and Indian Ocean with Ivan Seago and Page Hanson as her crew. She has enjoyed the chartering from the sunny Caribbean to the tropical Seychelle Islands to fascinating variety of the Mediterranean. The Rampant accommodates up to 6 guests in 3 cabins and has 2 guests heads.

Ring-Andersen: *Captain Rick Brendlinger, chef Louise Brendlinger*
Ring-Andersen combines old world elegance with new world comforts. An experience not to be missed.

Rising Sun: *Captain sRon Hale and Carolyn Murphy, Chef Paulette Dupuis*
An invitation for your palates delight from Chef Paulette, specializing in gourmet European cuisine...with added interest in Caribbean cooking. Rising Sun, a new powerful 64' Schooner custom designed for six passenger chartering. Rising Sun's exceptional sailing performance, a strong personable crew and recognized cuisine ensure unequaled memories.

Rising Sun 47: *Captain Brooks Kuhn , Chef sTuffis Byden and Brooks kuhn*
Island ways. Island dishes. Island life - that's why you choose the Caribbean. We give you a truly tropical (not topical) experience. Kingfish and fungi over beach campfire, wahoo and plantains, fresh coconut and sugar cane. Island friends, Island music, Island time. Swan 47 soon come.

Sandcastle: *Captain Rik Allen, Chef Ann Gracie*
A relaxed and carefree vacation awaits you when you step aboard "Sandcastle". Your crew, Rik, Ann and Robin, delight in the opportunity to sail with you. Their relaxed and easy going manner will ease you into the island pace. Sail azure waters, indulge in fine cuisine and enjoy invigorating water sports.

Scatteree: *Captain Charles Curren, Chef Peggy Curren*
You'll sail in style aboard "Scatteree" - a luxurious 70' new horizon ketch. Accommodates up to 6 guests in 3 private cabins. There's never a lack of things to do - windsurf, waterski, snorkel or just relax! Gourmet meals served by her professional, friendly crew, makes this vacation one of pure pleasure!

Schooner Windsong: *Captain Colin Day, Chef Karen Day*
A classic 50' wooden schooner "Windsong" has great deck space under a cloud of sail and an unusual 52 year history. Sail the ship's dinghy in quiet harbors and listen to guitar music under the stars. Enticing menus, huge cockpit, owners/crew Colin and Karen, warm and hospitable.

Scorpio: *Captain Arthur Desroches, Chef Patti Messersmith*
The 57' Ketch "Scorpio" was custom designed for comfort and performance. Her luxurious accommodations include 3 double staterooms complete with 2 hot water showers. Dining on board is a unique blend of exquisite food and unforgettable surroundings. From the moment you step aboard, the professional crew will see to your every need and desire.

Sea Cloud: *Captain Paul Preston, Chef Gregor Rohlsson*
Gregor Rohlsson is a 25 year old graduate of Johnson and Wales College who has worked in many fine restaurants in the USA. He is presently Chef on the Sea Cloud, an 85 foot Ketch, captained by Paul Preston. The Sea Cloud is one of the premier charter sailboats in the Caribbean.

September Morn: *Captain Jerry Dudley, Chef Jennifer Dudley*

Sheerwill: *Captain Peo Stenberg, Chefs Marilyn Stenberg and Peo Stenberg*
To sail a swan is to indulge in one of sporting's greatest privileges; to charter the Swan 65 Sheerwill is to create your own personal adventure. Your own private pleasure. Peo and Marilyn will ensure the cruise of a lifetime and tempt you with many dishes from their truly international repertoire.

Silent Joy: *Captain Herb Hale, Chef Mary Woods*
Silent Joy, newest and most deluxe of the Irwin 68's, welcomes you with first-class service and extraordinary cuisine prepared in our fully-equipped galley. Completely air-conditioned, 4 double staterooms with individual heads, and a spacious salon, add to your comfort. On-deck ammenities include, Jacuzzi, Wave Runner, Windsurfer, Waterskis, Third Lung Diving Apparatus, and a 14 ft. Zuma sailboat.

Skeets: *Captain Ted Carr, Chef Holly Carr*
Skeets is 64' Hinckley Ketch. She carries six guests and a crew of two. There is a large owners cabin AFT with one double and one single bed and a large head with shower. There are twin midship cabins with two single bunk style beds. Each has its own head and share a shower. Crews cabin is forward.

Skylark: *Captain Philip, Chef Patricia Bryant*
Skylark is a CSY 44 midcockpit cutter designed and constructed with the comfort and relaxation of our charter guests in mind. From visiting remote Island harbours and snorkeling brilliant coral reefs to windsurfing, shelling and enjoying tantalizing dinners under the starlight. YOUR VACATION NEVER ENDS ABOARD SKYLARK.

Sonrisa: *Captain Billy L. Cast, Chef Ann Landry Cast*
Just for two - a romantic, tropical cruise on a luxurious 44'yacht. We plan everything to suit your personal preference - the itinerary, the day's activities, the menu. Enjoy comfort and privicy in the spacious aft cabin with ensuite head and shower. Weddings and honeymoons are our speciality.

SS PAJ: *Chef Gillian Bethell*

Tara: *Captain Lee Liebig , Chef and Captain Bonnie Ratrie*

Tava'e: *Captain Gerald A. Condon, Chef Madou Condon*
Gerald and Madou left one paradise: the South Pacific, for another paradise: the Virgin Islands. Their souvenirs are Hiva Oa, Raiatea, Bora Bora, Easter Island, Sepik River, Pitcairn etc... Thanks to Tava, their 50' cold molded Ketch.

Tequila: *Captains Bob Belschner, Chef & Captain Didgie Belschner*

Tuff: *Captain Jim Oosterhoudt, Chef Nan Gee*

Vanity: *Captain Bob Robinson, Chef and Captain Jan Robinson*
Vanity is a luxurious 60' Motor Sailer. This owner/operated charter yacht is designed for privacy. Taking only four guests, Vanity assures you of individual consideration. Dine under the stars, enjoy international cuisine. Ten years of chartering give the Robinsons the knowledge of where the action is, and where serenity prevails.

Verano Sin Final: *Captain Ted Dixon, Chef Jane Dixon*

m/v Voyager: *Captain Peter Usmar, Chef Mary Usmar*
The sea, the sea, the ever free. Join us on this spacious, luxurious 66 foot Cheoy Lee.

Voyager: *Captain Tim Hurst, Chef Anne Hurst*
Voyager is a "NEW HORIZON 70 foot ketch accommodating eight guests in four equal double staterooms, with a crew of four. We are strictly a "DOWN ISLAND" boat whose crew enjoys the tranquility and adventure of the less developed Caribbean. Our dining table reflects the diversity of our cruising grounds.

Wishing Star: *Captain Tore Waagen, Chef Susan David*

ABOUT THE ARTIST

Our ingenious illustrator/artist, Raid (pronounced ray-eed) Ahmad, is part of the *Ship To Shore* cookbooks success.

He works with major publishers, newpapers and magazines. His illustrations may be found in some of the best publications including Cats Magazine. Raid has participated in international exhibitions for which he has won numerous awards.

Cruise through *Sea To Shore* with Ahmad's cartoon characters and their useful hints!

RE-ORDER ADDITIONAL COPIES

Quantity	Description	Price	Total
	Ship To Shore I	$14.95	
	Ship To Shore II	$14.95	
	Sweet To Shore	$14.95	
	Sea To Shore	$14.95	
	Sip To Shore	$10.95	
	Slim To Shore	$14.95	

AUTOGRAPH TO: _____

_____

SHIP TO: _____

_____

_____

_____

AUTOGRAPH TO: _____

_____

SHIP TO: _____

_____

_____

_____

_____

Call to order **TOLL FREE**
1-800-338-6072

6% Tax (N.C. Only)		
Gift Wrap $2.00 Each		
Freight $2.50/Book		
TOTAL		

Please charge my: ☐ VISA
☐ MasterCard   ☐ AmEx

Card Number:

Make **check** and **Money Orders** payable to:

SHIP TO SHORE, INC.
10500 MT. HOLLY ROAD
CHARLOTTE, NC 28214-9219

Signature:

_____

Expiration Date: _____

- -

RE-ORDER ADDITIONAL COPIES

Quantity	Description	Price	Total
	Ship To Shore I	$14.95	
	Ship To Shore II	$14.95	
	Sweet To Shore	$14.95	
	Sea To Shore	$14.95	
	Sip To Shore	$10.95	
	Slim To Shore	$14.95	

AUTOGRAPH TO: _____

_____

SHIP TO: _____

_____

_____

_____

AUTOGRAPH TO: _____

_____

SHIP TO: _____

_____

_____

_____

_____

Call to order **TOLL FREE**
1-800-338-6072

6% Tax (N.C. Only)		
Gift Wrap $2.00 Each		
Freight $2.50/Book		
TOTAL		

Please charge my: ☐ VISA
☐ MasterCard   ☐ AmEx

Card Number:

Make **Checks** and **Money Orders** payable to:

SHIP TO SHORE, INC.
10500 MT. HOLLY ROAD
CHARLOTTE, NC 28214-9219

Signature:

_____

Expiration Date: _____

PERFECT GIFTS
FOR ANY OCCASION
FREE!!!

Share the taste of the Caribbean with your Friends!
We will send your friends a FREE catalog.
Simply mail this form or call 1-800-338-6072.

Name:_____

Address:_____

City:_____State_____Zip:_____

Name:_____

Address:_____

City:_____State_____Zip:_____

SHIP TO SHORE, INC.
10500 MT. HOLLY ROAD
CHARLOTTE, N.C. 28214-9219

- -

PERFECT GIFTS
FOR ANY OCCASION
FREE!!!

Share the taste of the Caribbean with your Friends!
We will send your friends a FREE catalog.
Simply mail this form or call 1-800-338-6072.

Name:_____

Address:_____

City:_____State_____Zip:_____

Name:_____

Address:_____

City:_____State_____Zip:_____

SHIP TO SHORE, INC.
10500 MT. HOLLY ROAD
CHARLOTTE, N.C. 28214-9219